Also by Georges Lemaitre

FOUR FRENCH NOVELISTS

ANDRÉ MAUROIS

FROM CUBISM TO SURREALISM IN FRENCH LITERATURE

BEAUMARCHAIS

BEAUMARCHAIS

ENGRAVING BY SAINT-AUBIN AFTER A PAINTING BY COCHIN

Georges Lemaître

BEAUMARCHAIS

Alfred A. Knopf: New York

1 9 4 9

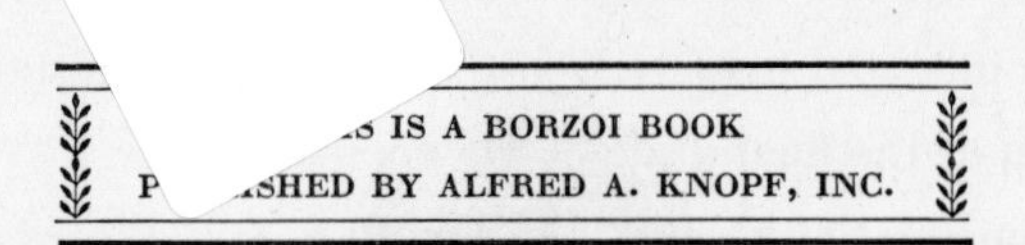

 Published simultaneously in Canada by McClelland & Stewart Limited. Manufactured in the United States of America

FIRST EDITION

PREFACE

THERE ARE no imaginary dialogues or anecdotes in this book. All the facts presented are strictly authentic, and all the conversations and remarks reported are directly quoted from reliable original sources.

I wish to express my sincere thanks to Herbert Weinstock, who gave me friendly advice and help and offered many invaluable suggestions throughout the composition of this work. Furthermore I am greatly indebted to Bart Keith Winer for his assistance in the preparation of the final draft of the manuscript.

My appreciation also goes to Dr. F. A. van Woerden, Consul General of the Netherlands in San Francisco, and to Dr. G. van Alphen of the Royal Library at the Hague for their kindness in providing me with information on certain problems connected with Beaumarchais' activities in Holland.

G. L.

CONTENTS

Contents

BEAUMARCHAIS

Chapter 1

A SHOPKEEPER'S SON

1. André Caron, Maître Horloger

LATE IN THE SUMMER OF 1722, a watchmaker's shop was opened on the busy Rue Saint-Denis, near the Rue Sainte-Catherine, in the very heart of Paris. Through the small square panes of the front window, the passers-by could see a large sign painted on the low ceiling: ANDRÉ CARON, MAÎTRE HORLOGER. In spite of its humble and rather gloomy appearance, the shop was the crowning achievement of its young owner's ambitions and his reward for tedious and arduous efforts.

André Caron's father, Daniel, had also been a watchmaker, plying his modest trade in the sleepy provincial town of Lizy-sur-Ourcq. For many years, Daniel Caron and his wife, *née* Marie Fortain, both of sturdy Huguenot stock, had led a wholesome and uneventful life there. They had not accumulated riches, but they had not known want, either. They had toiled stoutly side by side, and a lusty brood of fourteen boys and girls had grown happily around them.

Daniel Caron's death, in 1708, had brought an end to this familial paradise. His widow had moved to Paris, where it was easier for her to scrape together a living, and the children, striking out for themselves, had scattered far and wide.

André, under the name of Caron d'Ailly, had joined the dragoons. The dragoons wore a resplendent uniform, and prided themselves on being the *élite* of the French Army—and André, as a spirited lad would, entertained high hopes of grandeur and glory.

Soon, however, the gray monotony of barrack routine and the coarseness of his fellow soldiers turned his heart from his early dreams. He was not like one of his brothers, Caron de Boisgarnier, who had enlisted in the Régiment de Blaisois and become genuinely fond of military life. Caron de Boisgarnier, Caron d'Ailly—*noms de guerre* they had adopted when, in adolescent fancy, they had pictured themselves victorious generals, great and powerful lords—all that was now past and gone for André. He wanted to be plain Monsieur Caron, nothing else. He wanted to marry and raise a large family, as his father had done. He wanted to be a *bon bourgeois*, as his father had been.

Soon his daydreams centered upon a young and pretty girl, Marie-Louise Pichon, the daughter of a worthy, though not wealthy, Parisian bourgeois. How Caron managed to be received into their home has not been recorded and will never be known. Caron realized that Marie-Louise's dowry would be very small and that her worldly accomplishments were few. Friends did praise her high musical gifts, but the young dragoon had absolutely no ear for the high-flown music she played. Yet when he gazed at Marie-Louise sitting at her spinet, looking demure and sweet, he felt that there was hardly anything on earth he would not do to have her by his side all his life. And the girl did not remain unmoved by the handsome young man's mute yet eloquent worship.

They were both undoubtedly aware of the many almost unsurmountable obstacles that stood between them. André Caron was a Protestant, Marie-Louise Pichon a Catholic. André had no trade, no means of supporting a wife. Moreover, how could the daughter of a respectable bourgeois ever wed a soldier, a dragoon?

André Caron, however, seems to have called himself a Protestant mainly because of family loyalty: religious dogmatic subtleties held no appeal for him. He knew that if he became a Catholic, the Church would smooth the path before him. After some hesitation, his mind was made up. On February 5, 1721, thanks to ecclesiastical influence, he received an honorable discharge from the French Army, and a month later, on March 7, he solemnly abjured Calvinism. Immediately afterward, though he was nearly twenty-three years old—he was born on April 26, 1698—Caron was unquestioningly accepted as an apprentice by the Watchmakers' Guild of Paris. One year later, he asked the Conseil d'Etat that as a special favor, in view of his conversion, he be given the rank and title of master watchmaker. His request was granted, and on July 13, 1722, beaming with joy, he led Marie-Louise Pichon to the altar.

This bold start was followed by lean and difficult years. André Caron was a greenhorn in all business matters, and his hurried apprenticeship had no doubt left gaps in his technical knowledge of his trade. But he set himself grimly to learn. Every day, from dawn until dark, he sat at his workbench, huddled over his pinions, his pallets, and his wheels. After dinner, he wrestled with the theory of mechanics and pored over thick books, often late into the night.

Around that time, the close relationship between the branches of the Bourbon dynasty reigning in Spain and France had fostered cordial ties between the two nations. Every year, visiting Spanish noblemen and noblewomen flocked to the French capital, where they made many purchases. Eventually, some Spanish ladies discovered Caron's little shop. They spoke among themselves about the stalwart young watchmaker with such a martial bearing and such engaging, even downright gallant manners. From then on, André never lacked customers. A certain Countess of Fuen Clara grew particularly fond of him and for many years sent him tender messages from Spain.

Though these noblewomen and their husbands were lavish with their orders, they were less prodigal with their remittances. What with the Spaniards' natural inclination to put off until tomorrow all disagreeable tasks, and the aristocrats' lofty disdain for anything as trivial as a debt to a shopkeeper, poor Caron often had to wait for years to settle his accounts. How, indeed, could he effectively dun beautiful countesses or duchesses who lived far away in Madrid and who answered his polite reminders with still politer compliments or, even oftener, did not answer them at all?

André Caron, however, had also acquired a less brilliant but more reliable clientèle among the Parisian bourgeois. In spite of ever-recurring financial worries, mainly caused by unpaid bills, he now felt himself in an honorable and secure position. Thanks to years of hard, painstaking labor, he had become a truly skillful craftsman highly esteemed by the other members of his guild.

Furthermore, his study of the laws of mechanics had given him a more than average competency in that field. When, one day, the Governor of Madrid, who had probably heard of André Caron through his fair Spanish customers, officially sought the watchmaker's advice about certain technical problems connected with the dredging of rivers, the latter did not let any of his friends remain ignorant of the fact that his reputation as an expert on machines had spread far beyond the borders of the kingdom of France.

Caron's family was growing and thriving. His wife gave birth to ten children, and though four of them died in infancy, five girls and one boy remained to fill the small Caron house with happy noise and great hopes. The eldest girl, Marie-Josèphe, was born in 1725. Another girl, who, like her mother, received the name of Marie-Louise, came in 1731. On January 22, 1732, the Carons hailed the arrival of a son. The boy was christened Pierre-Augustin, after his godfather, Pierre-Augustin Picard, a friendly neighbor, a plain, honest candlemaker. Then three more daughters followed: Madeleine-Françoise, in 1734; Marguerite-Julie, in 1735, and Jeanne-Marguerite, in 1739. These long, hyphenated names soon proved to complicated and solemn for everyday family use and were replaced by shorter affectionate or fondly mocking pet names. Marie-Josèphe, who was much older than her brother and her sisters, was deservedly called "La Grande." Marie-Louise was dubbed "Lisette"; Pierre-Augustin, "Pierrot"; Madeleine-Françoise, "Fanchon." Marguerite-Julie, by far the unruliest and the brightest of them all, was nicknamed "La Bécasse"—the Wood hen—an appellation connotating both submissiveness and utter stupidity. And, after a while, the toddler Jeanne-Marguerite answered to "Tonton."

2. "*My youth, so gay, so mad, so happy.*"

SELDOM had a crowd of such mischievous little imps been assembled under one roof. The sedate Marie-Josèphe was, of course, nearly always busy helping her mother with the innumerable household chores. But from early morning until night, Lisette, Pierrot, Fanchon, La Bécasse, and Tonton made the upstairs rooms of the modest lodging ring with their laughter and cries. Their father had to remain all day long in his shop, engrossed as he was with his meticulous work, and could not control the rumbling, tumultuous din going on almost continuously above his head. The mother was tenderly beloved by all, but was much too gentle and weak to establish even a semblance of order among her gamboling young demons.

Whenever the weather was fine and warm, the children were herded into a tiny back yard. There they were joined by a few like-minded neighbors of their own age. Together, they would romp, run, jump, tumble, and fight with the exuberant, wholesome vitality of happy youth.

"*Ma jeunesse, si gaie, si folle, si heureuse,*" Pierrot wrote later, after he had become the celebrated and much maligned M. de Beaumarchais. He was then wistfully looking back at the first years of his life, which were certainly among the best he ever had and which powerfully shaped his character.

Indeed, Pierrot soon discovered that, in a group of high-mettled, boisterous youngsters, it did him absolutely no good to be compliant and meek. Whenever he yielded to his sisters' caprices and whims, the girls invariably overwhelmed him almost at once with new exigencies and claims. If, on the contrary, he rebelled against them and raised an even louder clamor than they did, he usually succeeded in carrying out his will, often in imposing it upon his playmates. Since, however, the girls were as headstrong as he was, his victories always proved short-lived, and for years he found himself involved in ever-renewed contests and wranglings.

But there was never any true gall in Pierrot's fights with Tonton, La Bécasse, Fanchon, and Lisette. Very much like playful, frolicking kittens pretending to bite and scratch, they pitted their young strength against that of their playmates, but they never meant to inflict any wound, and they loved one another dearly.

This lovable and lively atmosphere was doubtless the origin of that inexhaustible fund of optimism and gaiety which Pierre-Augustin retained during his worst trials. His first impression of the world was a free and happy playground, and he never altogether relinquished this superficial but highly pleasant view of life.

While Pierre-Augustin thus gained a radiant confidence in life, he also received the seeds of a more complex emotion. In his frequent squabbles with his sisters, he knew that he could count upon an unwavering supporter: *Maman.* Mme Caron was fair-minded and never deliberately pampered her son. Yet, whenever Pierrot, her treasure, ran to her after a quarrel with Lisette or Fanchon, his doleful face stained with tears, her heart welled up irresistibly within her breast, and she overwhelmed him with love.

And with sharp insight, he sensed that, whatever mischief he might perpetrate, his *maman* would always stand by his side.

Throughout his whole life, Pierre-Augustin retained in his mind an indelible image of his guardian angel, his mother. In his numerous love affairs, he invariably felt drawn toward women older than himself or with commanding stature. Beyond any doubt, he was always pursuing a duplicate of the figure of gentle strength who had shielded him in his youth against all fancied or actual dangers.

When Pierre-Augustin reached the age of nine, his father decided to send him to school. Up to then, his mother had taught him the alphabet and whatever else she knew, which was little indeed. But André Caron had high ambitions for his son. His business had been going well during the preceding few years. Perhaps, in a time not too remote, he would be able to raise the lad above the rank of a mere shopkeeper. He could not afford to place him in one of the best aristocratic *collèges* of the capital. There was, however, in a suburb of Paris—Alfort, near Vincennes—a boarding school with a good reputation and rates that would not too severely tax his limited means.

At home the little chap was getting more and more unruly, and André Caron thought it high time to subject him to discipline. When his wife mildly objected, he reminded her that the child would not in any way be cut off from the rest of the family. Every Sunday and every holiday, he would return to the Rue Saint-Denis house. It was also arranged that, on those days, on his way back he would stop at a certain monastery in Vincennes to be given qualified instruction in Church doctrine.

Pierrot was delighted. To him this meant, above all, a change of scene: new faces, new friends, new games—an adventure—though hardly an adventure in learning. His teachers tried to initiate him into the arcana of Latin grammar and prosody, but he nimbly eluded their efforts. Thanks to his quick mind, he was seldom punished for slackness, yet he never managed to master more than the rudiments of Latin. In French, his spelling remained strangely uncertain until the end of his life, and his punctuation, curiously erratic.

On the other hand, he learned from his schoolmates brand new deviltries that were infinitely more satisfying than the comparatively harmless pranks he and his sisters had indulged in at home. Of his visits to the monastery, he remembered mainly the good things that an old monk gave him to eat. He also later recalled, hanging in the vestry, a large canvas depicting the Last Judgment. But it seems that the angels painted on it inspired him more with amusement than with awe, and the devils more with curiosity than with horror.

After four years André Caron realized that his son did not have the makings of a scholar, and in the spring of 1745 Pierre-Augustin was taken out of school. He was only thirteen years old.

3. Revolt and Defeat

JUST as, twenty-five years earlier, the young dragoon, Caron d'Ailly, had surrendered his military dreams when they were balked by reality, so now the practical Monsieur Caron gave up his high-falutin ideas about his son's future. Not too grudgingly, he fell back on a modest program: he would teach the young boy the secrets of his craft. Someday Caron *fils* would succeed him in his shop. Someday Caron *fils* would probably be one of the most prosperous and honored members of the Watchmakers' Guild.

The first months Pierre-Augustin spent as an apprentice in the Rue Saint-Denis shop were trying indeed. The mild discipline of the Alfort school now seemed like unbridled freedom, in retrospect. He had to sit for endless hours at his workbench under his father's stern and vigilant eye. André Caron, however, was not unduly exacting. Perhaps he soon found out that demanding too much from the child inevitably resulted in bungled work. In any case, he allowed him fair spells of relaxation during which the boy could run freely about the house and unbend.

Pierre-Augustin and his sisters no longer capered and romped in the back yard as they had in their earlier years. Although they remained mischievous and merry, this stage of childhood had now passed for all of them. Marie-Josèphe had already reached the season of life when young girls' thoughts turn to matrimony. It was not long before she became engaged to an honorable, though not very prosperous, young man named Guilbert, a stonemason by trade. In 1748 they were married and, soon afterward, decided to try their luck in Madrid. Were they counting upon definite promises of help from some of André Caron's Spanish customers, or were they merely going in search of castles in Spain? In any case, on his way to fortune Guilbert dropped his humble title of stonemason and in the Spanish capital became an architect.

The Guilberts had taken another of the Caron daughters, Marie-Louise, with them to Madrid. Lisette was now at the age of golden adolescent dreams. Perhaps in her girlish fancies she could see the handsome, if imaginary, figure of a Spanish husband-to-be, an improved copy of the haughty and glamorous dons who had brought to her father's shop a glow of exotic romance.

Back home, the characters of Fanchon, Julie, and Tonton were assuming clearer, firmer outlines. Fanchon had grown into a shapely, fresh-complexioned lass with a precocious interest in the neighborhood boys. Julie, on the other hand, paid scarcely any attention to them. She had a long, pointed nose and, in spite of her large, bright eyes, looked rather plain; but she had a quick and lively mind. Constantly laughing and joking, she appeared merely lightheaded and giddy to outsiders when, in fact, she inwardly craved an intense personal attachment. By and by, she found an outlet for her feelings through ardent devotion to her brother. Tonton, the youngest and the prettiest of the Caron sisters, looked more refined and delicate than the rest of the family. In turn skittish, coquettish, or gracefully indolent, she thought that special privileges were due to her precious, fragile person. And the others, won by her appealing and coaxing ways, usually gave in to her whims and changing moods without much struggle.

Tonton had by far the best voice among the Caron children. Yet all of them had to a remarkable degree inherited their mother's musical gifts. In those days, playing some musical instrument was considered an essential part of a girl's education. André Caron encouraged this worthy accomplishment in his talented daughters and did not deny the same advantage to his son. But much to his dismay, his house, which a few years before had been a bedlam of childish cries and wails, now resounded with the doubtful harmonies or the downright dissonances of the harpsichord, the cello, the violin, and the flute.

The squeals of the violin and the moaning of the flute were

Pierre-Augustin's special, dismal contributions to the family concert. The boy, however, also had an amazing knack of catching and even inventing tuneful airs. Moreover he could learn with incrediable speed to perform on any instrument that struck his fancy. Music evidently provided him with an outlet for his pent-up energies. Like a young bird imprisoned in a narrow cage, he turned all his longing for freedom into frantic sound. Almost every night, along with his sisters, he filled the house with what seemed to his tired father a senseless hurricane of noise.

For a while, André Caron bore his musical trials patiently. But he could no longer share in the exuberance of youth. A quarter of a century spent in small hole of a shop had not improved his temper. He had become austere, even morose, in the last few years, and a backwash of his former Protestant puritanism seems to have swept over him. He now frowned upon the most harmless pleasures of life and looked upon every form of joy as sinful.

He was still a regular member of the Catholic Church. In fact, he observed ritual more scrupulously than ever. But there was a formal, almost mechanical element in his conception of religion that left little room for true spirituality. In order to compel his children to attend church on Sundays he had set up an elaborate system of fines, which he enforced pitilessly. "My father," his son explained many years later, "was inexorable about our going to High Mass. When I was late, and came after the Epistle, twelve sous were deducted from my monthly allowance of four livres. If I arrived after the Gospel, I would lose twenty sous; if after the Elevation, it was the whole of four livres; so that I often had a deficit of six or eight livres in my finances."

This system succeeded in forcing Pierre-Augustin to go more

or less regularly to church, but it utterly failed to inspire him with deep religious fervor. In his mind, religion always remained linked to an arbitrary set of penalties and orders. Though to the end of his life he retained an implicit belief in God, he derived no true help or positive guidance from this vague faith.

Pierre-Augustin was then entering the troublesome period of early adolescence and greatly needed both guidance and help. He fell in love with a girl much older than himself and in a spell of exaltation declared his passion to her. The girl was amused by the impetuosity of her fourteen-year-old lover and encouraged him for the fun of it. Then she married someone else. "I wanted to commit suicide," Pierre-Augustin wrote many years later when telling a friend the story of his grand amour.

Perhaps in order to forget, he flung himself wildly into mischief. After his day's work was over, he would go out, until late at night, with young scamps of the neighborhood. They were mostly apprentices like himself, honest enough, but turbulent and noisy. They rough-housed together, went places where they should not have gone, played tricks on sedate bourgeois, and more than once overstepped the uncertain boundary between jollity and disorderliness. Sometimes they organized a "concert." Then they would shout and sing, keeping all decent folk in the vicinity awake, and, whenever this took place in Pierre-Augustin's house, driving old Caron to frenzy.

Old Caron, however, forbore for a long time to interfere with this bunch of young rowdies and limited his disapproval to ill-tempered grumbling. But when he heard his neighbors complain and realized that the good name of his house was endangered, he strongly remonstrated with his son—to no avail. Evidently the lad did not care a straw what his father thought or said. His work in the shop became more slipshod every day. Admonition or punishment made him sulky, if not openly mutinous. For months father and son confronted each other tensely, challengingly, both feeling that a crisis was at hand.

The crisis came in 1750, when Caron discovered that Pierre-Augustin, apparently dissatisfied with his meager allowance, had not only purloined a few livres from a drawer at home, but had also kept the money paid by certain customers for repair work he had done on their timepieces. A violent scene followed, and when Pierre-Augustin refused to express regret or to make amends, his father threw him out of the house.

With the cocksureness of youth, Pierre-Augustin felt confident that, thanks to his "musical talents," he would now lead a much more pleasant, entertaining life than the one he had led at home. Later on, his enemies accused him of having been a mountebank, a street musician, even a beggar at this period of his life. There was probably some exaggeration in these statements, but perhaps a kernel of truth as well. It is practically certain that the young man tried, but without success, to join one of the companies of the Théâtre de la Foire, a low-brow, vaudeville type of show then popular in Paris. One may also surmise that he resorted to still more precarious expedients to keep body and soul together. At any rate, after a comparatively short time he had to admit defeat to himself.

Although he had come to the end of his tether, he did not dare to face his father's wrath. Some family friends, however, gave him shelter in their house and interceded for the now repentant young scapegrace. But stern old Caron was not to be mollified so easily. Not until his wife begged him with tears in her eyes to take their child back into their home did he finally relent, though not without making rigorous stipulations beforehand. With great punctilio, he insisted upon having the boy sign a regular treaty of peace. The boy was to declare himself vanquished and to pledge himself to fulfill certain definite clauses, which were then enumerated in six tersely worded articles.

"Know," a solemn preamble stated, "the conditions I place upon your return. I require full and complete submission on your part, and I want you to show me great respect in your words, in your actions, and in your whole attitude. Not only do I wish to be obeyed and respected, but I also want you to anticipate my desires in anything that you think might please me."

Among the various provisos of the treaty were:

"You shall rise in the summer at six o'clock and in the winter at seven. You shall work until suppertime at anything I give you to do, without showing any distaste for your task. I mean you to employ the talents God has given you so that you may become famous in your profession . . .

"You must never go out for supper parties nor go out at all in the evening. Such parties and entertainments are too dangerous for you. But I consent to your having dinner with your friends on Sundays and holidays, on condition that I know where you are going and that you never return home later than nine o'clock.

"You must give up your wretched music altogether and, above all, the company of young men, for I shall not tolerate either of them. Both have been your ruin. However, in consideration of your weakness I shall allow you the violin and the flute, but on the express condition that you never play either instrument except after supper on working days and never during daytime and that you do not disturb the neighbors' rest or my own."

Caron *fils* signed this capitulation and added at the bottom of the page: "It is fitting that I suffer this humiliation, which indeed I have deserved, and if this, in addition to my good behavior, will put me back in your good graces and win me your friendship, I shall consider myself as happy, indeed."

Caron *fils* did get back in his father's good graces and win his friendship again. In fact, almost immediately, the shiftless and rebellious youngster became a model apprentice and a deferential, dutiful son. He observed to the letter the rules set down in the treaty imposed upon him. Between the ages of eighteen and twenty-one he meekly bided his time and never even attempted to indulge in the escapades that often signify the natural surging up of the vital sap of youth.

This sudden and complete taming of a strong temperament was neither normal nor altogether wholesome. Something snapped within Pierre-Augustin when, in a decisive struggle against his father's superior strength, he was worsted and had to cry for mercy. As a result, during his most crucial years, when a boy ought to change into a man, his moral development was abruptly broken. Thus he never wholly succeeded in bridging the psychological gap that separates adolescence from manhood. Even though he soon outwardly appeared a sound and sane adult, he nevertheless always retained the emotional earmarks of adolescence.

This discrepancy between his full-grown, mature appearance and his immature, arrested emotional state eventually became a source of endless misunderstanding for his contemporaries, who, almost without exception, failed to put together the intricate yet correlated pieces of his mental pattern. Thus, retaining as he did the instability of the adolescent, he found himself almost to the end of his life unable to settle his affections, once and for all, on any one woman. He was always impelled to flit from one to the other. And in each of his love affairs he oscillated between physical pleasure and maudlin sentimentality. This typically adolescent disjunction of sentiment and senses invariably characterized all his adventures in love.

Adventures in love, adventures in almost every conceivable field of action—his whole career was a succession of disconnected, independent episodes. He could never set a long-range, self-justifying, life-unifying goal for himself. His curiosity and his enthusiasm for each and every facet of the world that caught his eye were intense, vivid, quickly exhausted. He always welcomed any new, fresh experience, only to pass on to the next, then to the next again. This lack of continuity of purpose and this state of constant expectancy are normal for a youth standing on the threshold of the universe. But as he grew older, they created an atmosphere of pointless, futile agitation about him when they failed to give way to the steadier, if narrower, outlook that usually comes with maturity.

Also traceable to his emotional immaturity were his unbounded generosity and his incredible selfishness. Almost without transition, he could be in turn open-handed and stingy, idealistic and cynical, naïvely trusting and deliberately hard. He never integrated into a consistent whole the contradictory impulses that welled up from the depths of his consciousness. Thus, his apparently chaotic behavior justified the opposite and extreme judgments that were passed upon him. Many of the people who came in contact with him would, according to their own temperament, overlook or overemphasize one side of his personality. So he found himself almost constantly extolled by his friends, vilified by his foes; but friends, foes, and puzzled onlookers alike agreed upon one trait of his character: his unpredictability.

Aware of the atmosphere of uncertainty around him and therefore feeling insecure, he stuck throughout his life to a typically adolescent chip-on-the-shoulder attitude. Yet there was no malice whatever in his aggressiveness. He could hit hard at an enemy, but he could also be easily pacified. His anger subsided before kindness as quickly as it was aroused by suspected antagonism. And his hostility and his goodwill alternated according to an accidental concatenation of the most casual circumstances or the mysterious rhythm of his moods.

In no case was this odd blending of animosity and genuine benevolence more strikingly shown than in his relations with his father. All his life he retained an unavowed, perhaps unconscious resentment against parental authority. In his clash with the strong-willed, ruthless old man, he had been too deeply wounded not to bear an indelible scar on his mind. Yet he knew that his father was not a tyrant or an ogre. André Caron had reacted violently when his supremacy at home had been threatened. But now that he was recognized as master of the household, he relaxed his severity and became pleasantly cheerful. Much to everyone's surprise, he even wrote light, frivolous pieces of poetry in his spare time.

Old Caron no longer objected to music being played in his house. Of course, Pierre-Augustin, Fanchon, Tonton, and Julie, who was no longer called "La Bécasse," now sang very agreeably and performed expertly on several instruments. To be sure, their father was not overfond of the elaborate modern music that the younger generation favored, but preferred old-fashioned, simple tunes. Yet he was now thoroughly happy and enjoyed the warm and friendly atmosphere of his home. He had a cloudless and calm affection for his wife, his daughters, and his son. And to outward appearances, his affection was heartily and sincerely reciprocated by all.

Yet an obscure desire for revenge remained hidden in Pierre-Augustin's heart. The best way for him to prove that he was a better man than his father was to beat him at his own game. André Caron prided himself on being one of the most skillful watchmakers in Paris. Pierre-Augustin threw himself into watchmaking, body and soul. His natural aptitude and his frantic application soon made him amazingly proficient in his work. He felt that he had outstripped his father, and the father was delighted with the young man's zeal.

4. *First Fight with Fraud*

ANDRÉ CARON often boasted of his knowledge of the laws of mechanics. Pierre-Augustin therefore plunged into the study of them. Soon he tackled certain difficult technical problems then taxing the ingenuity of watchmakers. Most vexing, perhaps, was the awkward, spherical shape of the ordinary pocket watch. The inner mechanism then in use was so complicated and bulky that all efforts to build small, flat timepieces had resulted in failure.

Pierre-Augustin felt that the crux of the problem was the cumbersome structure of the escapement, which contained too many parts. He undertook to simplify it drastically and, for that purpose, began a series of calculations, computations and experiments that absorbed all his free time and his scant financial resources.

He received little encouragement and no help at all in his work from his father. André Caron was content to stick to usual business routine. He shrugged his shoulders when he saw Pierre-Augustin waste his pocket money trying to invent a supposedly momentous, but probably impractical, contrivance. Though he did not interfere with his son's hobby, he also did not allow him to spoil perfectly good watches in futile experiments, either; nor did he purchase the expensive scientific books that Pierre-Augustin claimed were indispensable to his great work.

Eventually, however, Pierre-Augustin found that he could borrow nearly all the books he needed from a fellow member of the Watchmakers' Guild named Lepaute. A clever, successful businessman, somewhat unscrupulous and extremely ambitious, though outwardly obliging and kind, Lepaute had built up a considerable clientèle in both Versailles and Paris. He was acquainted with many important persons at court and was wealthy. He had power not only within his guild, but also within a broader circle, the influential *bourgeoisie* of the capital.

With an engaging, though superficial friendliness that was part of his stock in trade, Lepaute placed his library at young Caron's disposal. Although the young man did not give him any detailed information about the progress of his work, he talked to him about his goal, and Lepaute became aware that the humble apprentice was actually on the track of a sensational discovery.

At the beginning of July 1753, after many months of work,

Pierre-Augustin succeeded in solving the problem he had set for himself. On July 23, he candidly told Lepaute about the startingly simple escapement he had conceived, and asked his opinion of it. Lepaute, though impressed by the lad's cleverness, was not competent to judge the practical value of the mechanism without a test, and offered to try it on a clock he was constructing for a certain M. de Julienne. Naturally, he swore not to reveal the secret of the young man's invention.

Apparently, he found the new escapement an epoch-making improvement in the manufacture of watches, for, two weeks later, on August 4, 1753, without further ado, he sent the French Academy of Sciences a communication describing the new escapement that he, Lepaute, had invented. The stir in scientific circles was so great that the leading review, *Le Mercure de France*, carried a full-length account of the basic principles of the "Lepaute system" in its September, 1753, number. The invention created a still greater stir among the Paris watchmakers, who began discussing its advantages, its drawbacks, and the changes that it involved in their industry.

Pierre-Augustin had no difficulty in recognizing in the *Mercure* article the very ideas that he had expounded to Lepaute less than two months before. Lepaute, puffed up with glory and perhaps somewhat uneasy, refused to listen to young Caron's immediate and furious protest. There was no tangible proof of their conversation. If worst came to worst, who would take the word of a mere, unknown apprentice against that of a famous master of the Watchmakers' Guild?

The Caron family felt indignant yet worried. With so little prospect of victory, with so slender a chance even to get a fair hearing, was it wise to fight so powerful an opponent? But Pierre-Augustin, who had met downright injustice and fraud for the first time in his life, impulsively threw himself into the struggle. His complaint was brought before the Minister of the Royal Household, Comte de Saint-Florentin, who acted as referee in all serious conflicts between members of the Paris guilds. Obviously the Count could not overlook Lepaute's self-assurance and prestige, but he was also struck by the note of sincerity in the young apprentice's voice. Knowing nothing whatever about watches, he advised the youth to submit his grievances to the Academy of Sciences and promised to see to it that the case was investigated thoroughly and impartially.

On November 13, Pierre-Augustin Caron sent a petition to the Academy of Sciences and, soon afterward, he wrote to the *Mercure de France*, presenting his version of the facts. The *Mercure* published his letter at once. Soon all the Paris cafés and salons buzzed with *l'affaire Lepaute*. Was Lepaute, the great Lepaute, nothing but a scoundrel? Or was he the victim of a shameful attempt at slander and blackmail?

Meanwhile the inquiry conducted by the Academy of Sciences proceeded. Pierre-Augustin produced a long string of documents, projects, rough sketches, and calculations showing how the invention had grown and matured in his mind. Lepaute showed nothing but bluster and the escapement, which seemed somehow to have sprung, all of a sudden, fully perfected, from his brain. On February 23, 1754, the report of the investigating commission was read before the Academy. Its conclusions were categorical: Pierre-Augustin Caron, not Lepaute, was the sole inventor of the escapement.

Characteristically, Pierre-Augustin did not press his advantage against Lepaute. He did not sue him for damages before the regular law courts, and Lepaute was only too glad to sink back into obscurity and oblivion.

Pierre-Augustin was now in the full light of public interest and curiosity. His honest, decent bearing, his intelligence and his courage were praised by everybody. One day he was informed that Louis XV had commanded that the young inventor be presented to him at Versailles.

Great commotion went on in the Rue Saint-Denis house. Old Caron was bursting with paternal pride. Pierre-Augustin's sisters bubbled over with excitement and glee while his mother silently blessed her worthy child. Eager friends thronged the modest Caron home and neighbors showed ill-suppressed envy.

A special, elaborate costume had to be made hurriedly and at great expense for Pierre-Augustin's presentation to the King. When it was completed, everyone agreed that the young man had as fine appearance as any of the *grands seigneurs* at court. He was not tall, but he was well built, and had a frank, mobile, expressive face. His long stay in a dark Parisian shop had given him a pallor that usually went with refinement and culture. He did not have the easy manners of a courtier, but that could be explained by the natural, becoming shyness of youth.

Louis XV was thoroughly used to seeing the persons presented to him overcome with timidity and knew how to put them somewhat at ease. He was kind to the young man and asked him questions about his escapement. At once Pierre-Augustin found his self-assurance and spoke briefly, evenly, clearly. His Majesty was interested and even put a watchmaker's magnifying glass to the royal eye, to be able to follow the explanations the young apprentice gave him. His Majesty was amazed to hear him say that, thanks to his invention, he could build a watch small enough to fit into a lady's finger ring. The King immediately ordered such a watch in a ring for Mme de Pompadour.

When the audience ended and Pierre-Augustin withdrew, he was surrounded by a fluttering crowd of courtiers overwhelming him with congratulations and with orders for watches of the same model that had attracted the King's attention.

When Pierre-Augustin returned to the Rue Saint-Denis, he found his father not only awed by his triumph—and this was not the least pleasant aspect of the adventure—but also elated by the flood of orders the young man brought back from Versailles. Financially speaking, André Caron had never been more than moderately successful in business. At present he had at home three lively daughters approaching the age of marriage. He found it difficult to keep up with their natural requests for entertainment and for finery, and still more difficult to put aside, for each of them, the customary dowry that French girls and their husbands-to-be expected. So he raised no objection when his son, after delivering Mme de Pompadour's watch and taking the title "Purveyor to the King," went to Versailles again and again, to deliver other watches and to get other orders.

Pierre-Augustin still spent most of his time at his workbench in the Rue Saint-Denis shop, but his glimpses of the brilliant world of Versailles nursed an ambition that had long lain dormant in his mind: to be free of parental authority and to escape from the humdrum life of the Parisian shopkeeper.

The Carons' recent affluence, gained by orders for watches from Versailles courtiers, had smoothed out many wrinkles in the fabric of their family life. The strict discipline his father had once imposed upon Pierre-Augustin had lately become very mild, indeed. The three girls, their modest wishes now fulfilled, radiated happiness and hope. André Caron had ceased worrying over bills and was constantly in good humor. Mme Caron, invariably kind and sweet, though not always in good health, quietly enjoyed a last warm glow of contentment and comfort in her declining years. And Pierre-Augustin, through force of habit, allowed the days to pass by without outwardly showing any sign of independence or restlessness.

Chapter 2

LEAPS AND BOUNDS

1. *Marriage*

WHENEVER PIERRE-AUGUSTIN went to Versailles, he put on the court costume that gave him an elegant air. Many ladies at court noticed the prepossessing young man, but he was to shy to respond to their flattering hints. In the end, one of them, Mme Francquet, decided to take a broad step beyond coyness. She brought a costly watch for repair to the Caron shop on the Rue Saint-Denis and insisted that Pierre-Augustin himself return the watch to her at her own home on a definite day and at a definite time. Pierre-Augustin, who had to humor customers, promised to go. It goes without saying that the lady's husband happened to be absent from home when she received the young man. She was very pretty, arrayed in her best finery, and ready for all eventualities. Pierre-Augustin gaily took up her challenge.

Madeleine-Catherine Francquet was six years older than Pierre-Augustin and twenty years younger than her husband. During the year 1754, Pierre-Augustin came to know them both very well indeed. Francquet occupied an important position in France's military administration. He worked at the War Ministry and drew a large salary as Controller of the Military Chest. He was also a Controller of the Pantry of the Royal Household, which office brought him only small financial returns, but gave him access to Versailles and thus enabled him to keep in touch with influential men at court. In recent years, however, he had felt quite secure at the War Ministry and needed no outside political support. Also, he was no longer in his prime and suffered from rheumatism, and the long trek to Versailles from his house in Paris, on the Rue des Bourdonnais, bored and tired him immeasurably. What he now enjoyed more than anything else was to sit quietly by the fireside in the evening with his young wife in his vast, well-built, and well-appointed home.

Yet, even there, he felt at times somewhat forlorn and sad, and was delighted when his wife introduced her new acquaintance, M. Pierre-Augustin Caron, Watchmaker to the King, to him. Pierre-Augustin? Pierre-Augustin was M. Francquet's name, too! Wasn't this coincidence, thought M. Francquet, almost providential? Pierre-Augustin Francquet soon found that Pierre-Augustin Caron was always most respectful, most considerate; that he listened attentively to his stories, assented to his ideas, and laughed heartily at his jokes. A very charming and intelligent man, indeed. Moreover, the young man's sunny disposition filled the Rue des

Bourdonnais house with well-mannered and well-tempered gaiety. It was not long before Pierre-Augustin Caron became a sincerely welcome guest in the Francquet home.

Music provided the main pretext for Pierre-Augustin's visits. Often, in the evening, while M. Francquet dozed comfortably in his armchair, Mme Francquet and young Caron played the harpsichord together. Sometimes, their hands met, perhaps by accident, on the keyboard. The music stopped. Francquet, aroused from his slumber by the sudden silence, stirred, and the music started once more and went on until it stopped again.

Madeleine Francquet seems to have been deeply in love with the boy, and her protective, almost motherly concern for his welfare struck a hidden chord in him. Mme Francquet soon undertook to further her young friend's career. Her husband was considering giving up his position as Controller of the Pantry. The salary was only six hundred livres a year, and though Francquet had purchased a small estate not far from Versailles, at Verlegrand, so that he could go to the royal palace without much trouble, he felt there was more bother than profit for him in the whole affair. Why not, then, sell this office to M. Caron, who no doubt would be glad to pay a large life annuity to Francquet to obtain an official foothold at court?

Mme Francquet advanced this argument and evidently convinced her husband, for everything was arranged according to her suggestions. On November 9, 1755, a royal warrant appointed Pierre-Augustin Caron *Contrôleur Clerc d'Office de la Maison du Roi* in place of Pierre-Augustin Francquet.

The *Contrôleurs d'Office* were essentially bookkeepers, whose main function was to check the expense accounts of the royal kitchens at Versailles. There were sixteen controllers, divided into four groups, each group on duty only three months a year. On solemn occasions, when a *repas et festin extraordinaire* took place, a controller on duty had the privilege of joining the procession of court officials taking the meat to the King's table.

Thus Pierre-Augustin Caron began his career as a courtier. His regular appearances in public gave him self-assurance. He was keenly observant and soon learned the best society manners. The fact that he had definite duties to perform helped him find and keep his proper place. Soon the young watchmaker mingled freely with the greatest without showing any trace of embarrassment or awkwardness.

Pierre-Augustin's life was dramatically changed when on the morning of January 3, 1756, Francquet was found dead in a bedroom of his Verlegrand country house. Blood had trickled from his nostrils, and the doctors, after examining the body, stated that he had succumbed to a cerebral hemorrhage. But it happened that Pierre-Augustin Caron had come late to Verlegrand the previous evening to visit his friends the Francquets and spend the night in one of their spare rooms, as he often did. Finding the inner gates locked for some reason, he had had to sleep, most uncomfortably, in an outbuilding of the small estate. Many years afterwards, his enemies, remembering this coincidence, spread the rumor that he had murdered Francquet in his bed to avoid paying the annuity they had agreed upon. At the time of Francquet's death, however, nobody—Pierre-Augustin least of all—foresaw that such an accusation would be made against him.

Her husband's sudden death left Mme Francquet in a most embarrassing situation. His main source of income, his salary as

Controller of the Military Chest, ended immediately. Francquet also had all sorts of irons in all sorts of fires, but, in most cases, his surviving business partners were only too ready to take advantage of the helpless young widow's utter lack of experience. She knew nobody she could trust but Pierre-Augustin Caron. Pierre-Augustin also lacked business experience, but he had an exceptionally keen mind. After six months of hard work, he succeeded in untangling the threads of the Francquet situation. When everything was settled, Mme Francquet could no longer be counted among the wealthy. She kept the Rue des Bourdonnais house, where her idyl with Pierre-Augustin had begun, a modest income, and a few plots of land outside Paris.

Throughout the early period of Mme Francquet's widowhood, when her financial affairs were being adjusted, Madeleine and Pierre-Augustin were brought into even tenderer and closer mutual confidence than before. As an epilogue, in November 1756, barely ten months after Francquet's death, they were married in Paris.

Their marriage was not the result of financial calculations on Pierre-Augustin's part. Having helped Madeleine thresh out her problems, he knew better than anyone else that she now had but little money. Indeed, he took so little notice of the pecuniary aspect of their union that he neglected to have the property settlement provided by the marriage contract duly and legally registered. Madeleine held a strong personal appeal for him. The difference between their ages—she was thirty and he twenty-four—perhaps enhanced that appeal, for he was particularly susceptible to the charm of comparatively mature women.

But the marriage represented above all a chance for young Caron to leave the Rue Saint-Denis and to emancipate himself completely from his father. As a symbol of his break with the past, shortly after his wedding, he gave up the name of Caron and assumed the *nom de guerre* Beaumarchais. Beaumarchais, which seems to have been spelled Bois-marché originally, was the name of a small wooded property belonging to his wife. The custom of adopting estate names was then common in France, and young Caron was quickly accepted as Beaumarchais. But this change of name meant more to him than mere indulgence in a passing fashion. It meant an open rejection of his former defeated, humiliated self and the beginning of a new life.

André Caron had disapproved of Pierre-Augustin's marriage with a woman he considered slightly passée. He now realized that the young man would never succeed him in his shop. When his son discarded their honorable name, he resented it almost as a personal insult. Yet no violent scene took place this time in the Rue Saint-Denis house. Pierre-Augustin had learned at Versailles how to do whatever he pleased and how to treat possible meddlers—in the present case, his father—with an elaborate yet distant courtesy. If this outward, chilly politeness allayed their emotional tension, it accentuated the feeling of estrangement that developed rapidly between them. For several years they were almost completely separated from one another.

Because Beaumarchais had no special occupation during the nine months he was not on duty at Versailles, he began to haunt the literary cafés in Paris. He met a crowd of journalists, critics, poets, and philosophers there and became slightly acquainted with d'Alembert, Diderot, and other Encyclopedists, who were then at the height of their prestige. He secretly admired and envied their glibness, their wit, their ability to talk endlessly on every possible or impossible subject. He realized how woefully inadequate his own schooling had been. Hurriedly, he started reading all the books, old and new, that he heard mentioned around him. Thanks to his amazing facility, he succeeded in a short time in absorbing a large amount of knowledge. But it was too late for him thoroughly to assimilate a substantial classical culture. In this respect, he always remained an amateur. This added to his personal charm, perhaps, but it also prevented him from consorting on an equal footing with the full-fledged citizens of the *République des Lettres*. Aware of his inferiority, Beaumarchais adopted a defensive attitude toward them, and tried to hide his deficiency behind a barrage of sharp and caustic remarks. This aroused both resentment and distrust in his interlocutors. Even after he became one of the outstanding literary men of his time, he could never establish thoroughly satisfactory relations with most of his confrères. Throughout his life, he found the professional writers, critics, publishers, and censors arrayed, almost to a man, on the side of his enemies.

For the time being, however, Beaumarchais had few problems and enjoyed perfect matrimonial bliss. His not-so-young wife idolized him, showered him with delightful feminine attentions, and wrapped him in material comfort. Moreover, their genuine common love for music created a close bond between them. Madeleine was particularly skilled in playing an old instrument then having a vogue, the harp, and she taught Pierre-Augustin how to play it.

Probably the fickle Beaumarchais would have eventually tired of Madeleine. But suddenly she fell seriously ill. Beaumarchais called four of the best doctors in Paris to her bedside. She died nevertheless shortly afterward, on September 29, 1757. From the records kept of the symptoms of her illness, it is almost certain that she had an acute attack of typhoid fever.

Beaumarchais' enemies later whispered that he had poisoned his wife, presumably for her money. In fact, Madeleine's death was a hard blow to him, even financially. Because he had completely forgotten to have their property settlement legally registered, he was not entitled to any share of his wife's estate and practically everything went either to her own family or to her first husband's heirs. Beaumarchais made an amicable agreement with his wife's relatives and, without a struggle, gave up the beautiful house in which he had spent so many happy hours.

Beaumarchais did not go back to the Rue Saint-Denis house, however. Although his salary as *Contrôleur Clerc d'Office* was a mere pittance, he decided against a reconciliation with his father, for a return to his parents' home would have inevitably meant a return to the everlasting drudgery of a shopkeeper's life. Instead he took temporary quarters with a friend who lived in one of the humblest districts in Paris, the murky atmosphere of which well fitted his present somber mood.

To while away his sorrow, Beaumarchais started working on the mechanism of the harp, as he had worked, a few years before, on the escapement system of the watch. After a short time, he made a new pedal arrangement that was adopted at once by all the harp makers in Paris.

Just about that time, his mother became very ill and, on August 18, 1758, died. Her last months had been darkened by the cloud hanging over Pierre-Augustin's relations with his father. The two men became formally reconciled at her deathbed and from that time on saw each other regularly. But years elapsed before their previous friendliness was completely restored.

2. *Four Princesses*

BEAUMARCHAIS was rescued from loneliness and gloom by one of his court acquaintances, Charles Lenormant d'Etioles, Mme de Pompadour's husband. Lenormant's wife's close—much too close—connection with the King had made his position at Versailles equivocal and embarrassing, so he appeared there as little as possible and spent most of his time in the neighboring Château of Etioles. At Etioles he kept up an almost incessant round of shows, masquerades, and banquets in order to forget his painful and shameful matrimonial misadventure. To these parties, he invited mainly people who, like himself, wanted to escape from some inward, hidden distress by a merry whirl in frivolous company.

Soon Lenormant found Beaumarchais both a perfect guest and an ideal entertainer with an unexpected talent for improvising, on request, short, witty, saucy plays. Lenormant had had a stage built in one of the largest rooms of his château and loved to present farcical, even somewhat ribald comedies there. With incredible deftness, Beaumarchais could sketch a grotesque character, turn out a piquant dialogue, or compose a few tuneful and gay *chansons*.

Lenormant sometimes "borrowed" actresses from the regular Paris theaters for his private performances and often Beaumarchais coached them in their parts. After a while, it was rumored that one, then two, then three of these broad-minded beauties had briefly but intimately entered the life of the merry young widower.

At Etioles Beaumarchais came into contact with one of the most influential lords of the time, the Duc de La Vallière. A grand-nephew of the Duchess who had made the name of La Vallière famous under Louis XIV, the Duke had access to the highest court circles. He was a member of the small, restricted set that clustered around Louis XV's daughters. Mesdames Louise, Sophie, Victoire, and Adelaïde had reached, respectively, the ages of twenty-two, twenty-five, twenty-six, and twenty-seven and were still unmarried. Complicated reasons of state and their father's selfishness had always prevented marriages that might have enabled them to lead a more or less normal life. Furthermore, the coils of strict court etiquette, for many years wound tightly around them, had half choked their moral development and thwarted the growth of their characters. So much ceremonial attended their public appearances that little was known about them, even among the courtiers—except, perhaps, that Madame Victoire, who evidently ate too much, was beginning to get quite fat; that Madame Louise, who was morbidly shy, looked at people sideways, hen-fashion; that Madame Sophie seemed slow-witted and dull, as she indeed was. Madame Adelaïde alone possessed charm, beauty, and a quick temper. All of them were virtuous, pious, and bored.

One day, the princesses asked M. de La Vallière what had caused the recent vogue of the harp. M. de La Vallière confessed complete ignorance on that subject, but told them that his good friend, M. de Beaumarchais, a very charming young man indeed, was an expert on that instrument and could doubtless satisfy their curiosity. Would, then, M. de La Vallière bring that young man to Versailles and present him to them soon? M. de Beaumarchais would be profoundly flattered by such a great honor, the Duke assured the princesses.

Thus Beaumarchais was introduced, in 1759, to the daughters of the King of France. His personality and winning manners, probably as much as his explanation of the harp, made a vivid impression on the four young women, and they asked him to become their music teacher. His services, said Beaumarchais, were entirely at their disposal. But he shrewdly declined to ask the princesses for any remuneration whatever.

A strange association then began between the King's daughters and Beaumarchais. It lasted for four years. Regularly, every week, he was received in their private apartments. He did not display before them the brisk, boisterous quality that had made him so popular at Etioles. He showed only a discreet cheerfulness, carefully and cleverly tinged at first with that subdued melancholy, so becoming in a young widower, which women always love to dispel.

The princesses dispelled his melancholy, and he dispelled their feeling of loneliness. Once they had learned to play the harp, after a fashion, they wished to study the guitar, the tambourine, and then something else. With characteristic versatility, Beaumarchais was always ready to teach them anything they wanted to know. He wrote easy musical scores for their use, and whenever they came back exhausted from some wearisome court function, or when he intuitively felt that they happened to be in no mood to do any work, he spent their "lesson" playing or singing for them.

Little by little, a shade of protective, feminine tenderness crept into the princesses' attitude toward this talented, handsome, and modest-looking young man. On his side, Beaumarchais undoubtedly realized how enormously the King's daughters could influence his career. Somehow he managed to give each of the young women the impression that she alone occupied a special place in his mind, yet was careful not to bestow too much attention on any one of them, lest he thereby arouse the jealousy of the others.

He succeeded at this difficult, subtle game probably because his feelings were not actually feigned. He certainly found pleasure in the company of the four princesses, who, though lightheaded and capricious, were well bred and consistently friendly toward him. He made every effort not to show marked preference for any particular princess, but keen and malicious observers, who were not lacking at court, detected a distinctly affectionate quality in his attitude toward Mme Adelaïde. Mme Adelaïde's good looks are perhaps an adequate explanation of his predilection for her. Yet it may be noted that she was the eldest of the four princesses and that, compared with her submissive and yielding sisters, she alone displayed a strong will and had a somewhat imperious countenance.

However pleasant in itself and promising for the future, Beaumarchais' association with the King's daughters brought him, for the present, no tangible profit. Asking the princesses openly for money would have relegated him, in their eyes, to the class of fortune seeker and lost him his privileged status of friend. In fact, far from deriving any financial advantage from his intimacy with the princesses, he often had to lend them money. Living as they did in an utterly artificial, sheltered environment, remote from normal contingencies, the princesses could not imagine anyone permanently short of funds. Whenever they wanted to buy some expensive bauble and happened not to have the necessary cash at hand, they simply asked M. de Beaumarchais to make the purchase for them. They had every intention of paying him back sometime, but such trifles were utterly unimportant to them.

Beaumarchais' small resources were melting rapidly away when unforeseen circumstances suddenly gave him an opportunity to acquire wealth—wealth beyond his wildest dreams.

3. *A Modern Croesus*

ABOUT forty years earlier, four remarkably gifted and enterprising brothers, the sons of a humble village innkeeper named Pâris, had laid the basis of one of the most stupendous financial empires in the history of France. The three youngest had adopted different *noms de guerre*, so they might be easily distinguished from their elder brother, Antoine Pâris. For a quarter of a century already, his name as well as their names—Claude Pâris La Montagne, Joseph Pâris-Duverney, and Jean Pâris de Montmartel—had been whispered throughout France with a mixture of envy and awe. Their power seemed almost boundless and, at the same time, disturbingly mysterious. The Pâris brothers had risen slowly, carefully shunning publicity, but forging relentlessly ahead. Working independently yet in perfect agreement with each other, in the end they covered France with a network of commercial and industrial enterprises all neatly dovetailing. Their greatest stroke of luck had occurred when the daughter of one of their clerks, Jeanne Poisson, became the King's favorite as Mme de Pompadour. For fifteen years the close alliance between Mme de Pompadour and the Pâris brothers had constituted one of the main pivots around which the political and financial life of France revolved.

Among the shrewd and mighty Pâris brothers, Joseph Pâris-Duverney was probably the shrewdest and the mightiest. In the division of interests agreed to in their partnership compact, he had received as his share the supplies for the French Army and the all-important lumber trade. The Seven Years' War had been a source of colossal profits for him, and he was now immensely rich, enormously powerful, and yet unhappy. Indeed, though he was well over seventy, he had not yet been able to fulfill his greatest desire.

His ally, Mme de Pompadour, had for years hoped to play in Louis XV's life the same part Mme de Maintenon had played in Louis XIV's life. Mme de Maintenon had made Louis XIV build the famed school of Saint-Cyr for the daughters of the aristocracy, and Saint-Cyr was considered one of the finest achievements of the Grand Monarch and his consort. Mme de Pompadour wanted to attach her name to the founding of an outstanding school for young noblemen in Paris. But knowing that it was not easy to make Louis XV do great things, she decided to proceed in a devious, diplomatic manner. Confidentially she told her friend Pâris-Duverney of her ambition, and he agreed to build a military college on the Champ-de-Mars. The cost was no problem, and it would not be difficult, they thought, to have the King officially accept the school.

But within a few years, Mme de Pompadour lost practically all interest in her old scheme, while Pâris-Duverney became positively enamored of his new work. In spite of, or perhaps because of, his success in finances, Pâris-Duverney was lonely, not a little cynical, and felt surrounded by greed. Perhaps unconsciously he craved an ideal. His *Ecole Militaire* became his ideal. An imposing, truly magnificent building now stood on the Champ-de-Mars, and five hundred cadets received regular training of the highest order there. One of Pâris-Duverney's nephews, Jean-Baptiste Pâris de Meyzieu, efficiently ran the institution. Only one thing was lacking: personal recognition by the King. Pâris-Duverney knew that if he died before that recognition came, his school would be dissolved almost at once, and nothing of his would remain but money for his heirs to squander and a nameless, aimless, soulless building.

To please Pâris-Duverney, Mme de Pompadour made several half hearted attempts to induce Louis XV to visit the school. But she had bitter enemies at court, particularly in the royal family, certain members of which fiercely opposed the project precisely because they knew that it had been started at her instigation. As was his custom in all embarrassing situations, Louis XV did nothing.

Pâris-Duverney realized that Mme de Pompadour could not give him much help. She was now old and worn and barely hanging onto her questionable position. She could not risk an open conflict with the royal family for a school that now meant little to her. But the school meant a great deal to him, and he sought ways and means to circumvent the obstacles in his path.

Pâris-Duverney did not know Beaumarchais, but he had heard, as everyone had at Versailles, of his unusual situation in the princesses' circle. He approached the young man cautiously, letting him know that he was very much interested in him and his fortunes. He did not offer him a crude bargain. It was up to

Beaumarchais to understand—if he had wit—what the old financier wanted and—if he had wisdom—to respond to his advances.

Beaumarchais lacked neither wisdom nor wit. He suggested a visit to the military school to the princesses. The princesses, bored with the humdrum routine of Versailles, fell in enthusiastically with his proposal.

On the day of the escapade, the four young women enjoyed the trip, the change, and, above all, the parade of the stalwart, handsome cadets, all spick-and-span in their splendid uniforms. During the parade, Madame Adelaïde suddenly declared that she felt very tired and asked M. de Beaumarchais to lend her his arm. Thus, in full view of five hundred scions of France's noblest families, the former watchmaker stood proudly with the King's eldest daughter leaning familiarly upon him.

The princesses returned to Versailles and were still bubbling over with excitement when their father called to see them in their private apartments that evening. They gave him such a glowing account of their visit that he decided to see the school himself.

The King's visit, which took place on August 18, 1760, was solemn and formal and, for Pâris-Duverney, had the long-hoped-for result: a few days later, his *Ecole Militaire* was officially recognized as a royal school.

Pâris-Duverney felt an immense gratitude toward Beaumarchais, which was soon increased tenfold by the young man's modest and deferential bearing. "M. Duverney swears that he will treat me like a son," Beaumarchais wrote in a letter about his new-found protector. Indeed, a strange father-son relationship developed almost at once between them. Pierre-Augustin's feelings for André Caron, though definitely affectionate in some respects, had always been marred by an unavowed yet perceptible element of revolt. In Pâris-Duverney, Beaumarchais found personal dignity, superiority, and helpful guidance without any admixture of discipline or rivalry. In Beaumarchais, Pâris-Duverney found even more. The military school was practically off his hands now and was no longer his life's goal. Pâris-Duverney soon transferred all his interest to Beaumarchais, who seemed to him a replica of himself forty years before: a young man of common birth, with no other assets than his courage and an amazingly nimble mind, fighting his way upward in a haughty, hostile, aristocratic society.

Pâris-Duverney discovered that Beaumarchais had an extraordinary knack for grasping the most difficult financial problems. It became a joy for him to initiate such an apt, keen, eager disciple into the intricacies of big business. He was immensely proud when he saw his pupil, under his supervision at first, and then independently, make a few speculative coups, for they boded a most brilliant future success for Beaumarchais.

Before long the old financier and his ambitious protégé formed a close personal association. During the ten years this lasted, they exchanged more than six hundred letters. To communicate safely with each other, they invented a code they called their "Oriental style," which has remained up to now largely undeciphered. But if this correspondence fails to give us exact clues about their speculations, it bears witness to their intimate, continued collaboration and to their mutual trust.

Thanks to Pâris-Duverney's help, within a short time Beaumarchais became a very rich man. However, he retained his position as music teacher to the royal princesses, who, by the way, seem to have been hardly aware of the change in his fortunes. For them he was only the man who had brought a ray of sunshine into the gray monotony of their lives, and of whom they grew fonder and fonder.

4. Pinpricks and Swordplay

IN TIME, Beaumarchais won the favor of other members of the royal family as well. The princesses' brother, the Dauphin Louis, was often seen talking privately with him, and it was rumored that the heir to the throne had declared that M. de Beaumarchais was the only person who had never told him anything but the truth. One day, as Beaumarchais was playing the harp for the princesses, Louis XV himself entered the room, unannounced, through a back door. Beaumarchais did not notice the King's presence at first and remained seated, but when he became aware of his blunder, he rose at once in utmost confustion. The King, however, with a gesture of good-natured familiarity for which many a courtier would have gladly paid with his blood, put his hand on the young man's shoulder, pressed him down onto his armchair, and smilingly motioned to him to proceed playing.

Such marks of personal favor bestowed on an obscure commoner soon fostered dangerous feelings of envy and rage among the noblemen of the court. For a while they taunted him, more or less slyly, about his humble origin. Once a young fop came toward him, surrounded by a crowd of snickering courtiers, loudly praised Beaumarchais' skill as a watchmaker, and then begged him to find out, please, what was wrong with a watch he had just purchased. Beaumarchais, sensing the contempt behind this request, at first tried to excuse himself and go away. But the courtiers' guffaws put him on his mettle. With assumed modesty, he warned the owner of the watch that, for lack of practice, he had grown lately very clumsy. When the nobleman, however, ironically insisted, Beaumarchais consented to examine the evidently costly and delicate timepiece. Then, as though by accident, he dropped it upon a marble step near by. The watch broke into fragments, and Beaumarchais, bowing, withdrew while the onlookers jeered at the dumbfounded and discomfited owner.

Pinpricks having failed, Beaumarchais' enemies decided to test him with the sword. In March 1763, a certain Chevalier des C***, known as one of the best swordsmen in Versailles, under the flimsiest of pretexts passed such remarks about him that Beaumarchais had no choice, according to the code of honor of the time, but to follow his challenger to the dueling ground. The two went to a secluded spot behind Meudon. Beaumarchais had taken lessons in fencing, but was not in any way an expert swordsman. Yet either through sheer luck or thanks to his natural deftness and agility, he soon put a foot of cold steel into his opponent's chest.

Panic-stricken, Beaumarchais rushed to help the fallen Chevalier and tried to stop the flow of blood with his handkerchief. The Chevaleir des C*** was a gentleman and told Beaumarchais to leave him at once. Although the fight had been perfectly fair, his relatives would undoubtedly seek with all their power to avenge him. Beaumarchais, who felt utterly useless anyway, rode to Meudon as fast as he could, sought out a surgeon, and directed him to the place where the wounded man lay. Then he went to Paris and waited for developments.

The Chevalier des C*** was promptly found by the surgeon

and transported, almost dead, to Paris. He lingered on a week, but to the end steadfastly refused to name the man with whom he had fought, saying, according to witnesses: "I got what I deserved. To please persons for whom I have no esteem, I challenged somebody who had never given me any offense."

Beaumarchais was seriously worried, however. Public opinion, it is true, not only condoned fair single combats, but looked down upon any man who refused to defend his honor, arms in hand, as a contemptible coward. But the police ignored these niceties and strictly enforced the edicts against dueling, especially if powerful people secretly prodded the search for a weaker "guilty" party.

After some hesitation, Beaumarchais decided to inform the King's daughters of the whole affair. The princesses were thrilled to the marrow by his story and admitted that he could not have acted more honorably and bravely, under the circumstances. They promised to speak to their father on his behalf. Louis XV, as a gentleman, could not but approve of a young fellow ready to fight to the death, if provoked. As the King's attitude became known in Versailles, everybody, including the police, agreed that the wisest thing was to let the whole matter rest.

Attacks against Beaumarchais did not cease, however, but now took the form of insidious rumors whispered by slanderers. Beaumarchais, it was said, had been a street musician, even a beggar; he had accepted money from depraved, rich old women; he had murdered Francquet; he had poisoned his own wife . . .

Certain of these rumors had no foundation whatever. How disprove them? Others had their origin in facts so wildly exaggerated or distorted that it would have taken endless explanation to establish the truth. Moreover, explanation would merely draw public attention more forcibly upon these calumnies and not dispel the cloud of suspicion and doubt now forming around him.

Beaumarchais was more affected by this vague, anonymous, intangible hostility than he would have been by any direct aggression. Since he could not strike back at anyone, he grew distrustful of everyone. He became impatient at well-meant criticism, resentful at imaginary slights, irritable, fretful and sarcastic.

5. *Nobility*

BEAUMARCHAIS believed his common birth the main cause of his difficulties. Many commoners had, of course, risen rapidly at Versailles, through either merit or sheer intrigue, without encountering hatred. But as a rule these parvenus knew how to be compliant and unassuming when necessary. Beaumarchais, on the contrary, constantly felt that he had to assert himself. In the company of people who he knew liked and trusted him—the royal princesses or Pâris-Duverney—he was openhearted, affectionate and entertaining. In the company of others, he inspired mainly aversion and fear through his perpetual jocularity and his biting wit.

So far, Beaumarchais was no social *révolté.* Far from wishing to destroy nobility, he ardently wanted to be an integral part of the aristocratic system. So, on December 9, 1761, for 85,000 livres he bought from a certain Denis Janot de Miron the office of *Secrétaire du Roi.* As secretary, he had no work or salary, but automatically held the rank of *Ecuyer*—squire—the lowest degree in the French nobility. As *écuyer*, Pierre-Augustin now had the legal right to bear the estate name, de Beaumarchais, which till then had merely been a *nom de guerre*. But much to his surprise, Caron de Beaumarchais soon found out that his purchased nobility made no difference in his status at court. For most of the courtiers, he remained an obnoxious upstart, the son of that Caron who sold and repaired watches on the Rue Saint-Denis.

Beaumarchais had long been concerned about the appearance of his father's shop. Particularly, he imagined that the naïve but pretentious sign painted upon the ceiling made everyone smile contemptuously. Often he had begged his father—in vain—to erase it. Early in January 1761, when André Caron asked his son what he wanted for a New Year's present, Pierre-Augustin renewed his request, which was grudgingly granted.

Shortly after Beaumarchais had deserted the shop, in 1756, his sister Fanchon had married a young Swiss watchmaker named Jean-Antoine Lépine. Lépine was a skilled craftsman, a steady worker, and for a while André Caron had hoped that his son-in-law would fill the place left empty by Pierre-Augustin. But Lépine wanted to enlarge and modernize the shop, whereas Caron opposed any innovation and brooked no interference with his business. They separated on friendly terms, and Lépine set up his own business, which soon became very prosperous.

Caron found it ever more difficult to keep up with new and younger competitors. Once again he worried about bills. His health grew poorer. He was losing his grip and knew it, but proudly carried on. Several times, however, he had to accept large loans from Pierre-Augustin. These loans contributed more than anything else to reconciling father and son. The father could not but appreciate his son's open-handed generosity. The son felt happy to be able to lighten his father's financial burden and perhaps show him that he had, after all, not turned into a wastrel as the old man had predicted.

There was no question of André Caron's repaying these loans, and by 1762 they turned into regular subsidies. That year, André Caron had a long and painful illness. His life was in no danger, but his temper soured markedly, and his occupation as watchmaker became mere pretense.

At the beginning of 1763, Beaumarchais bought a large and commodious house, No. 26 Rue de Condé. Considering his social and financial position, he felt that he needed a handsome, substantial residence. He furnished it luxuriously, and it had a truly aristocratic air. It included an elegant reception room, a spacious dining room, many bedrooms, and extensive servants' quarters. Beaumarchais was now attended by a valet. A chef reigned over his kitchen help. A coachman and a groom looked after his carriage and his horses. Indeed, it was a gentleman's establishment. But the mansion seemed somewhat dull and empty, inhabited only by a childless widower. Then Beaumarchais thought of an arrangement that would solve both his personal problems and his family's. André Caron should give up his shop altogether and, along with Julie and Tonton, move into his son's house.

Certain doubts, however, hung for a time over Beaumarchais' mind. Wouldn't his father grow more and more surly and crabbed? Wouldn't he feel humiliated to be completely dependent upon his son's good will? This last doubt very probably betrayed in Beaumarchais' subconscious mind a secret desire to pay back the humiliation of his adolescent days by compelling his father to recognize his superior worth.

Beaumarchais wrote his father a letter frankly stating his

suggestions as well as his hesitations. Whether or not he realized it, this letter represented his counterpart of the treaty he had signed with his father thirteen years before.

André Caron gratefully accepted Pierre-Augustin's terms. "I must try to set the mind of such a decent and respectful son at rest by assuring him that he may expect nothing but kindness, courtesy, and the tenderest friendship on his father's part. In truth, the illness from which I am recuperating has been so painful, so protracted, and so undeserved that it is not surprising my temper has suffered somewhat . . . But is this a reason to conjecture that, once in the midst of the pleasant life your filial affection is preparing for me, I would disturb the quietness and the pleasantness of your own?"

André Caron was delighted with the prospect of retiring and spending the rest of his days in comfort and leisure. The idea of humiliation that had loomed so large in his son's mind had never entered his own. "From the bottom of my heart, I bless heaven for finding, in my old age, a son with such an excellent nature; and far from being humiliated by my present situation, my soul rises and warms itself at the touching idea of owing my happiness, after God, to him alone."

After this answer, the family was once more gathered under the same roof. At once Julie became lady of the house. She was now twenty-eight years old. She had not gained much in beauty, but she had lost nothing of her merry disposition and vivaciousness. Her admiration for her brother had lately grown into veritable worship, and she now tried to identify herself with him in every way. When, in 1761, Beaumarchais had become his official name, she had refused to be Mlle Caron any longer and had called herself

Mlle de Beaumarchais. She had no right to that appellation, of course, but she was a strong-willed young person. Mlle de Beaumarchais she was, and Mlle de Beaumarchais she remained.

After her sister had assumed an "aristocratic" name, Tonton decided that she could not stay plain Jeanne-Marguerite Caron, and she consulted her big brother on that important subject. An uncle of theirs, Caron de Boisgarnier, had recently died after an honorable army career. Why not revive his *nom de guerre?* And so Tonton became Mlle de Boisgarnier—a pretty, fluffy little thing, spoiled by everyone. With her youth and charm she graced the imposing residence of her brother, the wealthy, well-connected M. de Beaumarchais, Secretary to the King.

M. de Beaumarchais could look back with pride on the long way he had traveled the last five years. But he wanted to go still farther ahead. His job as Controller of the Pantry was, he now thought, altogether too humble. *Grand Maître des Eaux et Forêts* seemed much more suitable. This office would place him socially in a truly eminent position. The cost, of course, was enormous: half a million livres. But Pâris-Duverney was willing to advance that sum to Beaumarchais, and Beaumarchais, evidently not doing too badly speculating in military supplies, figured that he could pay back the whole amount within a few years.

At first, negotiations for purchasing the office of Grand Master of Forestry went smoothly and without a hitch. Thanks to the royal princesses' support, he even secured the King's assent and signature. But when everything seemed arranged, and only a mere formality remained—the acceptance by the other Masters of his appointment—he found himself suddenly and decisively checked. The Masters flatly refused to receive him. M. de Beaumarchais was of too low, too common birth. This was sheer pretext, as Beaumarchais pointed out at once in a sarcastic memorial. Indeed, many of the Masters were of no higher extraction than himself: one was the son of a secondhand jeweler; another the son of a wool comber; another, the son of a wigmaker. The truth was that Beaumarchais had offended too many people at court. Wise old Pâris-Duverney cautioned him against pressing his case: let him fall back on some other less spectacular position that would be honorable yet attract less antagonism and envy.

Raging, Beaumarchais fell back on a judgeship and, in 1763, became *Lieutenant Général des Chasses aux Baillage et Capitainerie de la Varenne du Louvre*. There was no difficulty this time. The appointment was subject only to the approval of the Captain General of the Royal Hunt, who happened to be the Duc de La Vallière, Beaumarchais' friend.

For twenty-two years, with only two short interruptions, Beaumarchais sat every week as a judge in the Louvre. His jurisdiction covered all violations of the game laws within a radius of about fifty miles of Paris, particularly in the royal preserves. His judicial duties consisted in enforcing a multitude of ordinances, statutes, edicts, and rules generally dating back to the Middle Ages. Most of them were plainly antiquated in spirit; all had to be applied to the letter, regardless of circumstances. The procedure at the Louvre tribunal was narrow, traditional, and formal. The penalties meted out, usually extremely harsh, seem to a modern mind shockingly out of proportion to the offenses committed: shooting or trapping a rabbit out of season or in a forbidden zone, erecting or pulling down a fence or a wall without the consent of the proper authorities.

Beaumarchais' close contact with the workings of "justice" dealt a hard blow to his respect for the social system of the day. Before his amazed eyes the majesty of law dissolved into petty squabbles on minute points about things that did not really matter. Year after year, he had to listen to endless disputes on the interpretation of obscure texts, the whole meaning of which was changed by the position or the omission of a single comma. Time and again he noted the peculiar twist in the lawyers' mind that made them pin their argument on a technical detail and, with a perfectly tranquil conscience, disregard moral right and wrong. Slowly he began to see that many elements of the prevailing regime were ridiculously obsolete and that basic reforms were advisable—nay, inevitable, and in the very near future.

For the time being, whatever he may have thought, he always took great care to discharge his duties with utmost earnestness. On no occasion did he show himself slack, indifferent, or bored. In fact, he seems to have enjoyed having two authentic blue-blooded aristocrats, the Comte de Rochechouart and the Comte de Marcouville, as his subordinates. The Duc de La Vallière, officially Chief Justice of the Louvre Tribunal, practically never came to the court over which he was supposed to preside, so Beaumarchais regularly substituted for him and relished the prestige that such a situation gave him.

6. *Love and Hope*

BEAUMARCHAIS seemed most auspiciously and securely launched in his career. All he had to do now was to settle down and marry a girl of suitable condition and age. Soon he found one who seemed to fill the necessary requirements. Pauline Le Breton came of a wealthy family of French planters from the tropical island of Santo Domingo, and her fortune was evaluated at two million livres. Her parents had died while she was still a child, and unscrupulous relatives had for many years managed her properties more to their advantage than to her own. Finally, she had come to Paris to get help in fighting the legal administrators of her domains and probably also to find a husband.

Pauline was sixteen years old and lived with an old aunt who happened to be one of Pâris-Duverney's friends. The old aunt heard that Beaumarchais had met M. Jean de Clugny, the Governor of Santo Domingo. Would he do the girl the favor of writing to that important official, asking him to look after her interests in the island? Beaumarchais, unfortunately, was only casually acquainted with Clugny. The King's daughters, however, knew him very well. A recommendation from them would doubtless carry weight with the Governor. Beaumarchais spoke to the princesses of the orphan's case, and they not only promised their assistance, but even bade him bring his young protégée to Versailles and present her to them.

For two years Beaumarchais gave Pauline Le Breton both advice and help. He tried to straighten out her unbelievably tangled financial affairs. He lent her large sums of money when cash was needed to take action in Santo Domingo. In the end he decided to send his cousin, Pichon de Villeneuve, to the island to investigate ways of rehabilitating her huge, though evidently run-down, estate.

Pauline Le Breton was frequently seen at the Rue de Condé house, where she had been heartily welcomed by Julie and Boisgarnier. But it soon became obvious that she was attracted there mainly by the presence of their brother. When she had first heard that Beaumarchais was one of Pâris-Duverney's friends, she had pictured him as an old man, forbidding in appearance, standoffish, and dry. Instead she had discovered a handsome young fellow, always elegantly dressed, always perfectly mannered, yet vital, genial, and kind. He had a wide brow, intelligent gray-blue eyes, a fair complexion, a firm chin—a keen and forceful face. He was a man to whom it would be pleasant to be married, a man not difficult to love.

Beaumarchais, on his side, had found an engaging personality in Pauline, though not the type that had most appealed to him in the past. He was now thirty-one years old; she barely eighteen. She looked helpless and sweet. Not by any stretch of the imagination could she play a motherly, protective rôle for a man. Born in the tropics, she breathed a fragrant, exotic charm. What adolescent boy has not dreamed of a wonderful tropical island with a long, narrow, golden beach lined with tall, swaying palm trees? In Beaumarchais' still adolescent mind, the magic of the faraway blended with the fascination of the girl's blooming youth and her comely shape. How could he fail to be drawn to this voluptuous-looking creature with soft, submissive eyes? She allowed him a few liberties, and Beaumarchais, a widower for more than six years, felt his blood coursing wildly through his veins.

Was this love? Very often, little more is needed to bring about a marriage proposal. Yet Beaumarchais wavered. Soon the girl had misgivings about him. Pierre-Augustin puzzled her. He would pass from one mood to another with disconcerting suddenness. At times he was burningly passionate; then a casual remark, a single word, perhaps, and he would launch into explanations about finances, juggling large figures, his mind keen, hard, and cold. Then he turned to poetic evocations of the tropical moon or became sentimental about palm trees.

Pauline was not particularly interested in the tropical moon and had no enthusiasm for palm trees: they were commonplace to her. She hated business and considered figures a nuisance. As for the rest, she was not in any way frigid, yet she often felt ill at ease before the young man's spells of impetuosity and somewhat abashed by his boldness. Then, when she discreetly tried to guide their conversation toward church and wedding bells, she could not help but sense his shying away.

At that time, the Rue de Condé house seethed with romance. Boisgarnier had a worshipful slave almost constantly at her feet, Octave Janot de Miron, from whose father Beaumarchais had purchased his office of Secretary to the King. His good qualities could be measured by the bushel: honesty, decency, sincerity, constancy, propriety, reliability, devotedness. As a husband, he would have been perfect. As a lover, Boisgarnier found him dull, so she teased him, tormented him, and played with him artfully and gracefully, as a kitten with a mouse. She would pretend to be difficult to please, and utterly indifferent to him, and he would go away in despair. She would let him run free for a while, then quickly catch him again and triumphantly bring him back.

Julie also had a steady admirer, the Chevalier de Séguirand. Like his friend Miron, Séguirand was a lawyer and he too had far from an easy time with his capricious lady love. By a strange coincidence, he and Pauline Le Breton came from the same district in Santo Domingo, though he had not been acquainted with her before his visits to the Beaumarchais house. Julie de Beaumarchais made up for her lack of classical beauty by her striking appearance. She was tall and slender and had large, dark, expressive eyes, but her main charm lay in her scintillating wit and her constant liveliness. She made sport of her Chevalier somewhat more harshly than her sister did of her faithful Miron, for at bottom Julie was not truly in love with him. Her whole capacity for deep affection was already centered, perhaps unbeknown to herself, upon her brilliant brother, but she found it fun to keep an eligible man dangling. As long as he lent himself willingly to the game, everything was for the best in the Rue de Condé house as far as Julie was concerned.

"Our house," Julie wrote to a friend at that time, "is a regular dovecote where everyone lives on love and hope. I am the one who laughs most because I am least in love . . . Beaumarchais is a naughty fellow who worries and grieves Pauline by his levity. Boisgarnier and Miron discuss sentiment breathlessly and by orderly degrees rise to the height of sublime disorder. As for the Chevalier and me, it is even worse than that. He is as loving as an angel, as ardent as an archangel, as impassioned as a seraph, while I am as gay as a linnet . . . and as mischievous as a demon. Love does not make me go *lon-lan-la* like the others. Yet, in spite of my madness, I could not keep from tasting it."

This atmosphere of love eventually affected even old Caron. With a mixture of amusement and amazement, Beaumarchais, Julie, and Boisgarnier noticed that their father had also fallen victim to Cupid's archery. A widow of the neighborhood, a Mme Henry, was the object of his devotion. Like a timid swain, he sighed for her. His temper, until lately so morose, changed suddenly and completely. A streak of frivolity that had been faintly perceptible in his character at last broke into the open. He did not make a long face now at the gaiety of youth. He encouraged it, he partook of it as much as his age allowed, and perhaps even more.

Beaumarchais could not help smiling when he remembered the fine moral sermons his father had delivered to him only a few years before. Yet, despite a certain irony he felt within, he was genuinely fond of the old man. He was glad to see him enjoy himself and delighted that he refrained from spoiling the good time everybody else had. And, indeed, in the year 1763, a thoroughly good time was had by all in the Beaumarchais house.

Chapter 3

ADVENTURES IN SPAIN

1. A Maiden in Distress

In February, 1764, André Caron received distressing news of his daughters living in Spain. His son-in-law, Guilbert, had encountered serious difficulty in establishing himself as an architect in Madrid. During the initial struggle, Marie-Josèphe, with her sister Marie-Louise's help, had opened a small millinery shop. Eventually her "French" hats sold so well that the family attained an honorable position and modest comfort. The Guilberts had two sons and could afford to send the elder to a boarding school in Paris. Moreover, in their home on the Vía Jacometrens they regularly received a few Spaniards of somewhat higher rank than their own: army officers, successful writers, and dignitaries of the Church. All this was satisfying, but did not in any way measure up to their earlier dreams of fortune.

Lisette's dreams had suffered an even worse fate. The Spanish husband of her girlish fancies had postponed his appearance from year to year. She was now thirty-four and still a spinster. However, a young man from the Canary Islands, Don José Clavijo y Fajardo, had wooed her for a long time, not altogether in vain. Clavijo was a journalist and an author who had come to Madrid with great ambitions but little money. For many years he was so poor that the lovers agreed not to announce their engagement until he acquired the means of supporting a wife. In time, he became the editor of a successful periodical, *El Pensador*. Recently he had been appointed Keeper of the Crown Archives, and this eminent, well-paid position undoubtedly enabled him to marry Lisette, yet she was left waiting.

The delay in their expected wedding caused a great deal of whispering and tittering in Madrid's French colony. Evidently the Spaniard intended throwing over the French girl, if he had not already done so. But why should he jilt her after six years of open and constant courtship?

Lisette, aware of these rumors, saw her chances of marrying someone else dwindle daily. Besides, she was fond of the man, though she hated him for the shameful way he had treated her. She now sat all alone in her room for hours on end, crying. A poor, helpless girl in a foreign country, with no man to defend her honor —Guilbert was evidently well meaning, but utterly ineffectual— she thought herself completely ruined through Clavijo's villainy.

When Beaumarchais heard of these circumstances, he impulsively resolved to rush to his sister's aid. He had no difficulty in obtaining the princesses' permission to absent himself from their service for so noble a task as rescuing a maiden in distress. They even insisted upon procuring him a letter of introduction from Prime Minister Choiseul of France to Prime Minister Grimaldi of Spain. M. de La Vallière offered no objection to someone's substituting for his substitute at the Louvre tribunal and, along with his best wishes, gave Beaumarchais the leave he had asked.

When Beaumarchais spoke to Pâris-Duverney of going to Spain, the old financier considered the matter from a different angle. The Seven Years' War had just ended disastrously for France. By the Treaty of Paris (1763), France had been stripped of practically all her colonies. The public at large was not yet aware of the seriousness of the loss, but it would undoubtedly bring about a grave economic crisis within France very soon. The Spanish colonial empire, however, had remained almost intact. Indeed, to compensate Spain for the cession of Florida to England, France had given her Louisiana.

Would it be possible, Pâris-Duverney wondered, to obtain—amicably, of course, and unofficially, perhaps—economic arrangements from the Spaniards that would make up for the losses sustained by the French? Spain had passed the peak of her colonizing power and was not particularly interested in Louisiana, where so many French interests were vested. Why not create a company, with French capital under a Spanish name, that would give France an opportunity to keep her trade connections with that colony? Then there was the African Negro slave trade. The Spanish possessions all over America badly needed slaves and Spanish slavers seemed unable to bring them in adequate numbers. French shipping could be used for that purpose, to the great advantage of all parties concerned.

These delicate questions could not easily be discussed through ordinary diplomatic channels. But a clever man speaking for responsible persons in France might pave the way toward a satisfactory understanding—especially if he had persuasive personal arguments in abundance in his pockets. Pâris-Duverney entrusted Beaumarchais with two hundred thousand livres' worth of persuasiveness.

Beaumarchais left Paris by stagecoach on May 1, 1764, and reached Madrid about two weeks later. He went directly to the Guilberts' house. To his astonishment, he found Lisette almost engaged to another man. A middle-aged, respectable, well-to-do French merchant named Durand had unexpectedly proposed to her. The girl had not refused his offer, but she still thought of Clavijo and did not know whether she wanted to marry Durand or punish the beloved rascal.

In any case, early the following day Beaumarchais called at Clavijo's residence. Clavijo was temporarily occupying a sumptuous mansion belonging to a high official who had gone to the country for a rest. Beaumarchais did not let him know at first that he was Lisette's brother, and Clavijo hospitably invited him to share his morning breakfast. Clavijo did not look like a heartbreaker. He was short and fat and had a round, jolly face. He seemed a Sancho Panza: practical, cheerful, sensuous, and eager to avoid conflicts. But he was endowed with a great deal of common sense and cunning.

When Beaumarchais revealed his identity and the purpose of

his visit, a tragicomic scene developed between the two men. In the end, Clavijo signed a declaration confessing that he had promised to marry Mlle Caron and had failed to keep his pledge. He also stated that the lady had, according to his own expression, "always been pure and without blemish." The document ended with the promise to give her "any reparation she desired."

Shortly afterward, Clavijo called at the Guilberts'. Lisette ran to her room, locked herself in, and refused to see the traitor. Then she relented, and the lovers became completely reconciled.

The news of the forthcoming marriage of Doña María Caron and Don José Clavijo, Keeper of the Crown Archives, spread like wildfire throughout Madrid. Clavijo and Beaumarchais were often seen together, and Beaumarchais grew genuinely fond of his prospective brother-in-law, for despite his appearance, Clavijo was very far from mediocre. Very much like Beaumarchais, he had a hair-trigger mind; when he wanted to, he could display the most ingratiating manners and be entertainingly witty.

Then one day Clavijo disappeared. But the Keeper of the Crown Archives could not easily vanish in Madrid. Beaumarchais soon found his new lodging. Clavijo offered embarrassed, though plausible explanations for his flight: the high official in whose house he had lived had expressed such disapproval of his engagement to Doña María that he had had no alternative but to change quarters at once. He now had rooms in the house of another state official, one of his personal friends.

A few days later, Clavijo disappeared again. Beaumarchais discovered him in a small inn on the outskirts of town. The King of Spain, Clavijo explained this time, provided Clavijo's friend, the state official, with free lodging on the express condition that he live alone. When Clavijo had learned the royal stipulations, he had naturally moved immediately.

Beaumarchais was becoming suspicious and tried to make Clavijo sign his marriage contract with Lisette without further delay. Much to his regret, this was impossible, Clavijo said, for he had just taken medicine. According to Spanish law, a marriage contract was automatically void if signed on a day when one of the two parties had taken medicine. Beaumarchais could not believe his ears. Well, let him inquire. He inquired. It was true.

A few days later, Beaumarchais went to an apostolic notary to obtain Clavijo's signature on the marriage contract. But it then came out that Clavijo had previously promised to marry a chambermaid. He could not legally marry anyone else until the chambermaid renounced her claim on him, which she was not prepared to do—or until she died, and she turned out to be quite young.

People in Madrid now delightedly followed the game of hide-and-seek played by the Keeper of the Crown Archives and the excitable young man from Paris, with a forlorn damsel as the stakes. Beaumarchais, feeling himself hoodwinked, no longer tried to force Clavijo to marry Lisette. The man was evidently a scoundrel. He should be made to marry the chambermaid and thus be ruined forever.

The French Ambassador to Spain, the Marquis d'Ossun, was worried about the feud. Clavijo had many influential friends at the Spanish court. On the other hand, Beaumarchais had good connections at Versailles and intimately knew the powerful Pâris-Duverney. Beaumarchais had told everybody the story of his association with the King's daughters, and the story had undoubtedly lost nothing in the telling. A head-on conflict between Beaumarchais and Clavijo might place the French Ambassador in a most awkward position. Mlle Caron's "honor" seemed a trivial matter to him. The best thing was to end the whole affair by scaring the troublesome brother away.

The Marquis wrote Beaumarchais that Clavijo had gone to the police, complaining that the Frenchman had forced him at pistol point to sign a promise of marriage to his sister. The police were taking an extremely serious view of the accusation. The Ambassador felt powerless to protect M. de Beaumarchais from the "disagreeable and distressing consequences" that would probably ensue.

Almost simultaneously, an army officer with whom Beaumarchais had become slightly acquainted at the Guilberts' warned him that Clavijo had secured a warrant for his arrest. If he did not want to be thrown into jail and left there to rot, he had better flee immediately to France.

Beaumarchais' fighting instinct was now thoroughly aroused. Instead of running away, he drove straight to Aranjuez, the seat of the royal court. He first went to see the Marquis d'Ossun. The Marquis gravely told Beaumarchais that he was in great danger of being arrested and deported, without trial, to an African penal colony. The Ambassador, however, had intervened with Prime Minister Grimaldi and obtained, he said, a stay of execution, though not a cancelation of the deportation order. Beaumarchais must leave Spain. The Ambassador would gladly put a carriage and six mules at his disposal if he returned to France as quickly as possible.

On hearing such words, Beaumarchais for a while remained "stupid and struck dumb," according to his own testimony. But he was not daunted. In spite of the danger of continuing a seemingly hopeless struggle, he resolved to use his last weapon: Choiseul's letter of introduction to Grimaldi.

On the following day, he went to the royal palace and asked an audience of the Prime Minister. As he was kept waiting for an answer, his hopes sank lower and lower. Grimaldi had to receive him courteously because of Choiseul's letter, but would he lend a favorable ear to his plea?

While waiting, he heard someone mention Señor Whal's name. Señor Whal was a very old man who had held high positions in the Spanish government and was widely known as an ardent Francophile. With no other recommendation than being a Frenchman, Beaumarchais called on him at once. Trembling with emotion, he told him of his sister's predicament and of his own. Touched by his obvious distress, Whal took him to see no less a personage than Charles III, King of Spain. Once before the King, Beaumarchais spoke so convincingly and movingly that, after looking over the documents the young man had brought, His Majesty then and there ordered Clavijo dismissed from his post as Keeper of the Crown Archives and declared ineligible to occupy any government position in the future.

Beaumarchais went back to Madrid in a daze. Only after a few days did he fully realize his triumph. His adventures were the talk of the town. Everyone now praised the gallant young man who had come from France to vindicate his sister's honor; who, alone in a foreign country, had singlehandedly attacked a powerful, dangerous man; who had fought his way into the King's presence, and who, through sheer sincerity and the justice of his cause, had won.

Naturally, the French Ambassador made a diplomatic *volte-face.* He sent Beaumarchais his heartiest congratulations and an invitation to dinner.

2. *Marquise de La Croix*

For many months Beaumarchais remained a social lion in Madrid. He was made particularly welcome by the diplomatic corps. Foreign diplomats in Spain led a dull and boring life. Beaumarchais was amusing and lively, knew the latest Versailles gossip, and could tell countless anecdotes about the celebrities he had met there. His personal radiance and brilliance could turn a languishing social function into a successful party. Soon he found himself eagerly sought after by the most exclusive hostesses. He became a constant visitor and guest in the house of the Russian Ambassador and his wife, who had one of Madrid's gayest salons. He struck up a close friendship with the English Ambassador, Lord Rochford. Lord Rochford was approximately his age and, like him, was fond of light vocal music. The two often sang duets together, but they enjoyed their little private concerts most when their duets turned into trios with the addition of the Marquise de La Croix.

The Marquise de La Croix belonged to a distinguished, though impoverished French family. She was the daughter of the Marquis de Sénac and the niece of Monseigneur Jarente, Bishop of Orléans. While still in her teens, however, she had drifted into the most irregular sort of life. Eventually she had married the Marquis de La Croix, who had tolerant ideas about the binding value of matrimonial ties. The Marquis was an army man, a specialist in artillery, and something of an adventurer. He had recently entered Spain's service, but had not progressed in his new career as rapidly as he had hoped. Husband and wife had been living in Madrid for well over a year and both felt disappointed and bored. The Marquise had not yet been presented at court. Although she was received by a few broad-minded aristocrats, she remained on the outer fringe of the haughty, conservative Spanish society.

One of the Marquise's best friends in Madrid was the Countess of Fuen Clara—the same countess who, thirty years before, had cast an appreciative eye upon the young Parisian watchmaker, André Caron. The Countess of Fuen Clara was an old woman now and lived mainly on past remembrances. When Beaumarchais called at her house to pay his respects—his father had given him her address—she welcomed the son of her former French flirt familiarly and wistfully.

But the magnet which drew Beaumarchais day after day to the Countess of Fuen Clara's house was the Marquise de La Croix. The Marquise was a luxurious blonde, a little past her prime, perhaps, but still desirable. She had charm, poise, and an imposing dignity. A contemporary said that she was "the essence of majestic beauty and the ideal of a Roman empress." How different from the timid, cringing Pauline Le Breton! After only a few weeks' separation, Pauline had almost completely faded from Beaumarchais' mind. His thoughts were now concentrated on this resplendent woman, who corresponded so closely to his feminine ideal. She did not insist upon complicated or long preliminaries before she gave full satisfaction to what they both soon called their love.

The Marquise was no longer bored with Madrid. Her spirits, which only the day before had flagged so dismally, soared to new adventurous heights. As for Beaumarchais, he now found Spain perfect. He adopted Spanish dress, complete with sombrero and cape, and drove through the streets in a mule-drawn carriage to the sound of jingling bells. He was young, popular, in love, and enjoyed life to the full.

Beaumarchais did not forget Pâris-Duverney's financial plans, but he now wondered if they were not small items in a much bolder and vaster scheme slowly taking shape in his and the Marquise's daydreams. The King of Spain, Charles III, then around fifty, was friendly, even jovial, and well meaning, though endowed with only average intelligence and rather weak will power. Since his wife's death four years earlier, he had been lonesome and restless. The part Mme de Pompadour played in Louis XV's life and in France's political affairs set Beaumarchais and the Marquise thinking. Why couldn't the Marquise de La Croix become Spain's Marquise de Pompadour? And then, with her help, what position in Spain would be beyond Beaumarchais' reach?

Beaumarchais approached an Italian named Pini, who ministered to the King's private pleasures, on that subject. Pini said that such an arrangement was well within the field of possibility. Yet, in those days, the choice of a royal favorite was truly an affair of state. There would be a great deal of plotting and counterplotting among the Spanish courtiers, and serious obstacles would have to be overcome. But if an important party at court, say the pro-French party, backed the Marquise strongly, she would have a good chance, Pini admitted, of reaching her goal.

How could Beaumarchais enlist the pro-French party's support? Boldly, he wrote to Choiseul, pointing out the advantages to France if a Frenchwoman occupied a key position in Spain and if a Frenchman—Beaumarchais, naturally—remained at her side as political guide and adviser. Everyone knew that Choiseul had held onto his position as Prime Minister of France mainly through Mme de Pompadour's friendship. Beaumarchais therefore believed Choiseul would understand his point of view and help further his scheme.

Choiseul, however, neither understood nor helped. Perhaps moral scruples set him against Beaumarchais' cynical proposal. Perhaps he merely objected to the plan because Beaumarchais did not belong to his clique at Versailles. In any case, he did not vouchsafe Beaumarchais' memorial even the briefest answer, but merely wrote in the margin: "It is absolutely essential that this individual hereafter be excluded from our correspondence with Spain."

While waiting for a reply that never came, Beaumarchais started working on the missions entrusted him by Pâris-Duverney. The most important of them was connected with Louisiana. Beaumarchais suggested that the Spanish authorities create a stock company with a trade monopoly in Louisiana. The French would gladly assist their allies and friends, the Spaniards, with money in the venture and so receive a share in the enterprise. Beaumarchais, however, encountered only courteous indifference and apathy from Spanish officials. He persisted, but nothing happened. He appealed to public opinion and even went to the length of writing and printing a memorial entitled, not too accurately, "Patriotic Reflections of a Spanish Citizen on Louisiana." The public gave him no more response than the government.

Beaumarchais next put forward a comprehensive plan to transport large numbers of African Negro slaves on French ships to the Spanish American colonies, and this fared no better. He then turned to military supplies for the Spanish army, offering to reorganize and modernize the whole system and to run it efficiently. The Spaniards did not seem interested in reorganization, modernization, or efficiency. Almost every week Beaumarchais conceived a new plan and proposed it to the Spanish ministry: to repopulate the almost deserted Sierra Morena region; to revive Spanish agriculture; to stimulate dormant Spanish industries. Some of these plans were sound and practical; others, absolutely fantastic. But fantastic or practical, they were all ignored by the Spanish officials. Half asleep, they watched the little French mosquito buzz around with his projects and schemes for a while, then turned over and, hardly disturbed, went ahead with their administrative siesta.

After six months of vain agitation, Beaumarchais realized that he was not accomplishing anything. At the same time, all sorts of sorrows and difficulties assailed his family in both Spain and France. In Madrid, the house on the Vía Jacometrens became depressing and mournful when the Guilberts heard that their son, whom they had sent to a Paris boarding school, had died there after a short illness. Lisette, furthermore, had gained nothing from Clavijo's disgrace and was silent and moody most of the time. She had turned down a second proposal of marriage from Durand.

Beaumarchais was trying to comfort Durand, when he received word that his sister Boisgarnier had broken with Miron. It was nothing more than one of their usual tiffs, but Beaumarchais, believing the break serious, hit upon the idea of making everybody happy by arranging a marriage between Durand and Boisgarnier. Durand eagerly accepted, though he had never seen the young woman. But Miron was furious and wrote at once to Beaumarchais, telling him in no uncertain terms what he thought of his meddling. Beaumarchais apologetically withdrew his suggestion, and then Durand pulled a long face.

Soon Julie's letters, usually so cheerful, began to show worry. At the time of Beaumarchais' departure from Paris, his engagement to Pauline Le Breton had been considered practically settled by the whole family. Shortly after he had left, Pauline had written to him: "Good-by, my love! Good-by, my soul! Good-by, my all! When you come back, it will be the sunrise of a wonderful day indeed for me! Good-by!" But a few months had barely elapsed when a serious flirtation between the young girl and the Chevalier de Séguirand developed. Perhaps the Chevalier had tired of Julie's teasing; in any event, Julie felt jilted.

Julie also reported that their father was more enamored of Mme Henry than ever and had declared his intention of marrying her. But his health was not good, and his craving for new conjugal ties bore the unsavory marks of senile passion. The widow seemed a decent and sensible person and, so far, had given the old Lothario little encouragement. Yet women were notoriously weak when facing a marriage proposal; wedding bells might ring out for Caron *père* almost any day now. Julie added wistfully that, after all, this solution might be the best. Beaumarchais concurred in this, though he felt somewhat annoyed by the affair.

Then, official notice reached Beaumarchais that his cousin, Pichon de Villeneuve, whom he had sent to Santo Domingo to investigate Pauline Le Breton's problems, had suddenly died. Foul play was suspected, but Beaumarchais refused to believe it. All this bad news, coming almost at the same time, convinced him that he should return to Paris.

Parting with the Marquise de La Croix was easy. She now

had hardly any chance of becoming the official royal favorite, though with Pini's complicity she had had one private interview with Charles III. The interview must have proved particularly satisfying to the King, for, a few days later, His Majesty granted her a substantial pension and conferred the rank of Commander of the Order of Santiago on her husband.

As for Clavijo, he had taken shelter in a monastery near Madrid which he did not dare to leave, terrified as he was at the thought of arousing his enemy's ire once more. Eventually he wrote Beaumarchais a piteous letter, throwing himself upon his mercy and counting upon his compassion. "He was right to count upon it," Beaumarchais wrote later. "I hated him no longer. In fact, I never hated anyone in my life." Beaumarchais went to Grimaldi and asked that Clavijo be pardoned. Clavijo was immediately reinstated in his functions and dignities and thenceforth had a successful and brilliant career.

Beaumarchais left for France at the end of March 1765. He stopped a few days at Bordeaux for business and reached Paris in May. His adventures in Spain had lasted almost a year. They had brought him excitement and fun, but he had achieved nothing. He had failed to bring Lisette and Clavijo together. He had not been able to further Pâris-Duverney's plans. His association with the Marquise de La Croix had taken on the unpalatable flavor of low intrigue. His encounter with Clavijo was the only episode of which he could be truly proud. He had showed himself both resourceful and brave in an emergency. He had made his opponent crawl. Later he had held out his hand and helped him get to his feet again —fine gestures, boyishly chivalrous. But what had been the purpose of the whole fight?

Chapter 4

BUSINESS AND LITERATURE

1. Postwar Trouble

WHEN BEAUMARCHAIS arrived in Paris, he found his once friendly and familiar world transformed. For seven years France had been at war with England and Prussia. As long as the conflict had lasted, governmental authority had enjoyed a measure of respect. Moreover, the money lavishly spent to keep the armies in the field well supplied with food, clothing, and guns had fostered an artificial but profitable business boom. On the whole, in spite of the grave reverses the French generals had suffered in the last phase of the conflict, a pleasant, if deceptive feeling of well-being had pervaded the whole country.

The postwar period, however—the peace had been signed in Paris in 1763—brought about a slump in the people's morale and a collapse of the factitious prosperity created by wild government spending. The public began to realize the extent of the disaster that had befallen France. The supremacy the French had held in Europe since Richelieu and Louis XIV had obviously passed into the hands of the English. Strangely enough, hardly any resentment toward England was evident in Paris on that account. The war had been fought remarkably cleanly on both sides, with bitterness at times, yet without any of those atrocities which alone can breed deep and violent hatreds.

But soon a tremendous wave of anger rose, rolled throughout France, and finally broke against those held responsible for the catastrophe. Louis XV and his Pompadour were riddled by satirical pamphlets. The government at Versailles and the aristocratic ruling class became targets for sharp, barbed criticisms. For many years, the "philosophers" had asked for social and political reforms. In the past these requests had been considered an expression of the discontent of a limited intellectual group. Now it was evident that the régime was rotten through and through. Drastic remedies had to be applied at once if the nation was to be saved from utter decay.

The aristocrats, sensing this change in mood, reacted by taking a defensive stand. Up to that time, many of them had often welcomed in their midst those bourgeois with good manners and good money who knew how to take the proper, humble attitude when admitted into noble company. Feeling threatened, the noblemen now shut themselves up in their assumed superiority and class prejudices, held on fiercely to their hereditary privileges, and looked down with contempt upon all commoners.

When Beaumarchais became aware of the tense atmosphere at Versailles, he felt thoroughly perplexed. He had staked his success in life on making a brilliant career at court. He knew that his low birth was a serious hurdle in his path, yet he had hoped, somehow, to get over it. At present he found himself before an almost insurmountable wall.

Moreover, a few visits to the King's daughters made him realize that he could no longer count upon their help. While he had been in Spain, the princesses' brother, the Dauphin Louis, had unexpectedly died. The shock of his death crystallized all the morbid elements that had accumulated imperceptibly in their minds during years of artificial, abnormal life at Versailles. All of a sudden they cut themselves off from the rest of the court and, though they remained in the royal palace, withdrew into an austere, cloistered existence.

When Beaumarchais asked the princesses for an audience, they granted it to him immediately. The interview was woeful. They remembered a Beaumarchais ingratiatingly boyish, shy, and pale. What had that appealing figure of the past to do with this sturdy, self-assured, sun-tanned man, this stranger, who now stood before them and spoke so untimely about playing the harp, the guitar, and the tambourine?

The music lessons were, of course, not resumed. Beaumarchais called a few more times at the princesses' private apartments, as he had done regularly before going to Spain. For a while he was received politely, though more and more distantly. In vain he strove to maintain a personal contact with Mme Adelaïde, of whom he had always been especially fond. Then, one day, the Minister of the Royal Household, the former Comte de Saint-Florentin, who had inherited the title Duc de La Vrillière at his father's death, notified him curtly not to call at the princesses' again.

Beaumarchais was given a hardly less chilly welcome by his fiancée, Pauline Le Breton. Before he had left for Madrid, Pauline had pursued him with her love, and he had frequently grieved her by his indifference. Now it was her turn to be indifferent to him. He naturally found new charm in her. But Mlle Le Breton made no secret of the fact that she preferred the Chevalier de Séguirand. Enraged by this "betrayal," Beaumarchais wanted to challenge the Chevalier to a duel. His jealousy, however, was based exclusively upon wounded vanity, and the affair soon blew over.

Mlle Le Breton decided to marry the Chevalier de Séguirand almost at once. After receiving the news of the forthcoming wedding, Beaumarchais sent her a bill. He had lent her, in the past few years, 24,441 livres. He would be pleased to receive the money owed him as soon as possible. Truly a shopkeeper's revenge, thought Pauline, as she wrote to Séguirand: "M. de Beaumarchais may sleep peacefully. He will be paid."

As a matter of fact, Beaumarchais was never paid. The Chevalier died after only one year of marriage, and his widow struggled with inextricable financial difficulties for the rest of her life. Beaumarchais forbore from dunning her, but he kept a duplicate of his bill, perhaps as a souvenir. It was found among his papers, more than thirty years afterward, at the time of his death.

Meanwhile, André Caron had succeeded in persuading Mme Henry to follow him, on January 15, 1765, to the altar. Beaumarchais did his best to hide his instinctive, secret annoyance at seeing his father find a successor to his beloved mother. André Caron naturally left the Rue de Condé house and established his bride in a love nest paid for by Beaumarchais. He was blissfully happy, and Beaumarchais did not spoil his bliss.

The next matrimonial venture in the family was Boisgarnier's. In 1767, she decided that she had kept Miron dangling long enough. From her brother she received a generous dowry that enabled her to make one of her dreams come true: to set up an elegant salon. She gathered a group of writers of some note around her and for several years reigned as a capricious little queen over her small court of admirers.

For Beaumarchais, this series of unconnected events—the rapid deterioration of the political situation on France, the withdrawal of the princesses' support, Pauline Le Breton's change of heart, his father's marriage, Boisgarnier's departure from the Rue de Condé house—meant that the happy environment he had known before going to Spain was disintegrating. Evidently, certain liquidations were inevitable, and a fundamental readjustment of his life would soon be imperative.

2. Le Barbier de Séville

Beaumarchais liquidated his position at court. It was obviously futile for a man of common birth to attempt under existing circumstances to overcome the fast-increasing aristocratic prejudices. He sold his office of Controller of the Pantry, which had given him access to Versailles. He thenceforth ceased to be a courtier. Resolutely, though not without pique, he forever turned his back on nobility.

But Beaumarchais held on to his judgeship. The Louvre tribunal was not directly connected with the court, and it gave him an official standing that was a definite asset. In fact, his functions as judge gave him the opportunity of forming one of the most precious associations of his whole life.

Beaumarchais had to pass sentence in a case involving the Prince de Conti. The Prince, though a member of the Bourbon family, had made himself thoroughly unpopular in Versailles by his independent spirit and his advanced, almost revolutionary ideas. He boasted of being Jean-Jacques Rousseau's admirer, protector, and friend. A sincere, honest man at heart, he was a stickler for his rights. His main hobby was lawsuits, which he usually won because he was a prince of royal blood.

The matter that brought him before the Louvre tribunal was of trifling importance. His attendants had pulled down a wall, which the opposing party contended should have been left standing. Judge Caron de Beaumarchais ordered the Prince to rebuild the wall. As soon as the Prince learned the verdict, he rushed to Beaumarchais' house to argue the case with him. Hearing that Beaumarchais had just left to take part in a hunt, he drove at once to the hunters' meeting place, found his man, and started arguing then and there. After listening to his argument with the utmost attention and courtesy, Beaumarchais replied with such frankness, subtlety, and good humor that the two became warm friends on the spot.

Beaumarchais had not many such friends. The noblemen had not accepted him as a nobleman. The bourgeois did not accept him as a bourgeois. His long and close connection with the King's daughters, the manners he had adopted during his stay at court, even the cut of his fashionable clothes put an almost insuperable barrier between him and the plain, ordinary businessmen whom he occasionally met.

Fully aware of the ambiguousness of his social position, he drifted back into the most equivocal company he had known so far—the company surrounding Charles Lenormant at Etioles. He was welcomed with joy; yet the spurious gaiety of the place relieved his inward uneasiness only temporarily.

His last two years had been filled with abortive enterprises and mortifying events. To allay the tension caused by his subconscious sense of failure, he sought solace in literary creation. In 1766, he saw a private performance of *La Précaution Inutile*, by Noland de Fatouville, at the Etioles theater. Soon afterward, his imagination fired by some lively scenes in the play, his memory haunted by Lisette's sad, disappointed look in Madrid, and his mind obsessed by the unsavory circumstances of his father's recent marriage, he wrote the first draft of *Le Barbier de Séville*. The plot of this rather short sketch revolves around two distinct episodes: a barber comes to the rescue of a sweet and modest maiden separated from her ardent admirer; and a besotted, grotesque doctor, in spite of his old age, plays the young blade and hankers after matrimony. Thus Beaumarchais vicariously gratified two of his unfulfilled desires. In the play, the barber succeeded in bringing the two lovers together, whereas Beaumarchais had failed in a similar undertaking in Spain. On the stage, the cravings of the ridiculous, infatuated old man were thwarted, whereas in reality André Caron had won his bride.

The favorable reception the Etioles audience gave *Le Barbier de Séville* induced Beaumarchais to tackle a more ambitious program. After seeing a revival of Diderot's bourgeois drama, *Le Père de Famille*, he decided to write a full-length play in Diderot's sentimental vein. For his plot he took a seemingly trite theme: a young and innocent girl is duped into contracting a fake marriage by an unscrupulous wretch of high aristocratic birth. When the deception is uncovered, the girl, considering herself "ruined," sinks into despair. But her generous and heroic brother steps in, and the aristocratic wretch repents. In the end, the girl forgives her seducer and agrees to marry him, this time for good, and they live happily ever after.

It is not difficult to perceive in this melodramatic subject the general outline of the exaggerated but still quite recognizable Lisette-Clavijo-Beaumarchais episode, once more capped with a happy ending.

The feature of the play that struck Beaumarchais' contemporaries most was its abundance of sardonic remarks directed against the aristocracy. Beaumarchais had originally set his comedy in France, but his friends had strongly advised him to locate it in England so that his attacks against the nobility could be interpreted as applying to English nobility alone. Beaumarchais followed this advice. Nevertheless, many French noblemen who had known him at Versailles were not deceived. They were incensed at the impudence of this miserable playwright, who only the day before could have been seen at court currying favor and bowing, and who now brazenly assailed his betters. As for the professional writers and critics, they sniffed with contempt at the presumptuousness of M. de Beaumarchais, the courtier, who thought he could poach on their literary preserves. They would show him that it was not easy to become a regular dramatic author, and they did. His play *Eugénie*, named after its sugary heroine, was presented at the end of June 1767 at the Comédie Française. It survived only a few stormy performances.

3. Settling Down

A FEW days after *Eugénie*'s failure, Beaumarchais was visited by one of his friends, Mme Buffault, the wife of a wealthy Paris silk merchant. Mme Buffault was an inveterate matchmaker. Seeing the young man dejected and glum, she good-naturedly chided him for leading such a lonely, useless existence. Then she spoke casually of one of her former schoolmates, Geneviève-Madeleine Watebled. Geneviève had married a wealthy man named Antoine Lévêque, but he had died. Geneviève was very pretty. She was rich. She had a sweet temper. She would make Beaumarchais a perfect wife.

When Beaumarchais laughingly said that at the present moment he was in no mood to marry, Mme Buffault begged him to have at least a look at her protégée. She would ride with her the following day, during the afternoon, in an open carriage, along a secluded avenue near the Champs-Elysées significantly called l'Allée des Veuves. If Beaumarchais cared to be introduced to her, he might by chance find himself there also.

The next day, at the appointed time, Beaumarchais was on l'Allée des Veuves, prancing on his best horse. Soon the expected carriage with the two ladies in it appeared at the turn of the avenue. Beaumarchais rode up to them, paid his respects to Mme Buffault, and was presented to Mme Geneviève Lévêque. She made an extremely vivid impression on him, for she reminded him forcibly of Mme de La Croix. Like the Marquise, Geneviève was blonde, buxom, and statuesque; moreover she had a dazzling, clear, pink complexion. She was in her early thirties, and her widow's weeds lent her a melancholy dignity that went straight to his heart.

Beaumarchais was invited to join the ladies in their carriage. He accepted eagerly and left his horse in the care of a groom who had received orders to follow at a distance. Then, for two hours, he displayed all the wit and seductiveness he could. In the end, he asked the women to dine with him at his home. Geneviève at first coyly refused, but Mme Buffault prevailed upon her to consent, and from that time on things went rapidly between Geneviève and Pierre-Augustin.

Aware of Pierre-Augustin's powers of attraction, evidently through personal experience, Geneviève begged him to give her his solemn pledge to remain faithful to her and, as she expressed it, to promise never "to let her weep in a lonely bed." Their wedding took place on April 11, 1768, and in December of the same year a son was born to them—altogether too soon, the gossip-lovers whispered. He was christened Pierre-Augustin-Eugène.

The Rue de Condé house was now a true home again. Geneviève and Julie got along extremely well together. Furthermore, around that time, old Caron, a widower once more after two years of blissful marriage, came back to his son's house and completed the happy family circle by showing himself a perfect, doting grandfather.

Beaumarchais made up his mind to settle down as a regular businessman. Before his trip to Spain, he had been half speculator, half courtier. He had been successful in his speculations, as Pâris-Duverney pointed out to him, mainly because wartime conditions had been exceptionally favorable to quick and bold coups. But now it was necessary to use more conservative and laborious methods to obtain safe and steady returns from investments. The military-supply business that had given Beaumarchais and Pâris-

Duverney such handsome profits during the Seven Years' War was no longer remunerative. On the other hand, the lumber trade, always essential in a period of reconstruction, offered excellent opportunities to an active and enterprising man.

Beaumarchais signed a partnership contract with Pâris-Duverney for the purchase and exploitation of an extensive forest tract in the neighborhood of Chinon, in Touraine. Soon he had to go there to direct the felling of the timber. Before leaving Paris, he established Geneviève, whose health had not been good since the birth of their son, in a country house at Pantin, near the capital.

For many months Beaumarchais lived the rough yet wholesome existence of a general manager and Jack-of-all-trades in a remote and rather primitive lumber camp. He had more than two hundred workers under him. He provided them with food bought at near-by farms, listened to their complaints and arbitrated their quarrels, repaired old roads and built new ones, inspected carts and wagons, purchased oats and hay for the dray horses, constructed gates and sluices on streams, outfitted barges for transporting the wood to Angers and Nantes. He could not help contrasting the reliability, stanchness, and homespun but solid decency of most businessmen with the corruption, depravity, and perfidiousness of the fine gentlemen he had known at court.

When Beaumarchais returned to Paris, he resolved to write a play to illustrate the life of the businessmen of the time and particularly to emphasize the moral principles that the best of them followed in transactions and dealings. So *Les Deux Amis* came into being, a play in which two friends, both merchants, vie with each other in a spirit of lofty generosity and disinterestedness.

Unfortunately Beaumarchais knew his subject too well. In presenting the technical aspects of business he made so many references to specialized trade methods and practices that certain phases of the plot became all but unintelligible to the average layman. It is said that after the third act a wag sitting in the pit shouted: "Let's have the solution of the riddle in the next number of the *Mercure de France*, please."

Les Deux Amis limped through a few performances at the Comédie Française in January 1770 and then fell flat. The play has little interest in itself, but it reveals Beaumarchais trying to identify himself with the bourgeois group. Yet its failure was proof that he had not yet succeeded in striking a responsive chord in the bourgeois mind. In spite of his material prosperity, Beaumarchais remained isolated and distrusted by almost everybody.

When posters had been put up at the Comédie Française to announce the forthcoming performance of *Les Deux Amis*, an anonymous hand had added to one of them, "by a man who has none." This cruel witticism had run throughout Paris. Indeed, it expressed a tragic truth: apart from the Prince de Conti, his wife Geneviève, and his old protector, Pâris-Duverney, who was truly Beaumarchais' friend?

Chapter 5

TRIALS AND ERRORS

1. Falcoz de La Blache

Both Pâris-Duverney and Geneviève died in 1770, and their deaths inaugurated a chaotic period for Beaumarchais. For some time, Beaumarchais had noticed alarming mental changes in Pâris-Duverney. Pâris-Duverney was now eighty-six years old. His intellect seemed as keen and lucid as ever, but his will power weakened every day. One of his grandnephews, Comte Alexandre Falcoz de La Blache, of whom he had always been particularly fond, now controlled his actions almost completely.

La Blache had a quick mind and did not lack personal charm. An orphan when still a child, he had been brought up without moral discipline or emotional restraint. He was hard, cutting, and insolent toward inferiors, but fawned upon any person from whom he might obtain material advantages. When crossed in his ambitions he could stage furious, tempestuous scenes. He was completely devoid of scruples and used any means at his disposal to carry out his selfish purposes.

For a long time he had been jealous of Beaumarchais' intimacy with Pâris-Duverney. To break up their friendship, he had sent anonymous letters filled with the vilest insinuations about Beaumarchais to Pâris-Duverney, and about Pâris-Duverney to Beaumarchais. Pâris-Duverney and Beaumarchais, however, had showed each other these slanderous missives and had laughed at their childish crudeness. Beaumarchais did not know at the time who had sent these letters, but he sensed an undefinable yet unrelenting hostility in La Blache's attitude toward him.

In his will Pâris-Duverney had made Alexandre Falcoz de La Blache his main legatee and sole testamentary executor. Beaumarchais had strongly objected to this last clause: his own financial affairs were inextricably intertwined with those of Pâris-Duverney, and he was certain to run into serious trouble if he had to deal with La Blache in settling accounts after Pâris-Duverney's death. He had suggested as executor another of Pâris-Duverney's nephews, Jean-Baptiste Pâris de Meyzieu, with whom he was on very cordial terms. The weak and weary old man, however, did not alter his will. When La Blache heard of Beaumarchais' request, his enmity toward him turned into furious, passionate hatred, which he made no attempt to conceal. He declared to a friend, the Duc de Chaulnes: "I hate Beaumarchais the way a lover adores his mistress."

Beaumarchais then asked Pâris-Duverney to liquidate all their accounts immediately. Pâris-Duverney no longer dared to see

Beaumarchais openly for fear of La Blache's scenes. The two men, nevertheless, managed to meet secretly in March 1770 and come to an understanding.

On April 1, 1770, Beaumarchais drew up in duplicate a document detailing the financial arrangements upon which they had verbally agreed. Their business partnership was dissolved. Beaumarchais was to return 160,000 livres in Pâris-Duverney's notes of hand. On his side, Pâris-Duverney declared Beaumarchais free of all debt to him and acknowledged himself Beaumarchais' debtor for 15,000. Furthermore, he promised to lend to Beaumarchais 75,000 livres without interest for a period of eight years. The document was dated, signed, and sealed by Pâris-Duverney.

The last two clauses of this settlement—Pâris-Duverney's promise to pay 15,000 livres to Beaumarchais, and to lend him 75,000 livres—were not executed immediately. La Blache kept a watchful eye on Pâris-Duverney, and his vigilance made any transaction between his great-uncle and Beaumarchais complicated and difficult. Moreover, Beaumarchais was now engrossed with matters of infinitely greater importance to him than money. His wife, Geneviève, was expecting a second child, and her health had taken a dramatic turn for worse.

Geneviève was suffering from an acute form of tuberculosis of the lungs. Her once beautiful body had wasted away pitifully. Her soft blue eyes, ringed with deep, dark shadows, now looked immense in her worn, emaciated face. Beaumarchais spent most of his time at her bedside. When Pâris-Duverney died on July 10, 1770, Beaumarchais, filled with anguish for his wife, gave the octogenarian's death hardly more than the cursory attention due to normal, expected events. But when Geneviève and her newborn baby died on November 21, he realized that the best part of his world had crumbled under his feet.

Geneviève's personal fortune consisted mainly of a large annuity that terminated with her death. Although Beaumarchais' income was thereby markedly reduced, he took little heed of this aspect of his loss. He was now firmly established in business. Although he had but little liquid capital, he was well able to earn a regular and ample living. He was therefore not unduly disturbed when he heard that La Blache intended to raise questions about Pâris-Duverney's disposition of his property. Beaumarchais had expected them, but he felt thoroughly outraged by his opponent's contemptuous attitude. Finally, when he produced the settlement signed and sealed by Pâris-Duverney, La Blache, glancing at his great-uncle's signature, declared it a forgery. Beaumarchais bristled at the accusation and vehemently protested. "That man is insane," Beaumarchais declared before witnesses. "He wants to ruin me. But I shall be the one to ruin him." And he took the matter to the courts.

At just that time the judicial system in France was in the midst of an unprecedented crisis. After Mme de Pompadour's death in 1764, the party, headed by Choiseul, that had enjoyed her support during her lifetime had succeeded in maintaining itself in power. But the opposition groups were emboldened by the discontent created by the disasters of the Seven Years' War. The spearhead of the opposition was the highest tribunal in France, the Parliament of Paris. The members of the Parliament considered themselves guardians of the traditional laws of the kingdom and therefore entitled to present remonstrances even to the King. Lately, to the applause of the huge majority of the nation, the

Parliament had harried the Versailles administration with reproofs and rebukes on every conceivable pretext.

Choiseul, who was comparatively tolerant and liberal in his views, bore the brunt of these attacks without retaliating. In 1770, however, Louis XV, annoyed at the Prime Minister's meekness, turned him out of office and called upon a rival clique—backed by Mme Du Barry, who since 1769 had been royal favorite—to form another ministry. The Duc d'Aiguillon, Chancellor Maupeou, and Abbé Terray were the outstanding figures of the new cabinet. They were known to favor strong-arm methods and were soon nicknamed the Triumvirs.

One of Chancellor Maupeou's first moves was to strike at the Parliament of Paris. During the night of January 20, 1771, its members were arrested by armed musketeers; soon afterward they were sent into exile. The provincial Parliaments that protested against this arbitrary step were dissolved. Then the whole higher judicial system was reorganized on an entirely new plan and with new personnel.

The new plan contained many commendable points, but the new personnel was poor. Most of the judges appointed by Maupeou were political intriguers devoted to the Triumvirs' interests. Some of them possessed only the sketchiest knowledge of law; many had had a most questionable past. Almost to a man, the public took the side of the "old" tribunals. Reputable lawyers practically went on strike, refusing to bring cases before the "Maupeou Parliaments."

Beaumarchais' case was at first only indirectly affected by this scandal. Indeed, his lawsuit with La Blache was not within the jurisdiction of the Parliament of Paris. It was scheduled to come before a lower tribunal, the Cour des Requêtes de l'Hôtel. Yet, even there, exceptionally long delays were to be expected, owing to the general confusion in all legal circles throughout France.

Thus Beaumarchais was temporarily reduced to complete idleness, for he could not use his comparatively small liquid capital for any commercial venture until his litigation with La Blache was officially settled. Throughout the greater part of 1771 he found himself with absolutely nothing to do but kill time and brood.

This time Etioles failed to provide Beaumarchais with an escape into frivolity and fun. After becoming a widower by Mme de Pompadour's death, Charles Lenormant had, much to everyone's surprise, suddenly turned into an upholder of the strictest and most rigid rules of conventional morality. He had soon married again, this time a woman reassuringly plain and indisputably virtuous. He was now a devoted, faithful husband and a fond, dutiful father. Beaumarchais still visited his old crony occasionally and loved to play with his young son, Constant, but the Château d'Etioles was chillily respectable and oppressively dull.

Beaumarchais found a measure of diversion at the Mirons' house. His young sister's literary salon was now in full swing, and Pierre-Augustin there met a company perhaps not so brilliant as the high society he had known at Versailles, yet decidedly pleasant, congenial, and lively. In the first months of 1771, he became acquainted there with a man who was to become and remain for the rest of his life his *fidus Achates*. Paul Philippe Gudin de La Brenellerie came, like Beaumarchais, from a Protestant family that had for several generations been engaged in watchmaking. While still a child, Paul Gudin had lost his father and had grown up in the shadow of his beloved mother. His elder brother Jacques Jérôme Gudin, took their father's place in the family shop. Paul decided to go to Geneva to study for the ministry. In Geneva he lost his religious faith and fell under Voltaire's influence. He visited Voltaire at Ferney and, fascinated by his example, decided to become a writer. The tragedies he composed in Voltairean vein were all complete failures, but he was inordinately proud of the fact that one of them, *Lothaire et Valdrade*, had drawn the attention of the Inquisition and had been burned solemnly by the public executioner. He was now busy writing a heroicomic poem called *La Napliade*, based upon the conquest of Naples by Charles VIII.

Gudin read passages of his *Napliade* in all the literary salons in which he could find an audience and thus came to the Mirons' house. Beaumarchais was present at one of these readings. He enthusiastically praised Gudin's poetic gifts and humor and made a friend of him for life.

Paul Gudin was short, stout, and slow. With his old mother, to whose apron strings he was tied, he lived on the scanty income of a small inheritance that had come to him unexpectedly. He was unmarried and led a preternaturally chaste life. Yet, as often happens, his puritanical behavior was oddly combined with a salacious imagination, which, however, found an outlet exclusively in books. When he met Beaumarchais, he was past thirty and, having failed to do anything worth while with his life, felt like a lost dog hankering for a kind but purposeful master.

Almost at once he attached himself to Beaumarchais with total devotion. It would have been difficult to find two beings more completely dissimilar. It has been said that Gudin had the gait of a stolid plow ox, while Beaumarchais pranced and stamped around like a thoroughbred horse. Perhaps their very dissimilarity gave them the impression that they complemented each other. In any case, the harmonious relations that were established between them in 1771 lasted without a single discordant note for nearly thirty years.

Neither the friendship of the stanch and staid Gudin nor the geniality of the Mirons' house, however, was sufficient to occupy all of Beaumarchais' thoughts for months on end. He therefore undertook to turn the short sketch of *Le Barbier de Séville*, which he had written five years earlier for the Etioles theater, into a comic opera. Naturally he had to expand certain aspects of the rather bare plot, but he did not show great originality or inventiveness in this task. The French stage of the time offered him a whole array of stock situations about lovers thwarted by a suspicious old man, and whom a clever servant helps to elope after a succession of episodes enlivened by picturesque disguises. Beaumarchais docilely followed this traditional pattern, adding only a few new personal touches here and there.

As for the characters of the play, he stuck quite closely to his original creations. The barber Figaro remained the stage counterpart of his own versatile, resourceful, irrepressible self. The very name Figaro is a fanciful Hispanized form of "Fils Caron"—the final *s* of the word *fils* being silent in eighteenth-century French pronunciation. Similarly, Bartholo—the scolding, morose, crabby, crafty doctor who spends treasures of cunning in trying to imprison youth and love—bears more than a superficial resemblance to Beaumarchais' father as his son remembered him in the worst days of their conflict in the Rue Saint-Denis house. Furthermore, Bartholo's preposterous idea of marrying for love at his age evidently had its source in old Caron's late *grand amour* and matrimonial escapade.

For the musical score, Beaumarchais incorporated into his work popular tunes he had heard in Spain and composed a few melodies of his own. Finally, with his usual deftness, he succeeded in putting together a play filled with action, romance, color, and gaiety. Indeed, *Le Barbier de Séville* was essentially Beaumarchais' means of turning his sadness into laughter and fun. As Figaro—undoubtedly expressing Beaumarchais' own views—says in a terse sentence that has since become almost a proverb in France: "*Je me presse de rire de tout de peur d'être obligé d'en pleurer.*"

At the end of October 1771 Beaumarchais' lawsuit with La Blache was at long last taken up by the Cour des Requêtes de l'Hôtel. La Blache brought a countersuit against Beaumarchais, charging him with forgery and asking for payment of 139,000 livres. La Blache's main argument in contesting the authenticity of the settlement made by Beaumarchais and Pâris-Duverney was that Pâris-Duverney's signature on the document was much too clear and firm for a man of eighty-six. But other similar samples of the old man's signature were found among his papers. Moreover, La Blache's own attorney had tampered with certain documents pertaining to the case, deliberately to throw suspicion upon Beaumarchais' character. When the fraud was uncovered, La Blache's cause was for all practical purposes lost.

After long-drawn-out debates, a judgment was rendered on February 22, 1772; it dismissed the accusation of forgery against Beaumarchais. A second judgment, on March 14, ordered that the settlement of accounts between Beaumarchais and Pâris-Duverney be acted upon immediately. La Blache was to pay Beaumarchais

15,000 livres and refund the crown the cost of the action. La Blache filed an appeal with the Parliament of Paris, and once more Beaumarchais had to wait.

Then, all of a sudden a devastating hailstorm of misfortunes broke unexpectedly over Beaumarchais' head.

A few days before the Cour des Requêtes de l'Hôtel passed sentence, La Blache, hoping to influence the judges, had spread the rumor that Beaumarchais had been banished from the presence of the royal princesses because of immoral behavior. Upon hearing that slander, Beaumarchais communicated with the Comtesse de Périgord, lady in waiting to Princess Victoire, who had shown him friendship in the past. Mme de Périgord, on the Princess' behalf, wrote to Beaumarchais: "Mme Victoire has never said a word to anyone that could injure your reputation, for she knows nothing about you that could lead her to do so."

Thereupon Beaumarchais wrote and published a memorial in which he alluded to this letter. Although he did not quote its exact terms, he tended to represent it as proof of special favor and personal protection on the part of the four princesses. It was now La Blache's turn to complain of the King's daughters' intervention in his lawsuit. The King's daughters, annoyed at having their names mixed up with a sordid forgery case, issued an official communiqué: "We declare that we take no interest whatever in M. de Beaumarchais and his lawsuit. We have not given him permission to state in a printed and public memorial that he enjoys our protection." Beaumarchais had antagonized the only persons at court still well disposed toward him.

Shortly afterward news came from Madrid that Guilbert had gone insane and then died. Marie-Josèphe and Lisette had had enough of Spain and soon arrived in Paris with Marie-Josèphe's two young sons. All naturally expected to be taken care of by the wealthy Beaumarchais. He found room for everybody in his house, but the new inhabitants brought with them many problems and little cheer. Then, in October 1772 Beaumarchais' own son died unexpectedly at the age of four, and he felt more forlorn and despondent than ever.

About the same time, *Le Barbier de Séville* was rejected by the only theatrical company in Paris—Les Italiens—capable of performing a comic opera creditably. When Beaumarchais had first approached the actors about his play they had seemed favorably disposed toward him. But he learned that the leading man in the troupe had been a barber in his young days and did not want to have this "undignified" episode of his life recalled publicly on the stage.

With characteristic resilience and determination, Beaumarchais sacrificed all the music he had composed, brightened the dialogue with witty remarks, and added a few amusing byplays. He then offered the work to the Comédie Française. *Le Barbier de Séville* was accepted at once in its new form and scheduled to be presented on February 12, 1773. But before that day came, another catastrophe struck Beaumarchais.

2. *Alarums and Excursions*

AMONG the few aristocrats with whom Beaumarchais still consorted freely, the Duc de Chaulnes had by far the most colorful and striking personality. Although he was built like a Hercules, he had refinement and culture. He had been won to the new liberal ideas and proclaimed himself free of class prejudices. But at irregular intervals he would pass through cycles of black despondency and intense exaltation. When he was in one of his excited phases, the slightest annoyance threw him into fits of uncontrollable brutality. Once he had been involved in such a disgraceful brawl that the authorities had advised him to go abroad for some time. After an absence of five years he had been able to return to France. Then he openly took as his mistress Mlle Ménard, one of the prettiest actresses in Paris.

Mlle Ménard had started her own hectic career by selling flowers in the streets of the capital. She had had ambitions to go on the stage, and by dint of artful compliance and willful pertinacity she had eventually succeeded in playing small parts at the Comédie Française. She was good-natured, easygoing, yielding, and soft and she never professed herself a paragon of virtue. When the Duc de Chaulnes wooed her, she surrendered almost at once and soon bore him a child.

Mlle Ménard's liaison with the Duke, however, shortly became very stormy. He was insanely jealous of her past. In his better moments he showed himself affectionate and generous; but during his spells of anger he reviled her, insulted her, and even struck her cruelly. Eventually she tired of his erratic and violent temper. She longed for a protector who would be more considerate and pleasanter in his ways.

Beaumarchais was introduced to Mlle Ménard by the Duc de Chaulnes himself. They conceived an interest for each other that fast went beyond the stage of platonic friendship. The Duke did not fail to notice his lady love's growing warmth toward his friend and her increasing coldness toward him. He now avoided Beaumarchais' presence as much as possible, while his relations with Mlle Ménard waxed more tempestuous every day.

In the end, Mlle Ménard, probably acting upon Beaumarchais' advice, decided to make a clear-cut break with her lover. In December 1772 she stealthily left her house and went to the country by herself. From there, a few days later, she sent the Duke a letter. She had gone away for a much needed rest, she said, but would soon be back in Paris. She would be delighted to see him upon her return, but only as a friend. Strangely enough, the Duke did not answer this curt note with an outburst of fury. Mlle Ménard, believing the whole matter settled, returned to her lodgings in the city at the beginning of 1773.

The Duke was not resigned to her loss, however, and visited her daily. At first he implored her to reconsider her decision. Then he grew alarmingly agitated. Finally, he terrified her with wild scenes and threats. At the same time he happened to be engaged in a lawsuit about his mother's will and he published a pamphlet in which he showed little respect for her memory. This affair seems to have preyed on his mind and to have contributed in no small measure to his increasing unbalance.

After weeks of quarrels and wranglings, Mlle Ménard, the Duke, and Beaumarchais met for a final discussion. Almost at once the Duke burst into frantic vituperation, heaped contumely on the weeping girl, and reminded Beaumarchais that he was, after all, only a baseborn commoner. Beaumarchais did not answer immediately, but a few days later he sent the Duke a biting retort. In his letter, he started courteously enough with the assumption that Mlle Ménard and Chaulnes had definitively separated and he congratulated them on the amicable solution of their difficulties. Then he added: "I wish to pass in silence over the scene, horrible for her, disgusting for two men like you and me, where you so far forgot yourself that you reproached me with being the son of a watchmaker. Since I honor my parents—even in the face of those who imagine they have a right to outrage their own—you must certainly feel, Monsieur le Duc, how much more advantageous my position was, at that time, than yours."

This was no less than a declaration of war.

Early on the morning of February 11, 1773, Paul Gudin went to pay his respects to Mlle Ménard in her private dressing room, as was the custom in those days. The Duc de Chaulnes then arrived, obviously with the same purpose. When he saw Beaumarchais' *alter ego*, he started pouring out a torrent of invective against his false friend and his unfaithful mistress, who instantly melted into tears. The meek, harmless Gudin somehow managed to slink away, pursued by the Duke's oaths and threats against Beaumarchais: "I shall kill him! I shall kill him! I shall kill him!"

Gudin ran to the Rue de Condé to warn Beaumarchais. Beaumarchais was just leaving his house to go to the Louvre tribunal, for it happened to be a day on which he sat as judge. When he heard of the Duke's threat, he merely shrugged his shouldres and said: "He will only kill his own fleas."

His curiosity piqued, Gudin walked back toward Mlle Ménard's lodging. On his way, he met the Duke again. Chaulnes pounced on the little man like a bird of prey, threw him into a hackney coach, and shouted to the coachman to drive to the Rue de Condé.

"By what right, Monsieur le Duc," said Gudin, according to

his sworn testimony, "do you, who are always talking about freedom, dare to take mine from me?"

"By the right of the stronger!" roared the Duke. "You will find Beaumarchais for me or else—"

"Monsieur le Duc, I am not armed. Will you also murder me?"

"No, I want to kill only this Beaumarchais. After I have plunged my sword into his body and torn out his heart with my teeth, I don't care what becomes of that Ménard woman."

When Gudin went on protesting, the Duke added: "If you resist, I'll strike you."

"Then I shall strike you back, Monsieur le Duc."

"You would dare strike me!" *

Thoroughly enraged, the Duke flung himself upon Gudin and grabbed him by the hair. But Gudin was wearing a wig, and the wig ludicrously remained in the Duke's hand. Gudin shrieked at the top of his lungs. Chaulnes caught him by the throat, but when a policeman sauntered near, relaxed his hold on his victim. Gudin jumped out of the carriage and ran to his own house as fast as his short legs could carry him. There he spent several hours nursing his damaged dignity and his bruises.

On reaching Beaumarchais' house, the Duke learned that his enemy had gone to the Louvre. He ordered the coachman to drive there at once. He found Beaumarchais presiding over the court, surrounded with all the trappings of the law. He nevertheless interrupted the proceedings with wild gesticulations and cries. He had something important to tell Beaumarchais. Beaumarchais must come out immediately. Beaumarchais answered that he was per-

*** This dialogue is quoted verbatim from Gudin's *Compte rendu* to the Lieutenant of Police.**

forming a public function in the King's service and could not, at the moment, be disturbed. As Chaulnes went on raving and ranting, Beaumarchais suspended the hearing. He went to a small nearby room and asked Chaulnes what he wanted. Chaulnes said that he wanted to kill him and "drink his blood."

"Oh, is that all, Monsieur le Duc?" Beaumarchais replied, "I am sorry, but you must allow business to go before pleasure." Then he returned to the court room.

The hearing lasted two more hours, and the Duke did not dare assault a King's judge on the King's bench. He paced petulantly to and fro, asking loudly from time to time: "Will this last much longer?"

When the hearing was over, the Duke challenged Beaumarchais to a duel. Beaumarchais objected that he had only a parade sword with him and could not possibly fight with such an ineffective weapon. The Duke then suggested that they call at the house of a certain Comte de Turpin. They could borrow a sword from him and request him to be their witness. Whereupon he sprang into Beaumarchais' carriage, and the two men drove to the Comte de Turpin's lodging. But Turpin told them that he was urgently expected at the Luxembourg Palace, and left them to each other's company.

It was now well past dinnertime. The two Frenchmen agreed that the fact that they were about to cut each other's throat should not interfere with the enjoyment of what might be their last meal. They went to Beaumarchais' house, and Beaumarchais ordered a repast served them in his upstairs study.

When the Duke entered the study, he saw Beaumarchais' sword lying upon a table. Impulsively he drew the blade from the scabbard and lunged at his enemy. Beaumarchais dodged the sharp point and grappled with him. For a few minutes, the two men wrestled together, bumping against the furniture, kicking, biting, and scratching viciously. Chaulnes was much stronger than Beaumarchais. Nevertheless, Beaumarchais managed to grab hold of the servants' bell cord and pull it violently.

The servants ran in. Seeing their master's predicament, they attacked his assailant from the rear. Beaumarchais' cook had a substantial piece of wood in his hand and was about to smash it down upon the ducal skull when Beaumarchais stopped him. The servants succeeded in wrenching the sword from Chaulnes' hand, but dared not touch the rapier he wore at his side. Beaumarchais and Chaulnes fought savagely in the study and out. At the edge of the staircase they stumbled and rolled down a whole flight of steps.

They had scarcely picked themselves up on the ground floor when a polite knock was heard at the front door. Chaulnes rushed to the door and flung it open. There stood Gudin once more! Chaulnes drew his sword with a flourish and slashed wildly right and left, while everyone closed in on him. He carved a good slice from the scalp of one of the lackeys, split the coachman's nose, and wounded the cook's hand. In the end they managed to take his sword from him, pushed him into the dining room, and locked the door. In the dining room the table had been set, and the family dinner was ready. His anger turning into hunger, Chaulnes started at once to eat and ate ravenously.

Julie, utterly bewildered, had sent for the police. When Police Commissioner Chenu arrived, he was surprised at Beaumarchais' bedraggled look and at the disorderly appearance of his lodgings.

He ordered the dining room door opened. As soon as the Duke found himself face to face with his foe once more, he hurled himself at him and the contest—mostly fistic this time—was resumed with equal gusto on both sides.

Chenu eventually separated the champions. Beaumarchais was sent back to his study, and Chaulnes was again locked in the dining room, where he systematically started smashing everything breakable: glass, crockery, and furniture. When he felt better, he consented to return home—in Beaumarchais' carriage.

The evening of that same day, Beaumarchais went to a reception to which he had been invited and was the life of the party.

The news of the brawl took little time to become known all over Paris. The Minister of the Royal Household, the Duc de La Vrillière, greatly annoyed (for the affair threatened to cast further discredit upon the already criticized aristocratic class), asked Beaumarchais to leave Paris temporarily. The matter would be hushed up in his absence. Beaumarchais flatly refused to go. His going away, under the circumstances, would mean either a confession of guilt or an admission of fear. He was neither afraid nor guilty. He would stay. Peeved at Beaumarchais' stubbornness, La Vrillière formally forbade him to leave his house for the time being.

The tribunal of the Marshals of France, which arbitrated all *affaires d'honneur* between noblemen—Beaumarchais had been officially a nobleman since 1761—then took cognizance of the case. On their own authority, the Marshals placed both Beaumarchais and Chaulnes under home arrest. Then a swift but thorough investigation of the scandal was started; reports were made; witnesses were heard; and Chaulnes and Beaumarchais were allowed to present their versions of the facts. On February 19, a verdict was made public: Beaumarchais was declared free of all blame and the order of arrest issued against him was rescinded. The Duc de Chaulnes was held responsible for the whole affair and sent as a prisoner to the Château de Vincennes.

The Duc de Chaulnes did not remain in Vincennes very long, however. To obtain his liberation, he wrote Lieutenant General of Police Sartines a letter in which he solemnly gave his word never to molest Mlle Ménard or Beaumarchais again. He faithfully kept his pledge.

Beaumarchais did not bear the Duke the slightest grudge. Some time after the affair had been settled, he was invited to a dinner party where the Duc de Chaulnes was to be present. When his prospective host, the lawyer Target, asked him if he would be embarrassed to meet his former foe, he answered: "I shall not be in any way embarrassed to find myself with M. le Duc de Chaulnes. Of all the men who have hurt me or had hostile intentions toward me, M. le Duc de Chaulnes has been the least unfair because he was the one most moved by passion. Far from my having any aversion for him, he is one of the men I have most sincerely liked, and everything that has taken place between us cannot completely destroy my fondness for him . . . Therefore I shall have dinner with you tomorrow."

For a while Beaumarchais was worried about the sequels of the fight. Did the cancelation of the arrest ordered by the Marshals of France mean that the same order given by the Duc de La Vrillière was also cancelled? He went to La Vrillière's residence, hoping to obtain definite information on that point, but La Vrillière was not at home. Beaumarchais then consulted Lieutenent General of Police Sartines, who told him that, in his opinion, he was free.

When, however, the Minister of the Royal Household heard that Beaumarchais had left his house without express permission, he obtained a *Lettre de Cachet* from the King and, on February 24, 1773, had Beaumarchais thrown into jail.

3. *In Jail at For-l'Evêque*

THE jail to which Beaumarchais was taken—For-l'Evêque, on the Rue Saint-Germain l'Auxerrois—was one of the oldest buildings in Paris. Most of the cells were below the high-water level of the Seine, and dampness seeped in through the stone walls. Beaumarchais was not treated harshly or placed in solitary confinement, as often happened to political prisoners. He was generous to his jailers and thus was allowed to enjoy a few small material conveniences. Soon he was even permitted to communicate with his family and friends. But the news they sent filled him with consternation and dismay. In view of the Chaulnes scandal, the performance of *Le Barbier de Séville* had been postponed indefinitely. This was disappointing but not disastrous. A real disaster, however, threatened him from another quarter.

Comte de La Blache, hearing that Beaumarchais had been imprisoned, started pulling wires to have their lawsuit taken up immediately by the Parliament of Paris. It was customary in France at that time for the litigants in all civil cases to visit their judges before the trial and to present their own points of view in plain words. This system, which minimized the importance of formal debates in court, had no grave drawback and even offered certain advantages if the judges were honest and listened impartially to all arguments. It must be said that more often than not, the judges gave only perfunctory attention to the explanations of the litigants, and appointed one of their number to study the pros and cons of each case through the same method of personal, unofficial, but effective interviews. After hearing his report, they passed sentence, practically always merely endorsing the suggestions put forward by the *rapporteur*. Thus, in final analysis, the issue of a lawsuit depended upon the conclusions reached by one judge—conclusions that were, to a large extent, determined by private conversations held between him and the litigants.

Were Beaumarchais to be unable, because of his detention in jail, to present his case personally to the judges and particularly to the *rapporteur*, he would almost inevitably lose his suit. Apart from the important sum of money at stake, the accusation of forgery, if upheld by the tribunal, would forever ruin him.

Beaumarchais wrote to the Duc de La Vrillière, asking why he was kept in prison. Had he not been proclaimed innocent by the Marshals of France? He ended his letter with explanations of the important reasons why he wanted to be set free at once. The tone of his request was by no means humble. He was an honest citizen, the victim of an unjust, arbitrary measure. He demanded nothing but his right, but he demanded it firmly.

La Vrillière did not vouchsafe him any answer. He was not Beaumarchais' personal enemy, but as an aristocrat he felt a definite aversion for the lowborn upstart who had shown up a Duke and Peer of the Realm as a disgraceful bully. Let the man learn to be docile and modest, as befitted his rank.

Beaumarchais saw in the Duke's action a planned, perfidious, dastardly move. All noblemen, he fancied, stuck together. There was no vile slander, no shameful brutality, no flagrantly unfair trick that any of the great lords, a Comte de La Blache, a Duc de Chaulnes, a Duc de La Vrillière, would not use to crush him because he was a commoner. His sour feelings toward nobility turned within a few weeks into virulent hatred. He was no longer merely a disappointed social climber; he had become a social *révolté*.

A rebel, in jail, without support, all alone—Beaumarchais felt himself utterly forsaken. The Prince de Conti tried to help him, but he had no credit whatever in high places. Gudin, of course, remained faithful to him, but what could poor Gudin do for him in this harsh and ruthless world? Beaumarchais was abandoning himself to despair when a small but touching token of friendship gave him back his much needed courage. One day, a note from Constant Lenormant was handed to him along with a child's purse containing all the boy's savings. The note read: "I am sending you my purse because in prison one is always unhappy. I am very sorry that you are in prison. Every morning and every evening I say an *Ave Maria* for you. I have the honor to be, Monsieur, your very humble and obedient servant, Constant."

Beaumarchais replied: "My dear little friend Constant: I have gratefully received your letter and the purse you sent with it. I have divided everything fairly among my fellow prisoners and myself, according to our wants. For your friend Beaumarchais I have kept the best part, I mean the prayers, the *Ave Maria*, which I certainly greatly need, and I have distributed the money the purse contained to the poor suffering people around me. Thus, while intending to oblige only one man, you have earned the gratitude of many. This is the usual fruit of good actions such as yours. *Bonjour*, my little friend Constant." Then he wrote to the boy's mother: "The letter and the purse have made me as happy as a child myself. Lucky parents! You have a son of six capable of this action! I also had a son, and I have him no more. Yours already gives you such happiness! I share it with all my heart and beg you to go on loving the man who has caused this lovely spontaneous gesture in our darling Constant."

Mlle Ménard seems to have been the only person who took active steps to help Beaumarchais. She had first sought refuge with her child at the Couvent de la Présentation. The nuns, however, had agreed to take care of the child only. Utterly distracted, she then threw herself at Lieutenant General of Police Sartines' feet, and he succeeded in placing her in the Couvent des Cordelières, in the Faubourg Saint-Marceau. But she had little taste for convent life and, less than two weeks later, left of her own accord. She went to see M. de Sartines again. Mlle Ménard was not unacquainted with masculine weakness. M. de Sartines was not unappreciative of feminine charm. Under such circumstances, how could he turn a deaf ear to her pleadings and entreaties? She begged him to intervene in Beaumarchais' behalf.

The Lieutenent General of Police asked the Minister of the Royal Household to be lenient to Beaumarchais, pointing out that the loss of his lawsuit would be unmitigated disaster for him. The Minister of the Royal Household was adamant. "That man is too insolent," he is reported to have said. "Let him follow his affair through his attorney."

Then Sartines, probably urged by Mlle Ménard, sent Beaumarchais, on March 20, 1773, a brief but friendly unsigned note. He drew Beaumarchais' attention to the fact that, under an absolutist regime, no one could hope to obtain favor by taking a hostile stand against the authorities. Bowing to superior force was the only wise course to follow. Beaumarchais understood. He had to choose between humbling himself and incurring utter ruin. With rage in his heart, he humbled himself.

On March 21, Beaumarchais wrote the Duc de La Vrillière: "Despair broke me and led me to take steps that may have displeased you. I disavow them at your feet, my lord, and beg you to grant me a generous pardon. . . . The members of my family tearfully join their prayers to mine. Everyone, my lord, speaks of your indulgence and kindness of heart. Shall I be the only one to implore you in vain? With a single word you can fill the hearts of honest people with joy, and their gratitude will equal the profound respect with which we all are, and I in particular am, your very humble and obedient servant."

A complete moral capitulation by Beaumarchais was all the Duke's vanity wanted. At once La Vrillière gave him permission to leave prison whenever he had to interview the judges. But to save face, he decided that Beaumarchais had to be accompanied by a police officer and return every night to sleep at For-l'Evêque. These stipulations were only trifling hindrances to Beaumarchais' moves, but he had no time to lose. The legal proceedings had already started, and the final judgment was to be pronounced in less than two weeks.

At first Beaumarchais made his routine calls without difficulty. The lawyers' "strike" against the Maupeou Parliaments had fizzled out. Although the general public still greatly resented the new courts, the legal machinery now ran with normal smoothness. After ten days, Beaumarchais succeeded in obtaining short interviews from all his judges except one, Louis Valentin Goëzman.

Goëzman had the reputation of a bully and a grafter. After several years' undistinguished service on the bench of the Supreme Council of Alsace, he had come to Paris in 1765 as a free-lance lawyer. He had joined the clique of the Duc d'Aiguillon, who was then intriguing against Choiseul. Goëzman had helped the Duke by writing slanderous anonymous pamphlets against his enemies. At the same time, he had eked out a rather precarious living by taking on foul-smelling legal cases. When the Triumvirs came into power, he was rewarded, in 1771, with a judgeship at the Parliament of Paris for services rendered.

A short, heavy, thick-set, bearded man of forty-three, Goëzman was gruff in approach, uncouth and boorish in manner. He had recently become a widower and remarried. His second wife, *née* Gabrielle Julie Jamart, was young, pretty, temperamental, and stupid, but a master of the art of twisting her husband around her lovely little finger. Grasping and unscrupulous, she knew that he frequently accepted bribes and she even occasionally helped him collect them. She was later quoted as having said: "It would be impossible for us to live decently with the salary we get, but we know how to pluck the fowl without making it cry out."

On April 1, 1773, Goëzman was made *rapporteur* for the La Blache-Beaumarchais lawsuit. Beaumarchais now had to see him as soon as possible and speak to him at length about the case. He called again and again at Goëzman's home, but was refused admission each time.

Thoroughly perplexed by the *rapporteur*'s most unusual behavior, Beaumarchais dejectedly paced the streets. On April 2, shortly before noon, he thus found himself before the Lépines' house. He entered and found a group of people there, most of them personal friends of his sister and his brother-in-law. They welcomed him sympathetically. Among them was a certain Bertrand Dairolles. Rumor had it that Dairolles was attracted to the watchmaker's home mainly by his wife and that the still flirtatious Fanchon was not altogether displeased by his attentions. Dairolles, a bachelor of thirty-seven, had his fingers in many pies, being in turn or even simultaneously middleman, promoter, broker, and banker according to circumstances. Originally from Provence, he was, like many Southerners, excitable, talkative, officious, and somewhat meddlesome, and he knew everybody.

Dairolles knew particularly well a bookseller named Jean-Baptiste Le Jay, who had published Goëzman's pamphlets against Choiseul. Mme Goëzman often went to Le Jay's shop to gossip with his wife. Perhaps through her Dairolles would be able to arrange an interview with Goëzman for Beaumarchais.

Indeed, the afternoon of the same day, Dairolles brought back word to Beaumarchais that, thanks to Le Jay, he had communicated with Mme Goëzman. She had promised to see that Beaumarchais was received by the *rapporteur* that very evening, but it would cost him one hundred louis. One hundred louis—two thousand livres! Beaumarchais howled. He was not particularly indignant at the idea of a judge asking for a bribe, but he was incensed at the amount requested. Yet he knew that a *rapporteur* was not legally compelled to grant a litigant a private audience: it was merely a matter of custom. He gave in.

Since Beaumarchais did not have one hundred louis available in cash, he sent Gudin with an explanatory note to the Prince de Conti, and the Prince let him have the whole sum at once. Bertrand

Dairolles took the money to Le Jay, who took it to Mme Goëzman. According to her promise, late in the evening the door of the Goëzman residence was opened to Beaumarchais.

Beaumarchais was led by a servant to the *rapporteur*'s study. The *rapporteur* looked hostile and surly. He listened with an uninterested air to Beaumarchais' explanation of the facts, asked two or three casual questions, then declared the interview at an end. Beaumarchais was shown the door.

Beaumarchais was worried, for he suspected some dark maneuver by La Blache. He was sure that Goëzman had not been able, in the few minutes their talk had lasted, to get a clear view of the intricacies of the lawsuit, which was to come before the Parliament in three days.

On April 3, Beaumarchais asked Dairolles to find out if he could possibly see Goëzman again. Dairolles communicated with Le Jay, who communicated with Mme Goëzman, who said that another visit to her husband would cost Beaumarchais another hundred louis. But Beaumarchais could not or would not borrow another hundred louis from the Prince de Conti. He offered, instead, to give Mme Goëzman a watch, a superb diamond-studded watch, the last watch he had made.

Mme Goëzman took the watch. At the last moment, however, she also asked for an additional fifteen louis for her husband's secretary—so she said. Beaumarchais somehow managed to find fifteen louis. He handed them to Dairolles and was assured that Goëzman would receive him the evening of Sunday, April 4.

In the interval, on Sunday morning, La Blache—as was later proved—went to Goëzman's house. Evidently he offered the judge a larger bribe than Beaumarchais'. When Beaumarchais presented himself at the appointed time, he was told that the *rapporteur* could not see him.

A last and desperate effort on his part to establish contact with Goëzman in the morning of Monday 5, failed in a like manner. In the afternoon, the Parliament rendered its verdict. As could have been expected, the judgment of the court closely followed Goëzman's recommendations. The charge of forgery was not upheld, but, oddly enough, the settlement of accounts signed by Pâris-Duverney was pronounced void. Later, a complementary judgment ordered Beaumarchais to pay La Blache 56,000 livres and bear court costs.

Beaumarchais, who had been allowed to leave jail temporarily so that he might call on his judges, was now locked up again at For-l'Evêque. He remained there another month, until May 8, 1773. When at long last he was set free, he realized the extent of his plight. Since he had not been able to pay the 56,000 livres awarded La Blache, the latter had taken steps to seize his enemy's property. He had started with the Rue de Condé house and had sent men there to carry away the furniture piece by piece.

Beaumarchais' family had fled. His father had taken a room in a middle-aged spinster's house. Julie had gone to a convent in Paris. Marie-Josèphe and Lisette had withdrawn to the convent of Les Dames de la Croix, at Roye, in Picardy. After a short illness, Tonton had died while her brother was in prison. She had left a little girl, who, along with the two Guilbert boys, had found shelter with the Lépines. Beaumarchais now also went there and began to set his affairs in order.

4. *The Goëzman Case*

Through Le Jay, Mme Goëzman had voluntarily sent the hundred louis and the watch back to Beaumarchais, but she refused to return the fifteen louis allegedly given to her husband's secretary. Beaumarchais was in no mood for compromise. While detained at For-l'Evêque, he had written Mme Goëzman courteously but firmly, asking for the fifteen louis. He had not received any answer. After his release, he started a discreet investigation through one of his acquaintances, M. de La Chataigneraie, who knew the secretary, Claude de Saint-Simon. He thus learned that Saint-Simon had neither requested nor received the fifteen louis. Mme Goëzman had evidently pocketed the money and meant to keep it. She probably believed that Beaumarchais would be wise enough not to raise an outcry over such a paltry sum. Had he not, after all, attempted to bribe a judge? He would understand that he had better keep quiet.

Beaumarchais did not keep quiet. His fight with Chaulnes, his arbitrary imprisonment, his spectacular ruin, had aroused a great deal of curiosity in Paris. Many people wanted to hear what he had to say about all this, and he was only too ready to talk. Whenever he came to the fifteen louis, his story caused raised eyebrows and contemptuous sneers. Even those who smilingly condoned a big, bold swindle could only despise cheap, petty thievery.

Goëzman heard the disparaging remarks that were passed about him, and mentioned them to his wife. But she hoodwinked her husband into believing that Beaumarchais was a liar.

Goëzman was now convinced that absolutely all the money Beaumarchais had paid had been returned to him and that he was trying to work some sort of blackmail. Goëzman had seen many blackmailers in his checkered career and knew how to deal with them. The only thing to do was to stand firm and to scare them out of their wits.

On May 30, 1773, Mme Goëzman asked Le Jay to call on her about an urgent and grave affair. When Le Jay came, she complained that Beaumarchais was asking a second time for the money that had been returned to him. Le Jay, who had handed the hundred louis and the watch to Mme Lépine, rushed to her house. There he was shown a copy of Beaumarchais' letter to Mme Goëzman, asking for the fifteen louis which had never been refunded. Annoyed at having been sent on a fool's errand, Le Jay ran back to the Goëzman residence to give Mme Goëzman a piece of his mind.

Mme Goëzman did not receive him this time. It was late in the evening, and a servant took him directly to the judge's study. The room was dark and had a sinister look. Two dim candles stood on the desk, and behind the desk, wrapped in ominous shadows, sat Goëzman, silent and grim. Before Le Jay could compose himself, a hurricane of reproaches and threats broke over his head: He knew better than anyone else Goëzman's close link with d'Aiguillon, Terray, Maupeou—the omnipotent Triumvirs. The whole power of the law was arrayed behind the judge. That scoundrel Beaumarchais was to be crushed as he richly deserved. Did Le Jay want to take his side and share his fate?

Le Jay protested that he was utterly devoted to Goëzman and stammered his good will. Very well, then—let him prove his devotion and good will through acts. The hapless Le Jay, terrified by Goëzman's booming voice and menacing countenance, wrote under his dictation and signed with a shaking hand a statement that he, Le Jay, had, at Bertrand Dairolles' request, agreed "to speak to Mme Goëzman on his [Beaumarchais'] behalf and even offer to her one hundred louis and a watch set with diamonds, to induce her to intercede with her husband in favor of the Sieur de Beaumarchais." He formally declared that Mme Goëzman had "rejected the proposal unhesitatingly and indignantly."

Armed with this document, Goëzman went two days later, on June 1, 1773, to see the Duc de La Vrillière and Sartines, asking them to step on Beaumarchais once more. But the Duke, whose conscience was perhaps not altogether easy about Beaumarchais, flatly declined to do anything against him. Sartines was even more emphatic in his refusal to support Goëzman. Goëzman returned home discomfited and worried.

Soon the news of Goëzman's abortive attempt to strike at Beaumarchais leaked out and spread throughout Paris. The actual facts were wildly exaggerated and distorted. Everybody now talked about the mysterious bribery that the government was trying to hush up. The Minister of the Royal Household and the Lieutenant General of Police were afraid, it was whispered, to take action against Beaumarchais: he must have a pretty strong case. His opponent, Goëzman, was apparently thoroughly corrupt. What else could you expect from a member of the Maupeou Parliament?

The President of the Parliament, Berthier de Sauvigny, disturbed by these damaging rumors, called in Goëzman for an explanation. Goëzman assured him that he had never done anything in connection with the Beaumarchais lawsuit that could give anyone grounds to impugn his integrity. Sauvigny then ordered him to bring the matter into the open. He would thus clear his own name and bring confusion to the scandal mongers attacking the Parliament through him.

This was infinitely more than Goëzman had bargained for, yet he could not withdraw. With fear in his heart but an expression of righteous self-confidence on his face, he asked the Parliament for a legal inquiry. Was an attempt to bribe a judge's wife to be considered as contempt of court? The answer could not be anything but yes. The Parliament ordered that an official investigation into the particulars of the matter be made forthwith.

When Le Jay heard this he lost his head completely. Since the night he had signed his mendacious statement under Goëzman's pressure he had been in the throes of remorse. He consulted a lawyer, who advised him to disavow his former declaration and say that he had written it under duress. He consulted Goëzman himself, who advised him to leave France and go to Holland. But Mme Le Jay put her foot down on that scheme. When Le Jay was called in to give evidence, he blurted out the whole truth. He was arrested at once and indicted on the charge of being the self-confessed author of a fraudulent affidavit.

At long last Mme Goëzman then told her husband what had happened to the fifteen louis. Goëzman was thunderstruck. It was too late for him to go back on his previous statements. He knew that his wife, if called as a witness, would never be able to stand up under a searching, pitiless cross-examination. He then asked the government to issue a *Lettre de Cachet* ordering her temporarily confined in a convent. She would thus be automatically out of reach of dangerous questioners. But either Goëzman did not have enough influence to obtain such a favor or the government did not dare spirit away a key witness in an affair that was beginning to create passionate public interest. In any case, his request was denied.

Filled with dark forebodings, Goëzman tried to negotiate a private deal with Beaumarchais. He could no longer approach him personally, but communicated with him through one of their mutual friends, a man named Marin.

Marin was editor of the most important daily newspaper in Paris, *La Gazette de France.* A superficially friendly, jolly fellow, Marin was very popular in the literary cafés and among the "philosophers." He supported the Triumvirs' policies and sat on the Board of Censors. Moreover, he owned several tabloids—then called *Nouvelles à la main*—in which expert blackmailing was practiced as a regular, remunerative branch of journalism. He consented to serve as intermediary between Goëzman and Beaumarchais mainly out of vanity. It flattered him to be the important man called upon to settle grave and difficult affairs.

Marin knew Beaumarchais only slightly, but their relations had been decidedly cordial. As a member of the Board of Censors, Marin had shown himself broad-minded and accommodating in all his decisions on Beaumarchais' plays. Yet when he asked Beaumarchais if he could not possibly compromise with Goëzman, Beaumarchais categorically refused. Deeply offended, Marin turned against Beaumarchais. One of Beaumarchais' main witnesses, Bertrand Dairolles, was one of Marin's intimate friends; both came from the same region in Provence. Marin persuaded Dairolles to pass with arms and baggage into Goëzman's camp. Then he unearthed an obscure, second-rate writer, a pedantic and sanctimonious fool, Baculard d'Arnauld, who was ready to swear that he had with his own eyes seen Mme Goëzman refuse the gifts shamefully proferred to tempt her husband's integrity.

The case against Beaumarchais was now complete; the lines of battle were well drawn. In spite of a few weak points—the weakest being Mme Goëzman herself—the Goëzman-Marin side seemed by far the stronger. The most powerful and dangerous elements of the press, the widely read *Gazette de France* and the *Nouvelles à la main*, were arrayed in its support. The literary cafés, never favorably disposed toward Beaumarchais, campaigned more or less openly against him. Above all, the formidable might of the judicial system and, behind it, the tremendous power of an absolutist government stood poised to consummate his defeat. Against such odds, Beaumarchais' position seemed hopeless. He had just been condemned by the highest court of justice in the kingdom under circumstances suggesting that he was a forger. The present lawsuit had its awkward side, too, for if he carried his point—if he proved that Mme Goëzman had not returned him the fifteen louis—he would automatically prove that he had given them to her in the first place, in other words, that he had tried to bribe a judge.

Beaumarchais also had to contend with the often-whispered accusations that he had been a street beggar, had murdered Francquet, and had poisoned his first wife. Now a brand-new set of slanders appeared. Why had he gone to Spain? His sister had got into trouble there. What kind of trouble was, of course, anybody's guess. . . . His second wife had seemed in radiant health until shortly before her death. Had she not been put into her grave in the same manner as his first wife?. . . His first wife's relatives, with whom he had never had any quarrel so far, banded together and joined in the fray. They abrogated the agreement they had freely made with him fourteen years before and sued him for damages.

To defend himself against this host of enemies, Beaumarchais had but one weapon: his pen. The press systematically presented his case in the worst possible light. He decided to appeal directly to the public. On September 5, 1773, he published a memorial in which he explained in a clear, lively manner the tangled legal and factual aspects of the whole affair. After reading the memorial, many people began to feel that Beaumarchais had been harshly treated. The natural tendency of the French always to take the side of the weak against the strong brought him a widespread sympathy previously denied him.

Public opinion slowly veered in Beaumarchais' favor, and he knew why. As he said in a "supplement" to his first memorial, which he composed shortly afterward: "I have no illusions. For the public, to see me justified does not matter so much as to watch how an isolated man can stand against such a tremendous attack and repel that attack all alone."

This supplement rapidly eclipsed the first memorial itself. Indeed, Beaumarchais, relegating to a secondary place legal and factual considerations, now turned his argument into a most entertaining comedy. With amazing dramatic force, he conjured up in terse, clipped sentences the personality of each of his opponents, showing their typical gestures, making them strut, stride, or stroll for the reader as if they were upon a stage, suggesting their intonations, unveiling their intentions, and naturally implying that they were deliberate liars or shallow fools. The public was delighted.

Marin, Bertrand Dairolles, Baculard d'Arnauld, and Mme

Goëzman herself, thoroughly alarmed, replied to Beaumarchais' memorial with memorials of their own.

Mme Goëzman evidently received help from her husband in her work, for her memorial was long, pedantic, stuffed with Latin quotations, and loaded with ponderous discussions on minutiae of law. "The work of a German lawyer," Beaumarchais commented. Here and there however, a few shrill ejaculations, a few hysterical insults broke through the technical arguments laboriously pieced together; these were undoubtedly the lady's own contribution to the pamphlet published under her name.

Bertrand Dairolles did his best to be abusive, but he lacked literary talent, and his memorial turned out ineffectual and weak.

Baculard's production was pompous and oratorical. Throughout his long-winded, redundant periods, he maintained a highly moral and religious tone. He was boring and dull. But since many people consider dullness and boredom the earmarks of sincerity and depth of thought, his attacks were definitely dangerous to Beaumarchais.

Marin's memorials, cleverly written, entertaining, and witty, were by far the most dangerous of all. They were filled with venomous insinuations about Beaumarchais' past life. Marin had raked up all the available muck and now offered it to the public with the perfect craftsmanship of an expert yellow journalist.

Beaumarchais, assailed from all sides, violently struck back at his tormentors. On December 20, 1773, he published a third memorial under the title: "Addition to the Supplement." Following Marin's lead, he tore into the private lives of his opponents. One after another—"Your turn, Marin" . . . "Your turn, Dairolles" "Your turn, Baculard"—they were collared, pilloried, flayed, and then left exposed, limp, and panting, to the public's sarcasm and scorn.

In his anger, Beaumarchais, unmindful of the new antagonisms he might arouse, poked fun at the aristocracy as he had never dared before. "Do you know," he wrote, "that I can prove twenty years of nobility? And that nobility is my legitimate property, as a fine piece of parchment adorned with a large seal of yellow wax attests. My nobility—unlike that of so many other people—is not uncertain, something for which you have to take somebody's word. No one can challenge its authenticity, because I still hold the receipt for the money I had to pay for it."

As for Goëzman, Beaumarchais dug up a disgusting affair, absolutely unconnected with the bribery case, but which gave him excellent ammunition for their mud-slinging war. Goëzman had been secretly keeping a young mistress, who had recently given birth to a child. Goëzman had not recognized the child, but had acted as its godfather. After the baptism, he had written a false name and false address on the Church register, which was considered a legal document in France in those days. Furthermore, later on he had failed to support the baby or the unwed mother, and the baby's grandparents had sued him under his assumed name to compel him to contribute to the child's care. Goëzman's behavior was sacrilegious in the eyes of the Church, criminal in the eyes of the law, and revolting in the eyes of anyone with a modicum of humanity and decency.

The Parliament, however annoyed by the disclosure of this scandal, had no choice but to order an inquiry into Beaumarchais' charges. Finding them clearly substantiated, it suspended Goëzman from the exercise of judicial functions.

All Paris now talked of the Goëzman-Beaumarchais affair. In the cafés, in the salons, in the theaters, even in the streets, people excitedly discussed the facts and the personalities involved in the case.

Banking on the publicity given Beaumarchais' name, the actors of the Comédie Française decided to revive his old play *Eugénie.* It was presented on January 9, 1774, and this time the performance ended with a triumph—better still, with a riot. Why not, then, give *Le Barbier de Séville?* Marin himself had officially authorized the performance of *Le Barbier de Séville* a year before. There was no need for the actors to obtain any new, special permission. Soon rehearsals began. When the Triumvirs sent the police to stop them, the public grumbled. Even at Versailles, the young Dauphiness, Marie-Antoinette, who had read the play, said openly that she could see no reason why it should not be performed. The prohibition was raised, and *Le Barbier de Séville* was announced for presentation on February 12, 1774. But at the very last moment, when a huge crowd already stood outside the theater, orders forbidding the performance came once more from Versailles.

The government's arbitrary and erratic attitude drew more sympathizers to Beaumarchais' side every day. The unpopularity of the Maupeou Parliaments also worked strongly in his favor. People were repeating: "Louis XV destroyed the old Parliament; fifteen louis will destroy the new one."

Beaumarchais now enjoyed the fight thoroughly. He was no longer alone. At his headquarters, the Lépine house, he was surrounded by eager, devoted partisans. Julie had left her convent and had thrown herself with all her heart and soul into the struggle. Her sparkling wit, her sense of the dramatic, and her sharp insight into human character left many definite marks on Beaumarchais' memorials. Gudin was naturally at hand, ever ready to undertake any amount of research or preparatory work needed. A young doctor named Gardanne, originally from Provence, was an inexhaustible source for funny anecdotes about Marin and Dairolles. Miron's levelheaded judgment served as a useful check whenever Beaumarchais' or Julie's imagination soared too high or strayed too far. A lawyer, Falconet, took care of the possible legal implications in the various statements made. Lépine now and then added a word of encouragement or advice. Even old Caron nodded approvingly when his son read to the enthusiastic little group a newly composed passage that was particularly pungent or moving.

Beaumarchais' fourth memorial was published the morning after the day on which the performance of *Le Barbier de Séville* had been finally forbidden. Within three days, six thousand copies of it were sold. The fourth memorial was a literary masterpiece. Its subject was Beaumarchais' own life and character. Beaumarchais was clever enough not to draw an idealized portrait of himself. He painted a likable scapegrace, imprudent, impulsive, lightheaded, but warmhearted and generous.

In answering the besmirching stories circulated about his sister's behavior in Spain, he recounted his whole adventure in Madrid. He told it with so much gusto and pathos that in faraway Frankfort, Goethe, after reading the memorial, composed in a week on that theme one of his best-known plays, *Clavigo*.

Voltaire himself—certainly no mean connoisseur of polemics—said of the fourth memorial: "No comedy was ever more amusing, no tragedy more touching." Also: "What a man! He unites everything—humor, seriousness, argument, gaiety, power, emotion, every kind of eloquence, and yet he seeks none. He confounds his enemies and gives lessons to his judges. His naïveté delights me, and I forgive him his carelessness and petulance."

It can be said without exaggeration that the publication of the fourth memorial became a national and international event. Beaumarchais' name spread among the cultivated men of Europe. In Paris—nay at Versailles itself—the fourth memorial rallied round him hosts of people who had till then been indifferent or frankly hostile to him. Many now read his earlier memorials, which they had previously overlooked, or reread them in a new spirit. Louis XV read them and was amused. Mme Du Barry read them and had their main episodes made into short plays, which were acted privately before the King and herself. Beaumarchais fast became the most popular man in France.

In the meantime, the Parliament had officially examined all aspects of the case. Goëzman and his wife tried to shift responsibility for their misdeeds to the defenseless, pitiful Le Jay. These tactics deceived no one and antagonized everyone. Mme Goëzman revealed herself a silly, conceited, dishonest minx who systematically lied, became entangled in her own lies, contradicted herself, flew into rages when her falsehoods came to light, and then heaped vulgar insults upon whoever was at hand. When she confronted Beaumarchais on the witness stand, the result was pure high comedy. Beaumarchais was perfectly cool, imperceptibly flippant, elaborately courteous, and supremely entertaining. A judge asked Mme Goëzman if she had seen Beaumarchais previously.

"Certainly not," she said. "I don't know him and I have no desire ever to know him."

"I don't have the honor of knowing Madame, either," Beaumarchais replied, significantly eying her comely figure. "But after having a look at her, I can't help expressing a completely different desire from hers."

Gales of Gallic laughter shook the court room.

During the questioning, Mme Goëzman said that she had indeed been offered one hundred louis by Le Jay on Beaumarchais' behalf and had indignantly rejected the offer, but that she had never heard of the fifteen louis.

"Le Jay," she said, "never spoke to me of the fifteen louis and did not give them to me, either."

"Please observe," Beaumarchais retorted, "that there would be more merit in saying 'I refused them' than in maintaining that you knew nothing about them."

"I maintain, sir, that no one ever mentioned them to me. What sense would there have been in offering fifteen louis to a woman of my rank—to me, who had refused a hundred the day before?"

"The day before what?"

"Well, sir, the day before the day—" She stopped suddenly, biting her lips.

"The day before the day no one mentioned these fifteen louis, isn't it?"

"Stop this," she said furiously, rising to her feet, "or I shall slap you in the face! What did I care about those fifteen louis? With all your nasty, twisted little sentences, you are trying to confuse me and make me contradict myself, but I tell you I am not going to answer another word."*

* This dialogue is quoted word for word from Beaumarchais' Supplement to the first material.

For days and days the show went on.

Saturday, February 26, 1774, had been set as the day on which the verdict was to be rendered. Huge crowds milled before the Hall of Justice, and the police reported that the Parisians were in a riotous mood. For ten hours the judges discussed the matter among themselves. In the end they reached a conclusion through a curious compromise.

Le Jay, Dairolles, Baculard, Beaumarchais, and Mme Goëzman were fined three livres apiece and were stripped of most of their legal abilities and rights. This partial civic degradation was called a *Blâme* in the legal language of the day. Moreover, Mme Goëzman was to return the fifteen louis, which would be distributed to the prisoners in the Conciergerie. Goëzman was expelled from the Parliament. The four memorials published by Beaumarchais were to be torn up and burned by the public executioner. As a special punishment for writing them, Beaumarchais was to pay an additional fine of twelve livres, which would also be given as alms to the Conciergerie prisoners.

When the throngs which had gathered in the streets learned the sentences passed, they booed and hissed so violently that the judges thought it wise to slink out through a back door. For Beaumarchais the affair ended with a complete moral triumph. For two full days the street on which Lépine's house was situated was jammed with the carriages of the highest personages of the kingdom, who came to write their names in the visitors' book, which was usually placed in those days at the door of every substantial residence. Even the Lieutenant of Police came, though incognito and on foot. He left on the register a large *S* followed by three stars.

On February 28, the Prince de Conti gave in Beaumarchais' honor a large banquet which was attended by the most prominent people in Paris. Beaumarchais was radiant, exultant. When it was all over, Sartines said to him ironically yet kindly: "*Ce n'est pas assez que d'être blâmé, il faut encore être modeste.*"

Chapter 6

SECRET AGENT

1. Mme Du Barry's Honor

BEAUMARCHAIS WAS WISE enough to heed Sartines' advice. He realized that his name had now become a symbol of victorious opposition to the Maupeou Parliament—to the government's policies—and he did not want an open conflict with the government. The court's condemnation was a serious matter to him. He had naturally been suspended from exercising his functions as judge of the Louvre tribunal. Because many of his civil rights had been forfeited, he also found himself gravely incapacitated for any future judicial action he might want to initiate.

La Blache, taking full advantage of these circumstances, went inexorably ahead with his plans to ruin Beaumarchais. The actual sum Beaumarchais had been ordered to pay La Blache was not enormous, but he did not have enough cash to discharge the debt at once and could borrow only small amounts to cover current expenses. His credit as a businessman was now at its lowest ebb. La Blache therefore started proceedings to force the liquidation of all of Beaumarchais' enterprises. Beaumarchais tried to fight La Blache off with legal aid, and his lawyers bored into his affairs from all sides like termites. The whole structure of his fortune threatened to collapse.

Beaumarchais intended one day to appeal the sentence passed against him in his lawsuit with La Blache and felt confident that he could eventually have the judgment reversed. But what would be the use of winning his case in the end if, in the meantime, everything he owned went into legal costs and fees? He had to stop La Blache without delay.

Beaumarchais knew that the only power that could stop the course of "justice" was the King. When in favor with the royal princesses, Beaumarchais had often met the King. At that time, the King had shown him genuine kindness. Since then, Beaumarchais had never said or done anything to which Louis XV might take offense. He had mocked the aristocracy, but he had never directed his jibes at the monarch. Yet Louis XV had certainly been displeased by the commotion created by the Goëzman trial. Furthermore, when Beaumarchais now appeared in public, he received ovations and demonstrations that amounted to indirect attacks against the Versailles régime.

As a mark of good will, Beaumarchais decided to leave Paris quietly. He went to Flanders. By thus voluntarily removing a cause of serious embarrassment to the administration, he hoped to show that nothing was further from his mind than his being a source of difficulty for the King. At the same time, he appealed to the King through one of his friends, a wealthy businessman named Jean Benjamin de La Borde, who held the honorary position of *Valet de Chambre du Roi* at the court of Versailles. Beaumarchais wrote to him: "The thing that more than anything else in this sinister event has broken my heart is the unfavorable impression created about me in the King's mind. He has been told that I was trying to gain a seditious reputation; but no one told him that I only defended myself and that I never ceased pointing out to my judges what might result from this ridiculous trial."

La Borde relayed Beaumarchais' protestations of personal loyalty to Louis XV. Louis XV appreciated Beaumarchais' sacrifice in leaving Paris and now felt inclined to treat the affair with benevolence.

As a matter of fact, leaving Paris had meant a much greater sacrifice for Beaumarchais than the King could possibly have known. Immediately after the publication of the fourth memorial, when he was the idol of the capital, Beaumarchais had received a most bizarre request through one of his friends. A Mlle de Willermaulaz had accidentally damaged her harp and had sent it out for repairs. Would Beaumarchais lend her his harp? At first he turned down this bold proposal. But when he read unmentioned, though alluring possibilities in his friend's face, he added that if Mademoiselle wished to practice on his harp in his home, she would be heartily welcome. She accepted the offer.

Marie Thérèse Amélie de Willermaulaz was not a brazen hussy; she was merely badly love-struck. She belonged to a respectable, well-to-do family. Her father had come from Charmey, near Fribourg, in Switzerland. He had entered the service of the rich and influential Marquis de Dreux-Brézé, Louis XV's Grand Master of Ceremonies. Both her parents had died when she was very young, but she had been left well provided for. She had grown into a strong, healthy young woman with a somewhat heavy bearing and outwardly cold and distant manners. Inwardly, however, she was anything but well balanced and calm. She often was the prey to feelings of deep melancholy. This melancholy had its roots in endless daydreams and blossomed into a sincere longing for goodness and into impulsive outbursts of sentimentality. At the same time, there was in her a definite streak of revolt against conventions and rules. She wanted to be herself, to assert her personality, even—and preferably—if doing so meant breaking the accepted social code.

These views and feelings were not idiosyncrasies of hers alone; they were common among the members of her generation. They were the outstanding traits of a new conception of life and the world at large, a conception that later developed into the great movement of Romanticism. Yet Mlle de Willermaulaz' generation, and Mlle de Willermaulaz in particular, retained certain typical features of the eighteenth century. She was lightheaded and merry, though her lightheadness and mirth were perhaps only means to escape from the anguish that constantly gripped her deeper, tormented self. Beaumarchais' sister Julie summarized the contradictory aspects of her character by saying, with her usual incisive humor, that Mlle de Willermaulaz represented "French frivolity on a pedestal of Swiss dignity."

Mlle de Willermaulaz' outward dignity and majestic appearance corresponded closely to Beaumarchais' feminine ideal. And in her superficial gaiety, which covered a fundamental spiritual unrest, he found a sympathetic echo of his own inward disharmony. Finally, her desire to rebel against the rules and her craving for sentimental self-expression answered similar feelings in him. Thus, despite their disparity in ages—she was twenty-three and he forty-one—they had a strong affinity for each other.

After staying in Flanders only a few weeks, Beaumarchais received word from La Borde that the King had granted him a reprieve. This meant that the legal proceedings La Blache had initiated against him were brought to a standstill. But there was one condition unofficially attached to this reprieve: the King wanted Beaumarchais to accept a secret mission. Nothing could be mentioned in the letter, but M. de Sartines would tell him the particulars of the affair.

Beaumarchais rushed back to Paris and went to see Sartines. He learned from him of a French adventurer and pamphleteer in London named Charles Théveneau de Morande. Morande claimed to be a political refugee, but was in fact a professional blackmailer. At irregular intervals he published a sheet, *Le Gazetier Cuirassé*, that dealt with scandalous stories—imaginary or true—about prominent Frenchmen. He would stop his attacks against a person only if he were offered what he considered an adequate price.

Morande had just printed a pamphlet with the lurid title, *Secret Memoirs of a Prostitute*, which told in needless detail the life story of Mme Du Barry, Louis XV's official favorite. Louis XV was most eager to prevent the distribution of the pamphlet; enough mud had been splashed on the French throne. The French authorities had already communicated with the English authorities about the matter. The Minister of Foreign Affairs in London at that time happened to be Beaumarchais' former friend, Lord Rochford. Lord Rochford had the utmost contempt for Morande, but was powerless to stop him. The man could, of course, be hauled up before the English courts on a charge of libel, but the trial would only increase the scandal, not suppress it. London, however, had confidentially informed Versailles that if French agents, acting with utmost discretion, managed to arrest Morande on British territory and take him quietly to France, the English police would ignore the whole thing.

Consequently, French agents had been sent to England to kidnap the scoundrel. But the woman they had used as a decoy to trap Morande had informed her intended victim of the plot. Morande knew better than to ask for police protection. Instead he raised a loud cry: here was a free, honest political refugee whom a foreign power was trying to remove from the sanctuary of British soil. The British public responded at once to his call for help, and a guard of volunteers was formed to protect him. The French agents nevertheless made an attempt to take him away, but were met by stout-fisted Englishmen and barely escaped being thrown into the Thames.

Since that unfortunate episode, all of the French government's efforts to establish contact with Morande had failed. Morande evidently distrusted anyone having any connection whatever with Versailles. The King and Mme Du Barry were in mortal fear lest, at any moment, the *Mémoires secrets d'une fille publique*—which were known to have been printed for some time—be thrown on the market by Morande. The King wanted Beaumarchais to go to London at once and see to it that the libelous pamphlet was destroyed. His traveling expenses would be refunded and any "reasonable" price Morande asked would be paid. No definite promise was made Beaumarchais about his lawsuit, but Sartines explained that accepting this mission was a way—the only way, in fact—to regain the royal favor he so badly needed.

At first Beaumarchais protested: this was police work of the lowest kind. But he quickly understood that he was in no position to be fastidious. He asked only to be given a personal interview by the King. Thus he could consider himself a secret agent entrusted by His Majesty with a confidential mission. This face-saving suggestion was accepted, and the interview granted. In March 1774 he sailed for England with a passport bearing the name of Chevalier de Ronac, Ronac being an anagram of Caron, for the name Beaumarchais was now famous all over Europe.

Beaumarchais had reluctantly accepted Sartines' proposal, but once he found himself in the midst of the game he enjoyed it thoroughly. Dressed in his very best and putting on his most courtly manners, he first called on Lord Rochford, who received him cordially—indeed, like an old friend. Yet, with the discretion befitting a well-bred gentleman, the Englishman refrained from questioning him about the object of his trip to London. A little later, Beaumarchais, now dressed in shabby clothes and affecting familiar and democratic ways, went to Morande's rather sordid lodging. Morande had heard of the forgery and bribery cases in which Beaumarchais had been implicated and naturally surmised that his visitor was a man of his own sort. The two came rapidly and without difficulty to a perfect understanding.

Only a few days after leaving France, Beaumarchais was on his way back to Versailles. He had in his possession a copy of the pamphlet against Mme Du Barry and the manuscripts of two other pamphlets that Morande planned to publish. He also brought with him Morande's conditions for destroying the three pamphlets and his offer to go over, lock, stock, and barrel, to the government's side. Morande knew the other French pamphleteers plying their trade in London. He would act as informer against them and serve Louis XV faithfully.

Louis XV was amazed. Here was an affair the French secret service had tackled from all possible angles for months and months and, in the end, had hopelessly bungled. In the very same affair, Beaumarchais, within less than a week, had obtained results beyond hope. The King considered the problem solved, as far as he was concerned, and turned Beaumarchais over to the Duc d'Aiguillon for the settlement of the details.

The Duke had never met Beaumarchais before, but had seen many of his portraits, which had been in evidence everywhere during the Goëzman trial. When "M. de Ronac" was shown into his study, he looked at him wonderingly.

"You must be the devil—or M. de Beaumarchais," he said.

"M. de Beaumarchais only, at your service, my lord," the other replied good-naturedly.

The Duc d'Aiguillon wanted Beaumarchais to double-cross Morande: Beaumarchais was to take advantage of the confidence the blackmailer had in him, and have the man arrested as had been originally planned. Beaumarchais, however, flatly refused to do such a thing and appealed to the King. The King unreservedly backed Beaumarchais' stand. On April 8, Beaumarchais left Versailles for London, carrying 20,000 livres in cash from the

King's privy purse and a deed of annuity for 4000 livres in Morande's name. Morande was to destroy the three pamphlets and become the King's secret agent.

When Beaumarchais arrived in Calais, however, he realized that he was shadowed by suspicious characters, whom he guessed to be the Duc d'Aiguillon's emissaries. What fun Beaumarchais had playing hide-and-seek with them, throwing them off his tracks by clever, subtle moves, sailing across the Channel in a small boat at night, and reaching London safely and alone!

Morande was now elusive and distrustful, for he had received anonymous letters, originating from the Duc d'Aiguillon, advising him to be on his guard against Beaumarchais. Beaumarchais was therefore unable to conclude the expected agreement with Morande and returned to Paris for a showdown with the Duke. Once more the King was called upon to arbitrate their differences and once more he took Beaumarchais' side. Beaumarchais went back to London with greater powers and succeeded in persuading Morande of his sincerity. On the night of April 24, 1774, the pamphlets were burned by the two men in an abandoned limekiln near St. Pancras, and Morande received his deed of annuity as well as 20,000 livres in cash.

Beaumarchais remained two more weeks in the English capital. He visited Lord Rochford again and this time revealed the secret of his mission. Furthermore, on his own initiative he and Lord Rochford reached an understanding whereby Versailles and London promised to deal sternly with adventurers who might in the future, acting under cover as political refugees, attempt to blackmail either government. Then, with a draft of this agreement in his pocket, he sailed back hopefully to France.

But when he landed in Boulogne, on May 8, he learned truly crushing news: Louis XV had been stricken with smallpox. The King was dying.

2. *Back to the World of Make-Believe*

Louis XV died on May 10, 1774. Not only did Beaumarchais not receive any reward whatever for his work; still worse, the very fact that he had accepted a mission to save Mme Du Barry's honor was likely to prove a serious obstacle to his being in the new King's good graces. Indeed, young Louis XVI and his wife, Marie-Antoinette, were known to be bitterly hostile to the Du Barry clique. There was no question of Beaumarchais even being refunded his traveling expenses to London.

Théveneau de Morande never received any payment on the deed of annuity that had been given him as the price of his recantation and change of side, yet he bore Beaumarchais no grudge. Beaumarchais was evidently in no way responsible for their common disappointment. In fact, Morande remained Beaumarchais' faithful confederate in the shady deals the latter was to undertake in the following years.

When Beaumarchais went to see Sartines, he found him restless and worried. All the high administrative posts were evidently going to be shuffled around, and the Lieutenant General of Police was not sure he would keep the position he had held under Louis XV. He was sympathetic to Beaumarchais, but could not help him in the present circumstances. Antoine de Sartines had come from a family of French merchants established in Spain. He had started his career as a lawyer. Eventually he had entered the Department of Police, where he had been successful, thanks to his shrewdness, firmness, and adaptability. But years of police work had made him cynical about human nature. He did not expect absolute integrity or perfect righteousness from anyone. In fact, he would have been either suspicious or ill at ease if he had found an individual with these exalted virtues. But he was able to appreciate a clever, courageous, resourceful man who could be depended upon not to double-cross his friends. Beaumarchais was such a man.

As Sartines and Beaumarchais surveyed the new French political landscape together, Sartines hinted that the best way for Beaumarchais to win the new King's favor would be to render Louis XVI the same type of service he had lately rendered Louis XV. With this remark in his mind, Beaumarchais returned home. A few days later, he went back to see Sartines, bearing grave news. He had just received word from Morande, he said, that another libelous pamphlet was being prepared in London. The nature of the revelations it contained was such that the prestige of the Crown and the personal dignity of the King himself would be seriously impaired if it was ever published.

The background of these prospective unsavory disclosures was well known to Sartines. Toward the end of Louis XV's reign, the old King had become an object of almost universal hatred and contempt because of his immorality and sloth. Many people, while remaining attached to the monarchic principle, could not help comparing the Bourbons of France with the Bourbons of Spain. The Bourbon line in Spain, though not particularly brilliant, had at least shown a measure of decency and concern for the public welfare. Couldn't the Spanish branch somehow be substituted at

Versailles for the French branch? Louis XIV had solemnly renounced all rights of his grandson, the Duc d'Anjou, and the Duke's descendants, when the young Duke had been called to the throne of Spain. But was this renunciation valid?

Louis XVI and Marie-Antoinette had been married since 1770, and so far there was no prospect of their having an heir. It was even whispered that, after four years of marriage, Louis XVI was still—and would probably remain—only a husband in name to his lovely wife. *Le pauvre homme!* But wasn't this personal inadequacy of the present King's a providential opportunity for shifting the Crown of France to the Bourbons of Spain?

With more psychological insight than good taste, Beaumarchais decided to gamble on the King's sensitiveness about his conjugal failure. Brazenly, he concocted a spurious, though on the whole plausible, story. An Italian Jew named Guillaume Angelucci—alias William Atkinson—had composed, he said, a pamphlet entitled *Avis à la Branche Espagnole sur ses droits à la Couronne de France, à défaut d'héritier.* The pamphlet, to be printed soon in England and Holland, was supposed to be filled with intimate details of the King's and Queen's private life. Atkinson-Angelucci had no political aim; he was purely and simply a blackmailer. About the same time, Beaumarchais managed, thanks to Morande's help, to have several vaguely threatening short articles, signed G. A., published in English newspapers. This preliminary, indirect approach, typical of any well-conducted blackmail, seemed to confirm Beaumarcahis' warnings.

Was the Lieutenant General of Police taken in by this hoax? He does not seem to have scrutinized Beaumarchais' report very closely to see whether it was authentic. Sartines was above all eager to show the new King that he was vigilant and that keeping him as head of the police was essential to His Majesty's welfare and peace of mind. He knew that Louis XVI was not very perspicacious and had a morbid fear of any allusion to his matrimonial insufficiency. He had little difficulty in persuading the jittery and dull-witted young monarch that the Atkinson-Angelucci pamphlet seriously endangered his reputation. When he told him that M. de Beaumarchais could doubtless take care of the blackmailer, the King felt immensely relieved. When he suggested that Beaumarchais be sent at once to England with this mission, the King assented not only readily but gratefully.

On arriving in London, Beaumarchais went straight to the British Foreign Office. Lord Rochford, however, received him rather coldly this time. The Morande blackmailing case and Beaumarchais' subsequent negotiations with him for an agreement had not been altogether to his taste. He had never refused to oblige an old friend, but what if that old friend now made a regular practice of handling the kind of police work that ought to be left to low underlings? Moreover, Rochford was perceptibly skeptical about the very existence of Atkinson-Angelucci.

Beaumarchais immediately wrote to Sartines. Their credit with the King would be utterly ruined if he did not succeed in stopping Angelucci in time, but he could not proceed in his work without Lord Rochford's support. He absolutely had to have an order from the King's hand accrediting him as His Majesty's personal envoy. He included a draft of this "indispensable" order in the letter. On July 10, 1774, the gullible Louis XVI copied this draft word for word and added his signature: "The Sieur de Beaumarchais, entrusted with my secret orders, will leave as soon as possible for his destination. The discretion and energy that he puts into their execution will be the best proof he can give me of his zeal in my service. Louis."

When Beaumarchais received this paper, he fairly shrieked with joy. In his exultation, he wrote the King: "A lover wears the portrait of his mistress around his neck; a miser hangs his keys there; a devotee, his reliquary. As for myself, I have had a large, flat, oval gold case made. I have enclosed Your Majesty's order in it and suspended it about my neck with a gold chain—as the most necessary thing in my work and the most precious possession I have."

Beaumarchais had invented this Angelucci affair as a desperate expedient in desperate circumstances, but he had not been free from anxiety about the outcome of the adventure. Now, however, he could see how incredibly easy it was to fool anybody. It was a child's game, and a fascinating one. He flung himself into the game with all the recklessness of his ever-resurgent adolescent impulses. He reported to Sartines that he had established contact with Angelucci, had paid him £1400 to give up his scheme of blackmail, and had burned four thousand copies of the pamphlet in a London suburb on a moonless night.

But the game was not to end there. Another edition of the same pamphlet, he now declared, was ready for distribution in Holland. It had to be destroyed. Beaumarchais then sailed, supposedly in Angelucci's company, for Amsterdam. But in Amsterdam Angelucci ran away. The rascal had taken a copy of the libel with him, evidently to have it printed somewhere else, in Germany, in Italy perhaps.

"I am like a lion," Beaumarchais wrote Sartines. "I have no

more money, but I have my diamonds, my jewels. I shall sell everything and, with rage in my heart, pursue my travels posthaste. . . . I don't know German. I don't know the roads I have to take. But I have a good map. I see I must go to Nijmegen, to Cleves, to Dusseldorf, to Cologne, to Frankfort, to Mainz, to Nuremberg. Day and night I shall go—unless I drop from sheer exhaustion on the way."

And he went—hot on the tracks of the imaginary Angelucci.

On August 14, 1774, Beaumarchais was driving in a post-chaise through the forest of Neustadt, in Germany. Suddenly he told the coachman to stop. The coachman pulled up. He was used to having such requests made by travelers when they passed through deserted spots and was not surprised to see Beaumarchais dash into the woods. But after waiting for fifteen or twenty minutes, he began to fear that the Frenchman had lost his way amidst bushes and trees. He decided to walk in the direction he had seen the man take, blowing his horn from time to time on the way.

It was not long before the coachman found Beaumarchais—disheveled, distraught, his clothes torn, his face and chest spattered with blood. The coachman did not knew French, but Beaumarchais made him understand that he had been attacked by robbers. The coachman was dumbfounded, for he had never heard of robbers in that region. Beaumarchais was bleeding profusely, yet his wounds seemed only superficial. The coachman helped him back to the chaise, then, whipping his horses, drove at full speed to the nearest city, Nuremberg. Soon, however, worried and puzzled by his traveler's condition, he bent down to have a look at him through the front coach window. The traveler was quietly and calmly putting a razor into his bag.

They reached Nuremberg in the evening. Beaumarchais went to the best inn, Zum rothen Hahn, and had his wounds looked after. He bore a deep cut in the chin. His left hand had been slashed to the bone. A stab directed at his chest—"which might have pierced my heart," he later stated—had been providentially turned away by a gold case—the case containing the King's order—and had left only a long but harmless scratch. Beaumarchais seemed beside himself with excitement, and the innkeeper was glad when the foreigner, after taking a light repast, withdrew to his room, locked his door, and went to bed.

On the following day, Beaumarchais went to see the Burgomaster. The Burgomaster spoke French after a fashion, and Beaumarchais repeated his story about the robbers—with suitable amplifications. He also hinted darkly at a plot hatched by a certain Angelucci. If that individual was found, he should be arrested at once in the name of Empress Maria Theresa. He himself intended to proceed to Vienna without delay to confer with Her Majesty. The Burgomaster, though somewhat bewildered by this mixture of high-flown politics and highway robbery, promised to keep a sharp lookout for the sinister Angelucci. Beaumarchais sent his luggage directly to Vienna in the care of the coachman who had driven the chaise through the forest of Neustadt. The man would eventually bear witness, thought Beaumarchais, to the truth of his own account of the episode.

Beaumarchais then took passage on a boat at Ratisbon and sailed peacefully down the Danube to the Austrian capital, where he arrived on August 20, 1774. He took steps at once to obtain an audience from the Empress. He called on a minor official, von Neny, who screened the numerous persons seeking such a favor from Her Majesty. Von Neny, seeing an agitated foreigner with his face wrapped in bandages, who talked mysteriously about affairs of utmost importance but refused to state their tenor, at first flatly declined to forward his request. Beaumarchais, however, put on a bold front, and von Neny, afraid to take a responsibility beyond his powers, turned him over to Graf Christian August Seilern, Statthalter of Lower Austria.

Beaumarchais told Graf Seilern that he was the Chevalier de Ronac, a secret envoy of the court of Versailles. He was bringing momentous news concerning the Empress, but he could reveal it only to her. Graf Seilern was as perplexed at first as von Neny had been. In the end, he decided to take this strange personage to the imperial palace at Schönbrunn. There, thanks to Seilern, Beaumarchais was admitted almost immediately into Maria Theresa's presence. Maria Theresa, however, insisted that Seilern remain in the room.

Then Beaumarchais put on his best performance. He acted as though he were about to faint—presumably from sheer emotion or perhaps from weakness caused by his wounds. An armchair was promptly pushed forward, and he collapsed in it. After a few moments of suspense, he began to compose himself. The proper atmosphere for his scenario thus created, he dramatically took out the gold case containing the French King's order and identified himself modestly as the famous M. de Beaumarchais. Then, in a halting voice, he proceeded to explain the affair of the Angelucci pamphlet. Maria Theresa loved her daughter Marie-Antoinette dearly. She had already received disturbing reports about her well-meaning but inadequate son-in-law from her ambassador in France. She listened to Beaumarchais' story with obvious concern.

It was time now for Beaumarchais to come to the Neustadt forest "attack." He was following Angelucci's trail, he said. Suddenly he saw Angelucci himself, riding on horseback along the road. Angelucci, evidently afraid of being overtaken, pushed his horse into the woods. Beaumarchais stopped his own chaise and ran after the fugitive, pistol in hand. He soon reached him, caught him by the leg, and threw him to the ground. Then he searched the prostrate and trembling scoundrel's pockets and bags. He rapidly found the purloined copy of the libelous pamphlet, also the money that had previously been paid to the blackmailer on behalf of the French King. Beaumarchais took the pamphlet and half of the money to punish the man for his perfidy, but made him a gift of the rest of the money and his life.

Beaumarchais was going back to his coach, when he was unexpectedly attacked by two robbers. He defended himself heroically, but his pistol misfired, and he was stabbed twice—once in the face, once in the chest. He succeeded in knocking down one of his assailants and wrenching his knife from his grasp, thereby wounding himself deeply in the hand. He would undoubtedly have been killed by the other brigand if the sound of the coachman's horn had not put the robbers to flight.

Several times Maria Theresa, pressing her hands together in a gesture of admiration and surprise, had interrupted his story to ask: "But, Monsieur, how did you come to have such zeal for the interests of my son-in-law and, above all, my daughter?" When the story was ended, Maria Theresa asked many more questions, then dismissed him with utmost graciousness. He certainly would hear from her very soon.

Yet, as soon as Beaumarchais had left the palace, suspicions entered her mind. She decided to ask the advice of her Chancellor, Prince Wenzel Anton Kaunitz. Kaunitz was coolheaded and skeptical by nature and he did not believe a word of the cock-and-bull story the Empress related to him. The Empress, however, had recognized her son-in-law's handwriting; the King's order was certainly genuine. The French court was known for sending strange persons on strange diplomatic errands.

Kaunitz at once conducted an inquiry into the particulars of the story. The German coachman who had taken care of Beaumarchais' luggage was carefully questioned. He stated that he had seen the wounded traveler put a razor into his bag immediately after the alleged holdup. Kaunitz had no difficulty in guessing the truth: the supposed attack was a fake. Beaumarchais had slashed his own face, chest, and hand with his own razor. He was an impostor.

But there was still the matter of the French King's unexplained personal order of mission. Kaunitz decided upon a course of action that was both cautious and firm. The Empress would instruct her Ambassador in France to ask the Versailles government what the Sieur de Beaumarchais' standing was. At the same time, information would be sought in Nuremberg about the circumstances of the incident. Meanwhile, Beaumarchais would be kept under protective custody in his own lodging.

After his interview with the Empress, Beaumarchais, bubbling over with self-confidence, had returned to his room at the Dreilauferhaus in Vienna. He was about to go to bed when eight grenadiers, two officers and an imperial secretary came in. On being requested to offer no resistance, he answered melodramatically: "I have sometimes resisted highwaymen, but empresses, never!"

His papers were placed under seal, and a politely worded letter from Graf Seilern was handed to him: he would not be allowed to leave his room for the time being.

Beaumarchais had to remain in his room thirty-one days, or, as the former watchmaker calculated, 44,640 minutes—44,640 minutes of wretchedness and misery. Would he be found out and condemned to spend the rest of his days in an imperial jail? He wrote letter after letter to Maria Theresa, all in vain. Imperial grenadiers stood stolidly, inexorably, before his door and under his windows.

His only diversions were visits from a certain Joseph von Sonnenfels. Sonnenfels claimed to be a passionate admirer of everything French and displayed profound sympathy with Beaumarchais' predicament. He was a jurist of some importance, a writer of note—and an assistant to Kaunitz. Kaunitz had evidently sent him to worm the truth out of Beaumarchais.

Beaumarchais told Sonnenfels his adventures over and over again. There were suspicious variants in his versions of the attack, yet he so convincingly assumed the tone of an injured, sincere man that Sonnenfels—and Kaunitz—began to wonder if there was not, after all, at least a kernel of truth in his story. They came to believe that he had freely and lavishly embroidered upon the plain fabric of reality, but it did not seem conceivable that he had manufactured the whole material. How much of the reported events belonged to the original pattern? How much was embroidery?

The inquiry in Nuremberg gave negative and disappointing results. No trace of Angelucci had been found there, but no additional proof that Beaumarchais was a dissembler could be produced. On the other hand, the news from Versailles was definite and categorical. Louis XVI obviously believed in the Angelucci plot. He confirmed the fact that Beaumarchais was his trusted envoy. Moreover, Sartines could not but back a man he had warmly recommended to the King. Beaumarchais' story and stand were thus fully endorsed by the French government.

The Vienna government then came to the conclusion that a blunder had been made. On September 21, 1774, Beaumarchais was informed that he was free. The sum of one thousand ducats was offered him as an indemnity for his trouble, but he declared that he would not take money from a government that had treated him so odiously. Yet, in the end, since he had absolutely no funds for his return to France, he condescended to accept this gift from Maria Theresa at least temporarily.

On his way back, Beaumarchais stopped at Augsburg. He saw there a performance of the drama *Clavigo*, which Goethe had composed about his adventures in Spain. Although he did not understand German, he was shocked at the liberties Goethe had taken with the "Truth." "That German," he later wrote, "has spoiled the anecdote contained in my memorial by adding a duel and a funeral to the action—which showed him more empty-headed than talented."

Beaumarchais had no doubts about his own talents. He felt proud of his boldness and skill. A good deal of uneasiness, however, was mixed with this pride. For a while he had had the thrill of living again like a boy in the wonderful world of make-believe. He had played "robbers" and enjoyed it immensely. But the people around him had refused to join the game. He had been arrested, suspected of fraud; he had had the narrowest of escapes. Never again in the future would he take such a chance, he decided. Thanks to his astounding dexterity and cleverness, he had outwitted the King of France, the Lieutenant General of Police of Paris, and the Chancellor of the Holy Roman Empire. Maria Theresa herself had come as close to apologizing as Her Imperial Majesty could. But he would make her go much farther still. He felt that he could manipulate all the great ones of this world according to his will, if he only could get close enough to them. He would no longer waste the superior power of his mind on low police work, which was unprofitable, dangerous, and as Lord Rochford had hinted, degrading. High diplomacy would henceforth be his field.

Meanwhile, Beaumarcahis had to liquidate the Angelucci affair. As soon as he arrived in Paris, he went to see Sartines.

"*Que voulez-vous?*" Sartines said. "The Empress took you for an adventurer."

Was there not an amused twinkle in Sartines' eye? Sartines evidently did not object to a measure of adventuring.

Then Beaumarchais wrote the King a report in which he explained in a logical manner the most fantastic aspects of his "mission." Playing the part of the incorruptible man for all it was worth, he protested vehemently against the very idea entertained by the Vienna government that *he* would take money from them. "I might have considered a kind letter from the Empress, or her portrait, or any such honorable object a sort of flattering compensation for the error into which they fell in regard to me—but money, Sire! This was the acme of humiliation for me."

Good Louis XVI, touched by this display of noble feelings, started negotiations with Maria Theresa to have Beaumarchais return the thousand ducats to her. Her Majesty consented, but, not to be outdone in magnanimity, sent Beaumarchais in exchange a ring with an enormous diamond. Beaumarchais deigned to accept this present. From that time on, until the end of his life, he ostentatiously wore this diamond ring on his finger. Whenever the opportunity offered itself, he would tell the story of the origin of the magnificent jewel with all the flourishes and embellishments his fertile imagination could provide.

Beaumarchais had, of course, sent his regular bill of expenses to the French administration. He knew better than to make it a small one. Moderation in this case would have meant that he did not want to attract attention to himself, that he had something to conceal. He coldly asked for 72,000 livres. They were paid to him without the slightest difficulty.

3. Judging His Judges

BEAUMARCHAIS' credit in government circles stood higher than it had for years. One cause for this altered situation was that the change in personnel expected since Louis XVI's accession to the throne had at long last taken place. The corrupt crew headed by the Triumvirs had been eliminated, and the young King had called an almost completely new team of statesmen to power. Most of them were highly competent in their respective fields and enjoyed a reputation for strict personal integrity.

The two strongest personalities in the Cabinet were the Finance Minister, Jacques Turgot, a liberal reformer backed by the "philosophers," and the Minister of Foreign Affairs, Comte Charles Gravier de Vergennes, a levelheaded, farsighted diplomat. The Prime Minister, Comte Jean-Frédéric de Maurepas, was flippant and frivolous, but a *grand seigneur* to his finger tips, and his perfect tact contributed greatly toward maintaining an indispensable harmony among the vigorous men who had to work side by side under him.

Of the few members of the Louis XV administration who remained in power, the foremost was Sartines. The Lieutenant General of Police knew too many secrets about too many prominent people to be easily set aside. Moreover, he knew, when necessary, how to bend with the wind. He had relinquished his important post as head of the police without a struggle and had accepted, as compensation, the least sought after portfolio in the Cabinet, the Ministry of the Navy.

The French fleet had been badly battered by the English during the Seven Years' War. Choiseul had afterward done his best to rebuild its strength, but it remained ineffectual and disorganized, for it was a hornets' nest of conflicting theories and bitterly hostile groups. Sartines knew nothing whatever about the Navy. But precisely because he could approach its problems with an unprejudiced mind and because he was a stranger to the cliques whose rivalries had in the past impeded every program of reconstruction, he was able to cut straight through the difficulties he found before him. Thanks to his undeviating good sense and firm will power, he was to succeed within a few years in making the French Navy a redoubtable fighting force, which would play an epoch-making part in the history of Europe and America. For the time being, however, nobody was aware of the gigantic task he was performing. He had almost vanished from the public eye. The new Lieutenant General of Police, Le Noir, whom Sartines had recommended as his successor, was popular because of his liberal ideas. Thus, the present arrangement was considered as thoroughly satisfactory by everyone.

A new mood of confidence and hope prevailed throughout the country. Louis XVI was evidently a man of good will intent on solving the problems that had harrassed his kingdom for years. People believed that these problems could and would be solved. Tension between aristocrats and commoners relaxed markedly, and many noblemen, particularly those of the younger generation, took the lead in asking for reforms. Why shouldn't peaceful and progressive reforms restore health to the ailing but still strong body of France?

The first reform openly requested by the public was the dissolution of the Maupeou Parliaments. Maupeou himself had been ousted in August 1774. But purely and simply recalling the "old" Parliaments presented serious dangers. Often in the past, the "old" Parliaments, whose powers were ill-defined and extensive, had taken advantage of their prestige to create grave difficulties for the government. In many instances, their opposition had not been inspired by concern for the general welfare. Yet, practically everyone wanted their return. They would undoubtedly return, but under what conditions and when?

The Cabinet was split on that question, and Maurepas wavered. Sartines suggested to Maurepas that Beaumarchais, who had learned through bitter experience the inner workings of "justice," be asked to offer his views on the subject. Thus a most paradoxical situation ensued: a man who had been civically degraded was called upon to pass judgment on his judges. In his report to Maurepas, *Elementary Ideas on the Recall of the Parliament*, Beaumarchais concluded, as could be expected, that the Maupeou Parliaments should be suppressed. The proposals he put forward on limiting and regulating the powers to be given the judicial bodies that would replace them were truly remarkable for their soundness and impartiality.

After reading the report, Maurepas wanted to know its author better. He had previously met Beaumarchais at Etioles, but their acquaintance had been only casual. Now they held long discussions together, and it is difficult to say whether Maurepas was more impressed by his interlocutor's judicial sense or more delighted by the fireworks of his witticisms.

In any case, Beaumarchais' suggestions on the curtailment of the Parliament's political authority were not put into effect. The pressure of public opinion in favor of the immediate recall of the "old" Parliaments was too strong to be resisted. In November 1774 the Parliament of Paris was formally reinstated with its full, original powers.

Beaumarchais lost no time in petitioning the Parliament to annul the sentence passed against him in the La Blache case. Simultaneously, he published an aggressive memorial, as he had done so successfully only a year before. But the mood of the French people had altered completely. The bitter hostility that the Crown had inspired under Louis XV had given way to love for and trust in Louis XVI and Marie-Antoinette. Beaumarchais had been absent from France—while chasing Angelucci in England, Holland, Germany, and Austria—when this sudden reversal of feelings had taken place. He had not been in Paris long enough to be fully aware of the change, so he was amazed at the "fickleness" of the public when his diatribe encountered unanimous disapproval and its sale was forbidden by the police.

On January 28, 1775, nevertheless, the sentence passed by the

Maupeou Parliament in the La Blache-Beaumarchais lawsuit was declared void. A little later, the case was referred to the Parliament of Aix-en-Provence. This court, remote from the nervous French capital, would one day, it was hoped, end the affair with a minimum of commotion and trouble.

Beaumarchais now waited confidently for the issue of the contest. Thanks to the 72,000 livres he had been given for expenses in hunting the mythical Angelucci, he could now pay off the liens that had been placed on the Rue de Condé house. Early in 1775, the mansion was officially returned to him, and he moved back in almost at once.

Mlle de Willermaulaz, who had adopted the *nom de guerre* Mme de Villers, now received Beaumarchais' guests there with complete naturalness and perfect poise. Julie unconsciously receded into the background, but there was no conflict between her and the new queen of the house. Mme de Villers' outward placidity and Julie's deep love for her brother prevented their imperceptible rivalry from breaking out into the open.

Beaumarchais took his sister Marie-Josèphe's two sons into his house to bring them up as his own children. Marie-Josèphe and Lisette came back from their convent in Picardy, but Lisette died shortly afterward. Tonton's little daughter, who precociously showed her mother's charm and coquetry, was also included in the Rue de Condé family circle, while her father, Miron, was kept busy as *Secrétaire des Commandements* to the Prince de Conti—a post Beaumarchais had obtained for him recently from his friend.

André Caron naturally returned to the house and, to his son's dismay, went on the rampage again. He was more than seventy-six years old, twice a widower, and by no means attractive, but he had not yet given up gallivanting. The object of his senile affections was his "housekeeper," the middle-aged woman in whose house he had taken shelter during the La Blache lawsuit. The cunning beldame knew that the old fellow had no money, but she could see that Beaumarchais was prosperous. So she hung on to the aged philanderer, counting on his doting and his dotage to win her the arrangements she wanted. Beaumarchais only too well suspected this, but what could he do to stop his father's folly? Old Caron, aware of his son's disapproval, did not dare take any step to gratify his desires, for the time being. But behind him the housekeeper lay in wait.

The Parliament of Aix, probably acting on orders from above, postponed study of the potentially explosive Beaumarchais-La Blache case from month to month. Beaumarchais was getting restless, so, to kill time, he took up the manuscript of *Le Barbier de Séville.* He enlarged his old text and poured into it all his past rancors as well as his current worries. He altered the character of Bartholo, which had always presented a striking similarity to his father, to make it fit more closely the decrepit and unprepossessing appearance of Caron at seventy-six. Thus Bartholo was described in the new version of the comedy as "an old libertine, covered with pimples, boring, sprightly, as though in love from childhood, wrinkled, bleary-eyed, jealous, silly—a poor devil in turn coughing, spitting, growling, and whining. A widower for the second time and no longer a gallant novice, he wants to play the lively young blade all over again."

In the first version of the play there had been a music teacher named Bazile who had only a small part. Bazile now became an awe-inspiring embodiment of everything low, mean, corrupt, and contemptible. Several times Beaumarchais even struck out the name Bazile and replaced it by "Guzman"—a transparent allusion to Goëzman. In the end he decided to keep the name Bazile; but Bazile now stood as an almost epic personification of base venality and slander—a man who advocates calumny as a system and who is ever ready to surrender to the "irresistible arguments" any man may carry in his purse.

As Beaumarchais relived in memory the agonizing hours of the Goëzman trial, a mass of hidden and bitter sentiments surged up to the surface of his consciousness. Biting sarcasms, cynical remarks on life, love, and politics, attacks against nobility, tirades against corruption, startling paradoxes, and devastating jests crowded one another under his pen. When this emotional outburst was over, *Le Barbier de Séville* had grown from four to five acts and been turned from a mild, pleasant entertainment into a caustic, virulent satire.

Beaumarchais found no difficulty this time in obtaining official permission to have his play presented at the Comédie Française. But at the first performance, on February 22, 1775, most of the large crowd that had rushed expectantly to the theater, drawn by Beaumarchais' name, trickled away before the end, disappointed and bored. As was true of Beaumarchais' most recent memorial, the author's temper was not in harmony with the general public taste. The French people were temporarily passing through a phase of optimism and hope. They were in no mood for recrimination and mockery. They had groaned at Beaumarchais' ironical puns and yawned at his declamations against aristocracy. Even a few hisses had been heard, coming, symptomatically enough, from the pit.

Beaumarchais sensed the causes of his failure. With his amazing ability of adapting himself almost instantaneously to a new situation, he undertook to make all the changes in his play that he felt the audience wanted— and this within twenty-four hours. He eliminated all his recent additions, which reflected only his irritation with his father, from the character of Bartholo. He trimmed down the character of Bazile, allowing only two traits, love of money and love of slander, to stand out clearly. Then he cut out practically all his attacks against social order. He carefully kept these discarded passages in his files. One day he would find a more favorable atmosphere for their use. But, in the meantime, he was ready to make all the necessary sacrifices to please the theatergoing public. The public wanted at the moment to look only at the rosy aspects of life. Well and good. The public wanted to be amused and laugh. The second performance of *Le Barbier de Séville* was amusing and aroused laughter almost from beginning to end. It was an unqualified success.

Le Barbier de Séville placed Beaumarchais at the forefront of the playwrights of his days, and secured him an outstanding place among the best French dramatists of all times. While *Eugénie* and *Les Deux Amis* are today completely forgotten, except by scholars, *Le Barbier de Séville* permanently retains a broad popular appeal. Yet, its plot—the story of two lovers, Count Almaviva and the innocent orphan Rosine, separated by the jealousy of the girl's old guardian and overcoming the obstacles he throws in their path thanks to the wiles and wit of a clever servant—is artificial and trite. But Beaumarchais showed amazing skill in handling this hackneyed subject, and infused into it a new interest and a new life. What with the picturesque setting of a somewhat fanciful but colorful Spain, what with the pungent, incisive quality of the witty dialogue, the spectator finds himself carried away by the verve and gaiety that fill the play from the first curtain rise to the last curtain fall.

Even the stock stage types of the ridiculous guardian, Bartholo, who wants to marry his young ward, of the sly go-between and interloper, Bazile, and of the ingenious servant, Figaro, are endowed with well-defined psychological traits all their own. Thus Bartholo is at once suspicious and benevolent, sulky and short-tempered, gullible and crafty. Bazile is cunning, cautious, cowardly, "on his knees before a gold piece," and he reaches almost epic heights of villainy in his praise of planned and malicious slander. But the most original of all is undoubtedly Figaro himself, a jack-of-all-trades who was in turn and with equal gusto an apothecary, a veterinarian, a journalist, a playwright, and finally a barber. His tribulations have left him few illusions about his fellow men; yet he remains cheerful, carefree, independent, impertinent, full of generous impulses, full of mischievous humor, full of music, and full of fun. From the very start the character of this likable rogue struck the fancy of the French public, and it was obvious that Figaro would live as long as the French theater itself.

Yet Beaumarchais was not altogether satisfied with the final outcome of his dramatic venture. His "successful" *Barbier* was not a completely innocuous *Barbier:* in the first act, for instance, Figaro took a few digs at nobility, and more than half hinted that everything was not for the best in the social order of his time. Yet the play scarcely expressed what Beaumarchais still had in his heart.

It then occurred to him to present his ideas through the medium of a "philosophical" opera. Since people could not stomach plain, bitter truths, he would make them swallow the selfsame truths with a sugar-coating of music. He knew that he was not able to compose the complete musical score of a full length opera and needed the help of a professional composer. At that time, Gluck's reputation was at its zenith. Gluck had been in Paris since 1774. Beaumarchais began negotiations with him about his new project, and Gluck listened with definite interest. Then Beaumarchais set himself to write the first draft of his libretto, for which he selected the title *Tarare.*

Beaumarchais was quite advanced in his work when Maurepas unexpectedly called upon him to help the government in a problem that had taxed the ingenuity of the Ministry of Foreign Affairs officials for years and which now threatened to become a national danger.

4. *Man or Woman?*

THE center of this baffling problem was the Chevalier Charles Geneviève d'Eon de Beaumont. This strange being had arrived at the court of Versailles twenty years before surrounded with a halo of mystery. Was it man or woman? On the one hand, Charles D'Eon—introduced as the son of a nobleman of Tonnerre in Burgundy—was a scholar of parts, an expert in law, and a writer of no mean talent. Moreover, he was a skillful swordsman and soon acquired the reputation of being one of the most dangerous duelists of his time. On the other hand, Geneviève d'Eon looked like an extremely pretty woman. Her features were soft and sweet. Her pink cheeks bore no beard. Her voice was crystalline and pure. Her body offered plesantly suggestive, rounded contours. To cap the enigma, this ambiguous person—who was twenty-two years old—led a perfectly chaste life, even at the court of Louis XV. No indiscretion or intimacy of any kind could cast a decisive light upon his or her actual sex.

Then, in 1755, Louis XV had selected the Chevalier d'Eon to be the protagonist in one of the most bizarre and daring stratagems in modern diplomatic history. A serious state of tension existed at that time between Russia and France. The reigning Tsarina, Elizabeth, had a strong penchant for everything French, but her clever and influential Chancellor, Alexis Bestuzhev-Ryumin, had succeeded in keeping Russia in the English diplomatic camp. The French Foreign Ministry, feeling a general European war imminent, wanted, at almost any cost, to detach the somewhat inorganic but enormous Russian power from the English alliance. But every attempt by French diplomacy to play upon the Tsarina's well-known pro-French feelings had been forestalled by the Chancellor's vigilance.

During that period Louis XV had throughout Europe a network of secret agents whom he entrusted with his personal messages and who carried out—sometimes unbeknown to the French Foreign Minister himself—the monarch's own foreign policy. He decided to send to St. Petersburg the young Chevalier d'Eon—dressed as a woman. Bestuzhev-Ryumin saw to it that no Frenchman could approach the Tsarina, but no one in Russia in those days would have thought of drawing an iron curtain against a pretty French girl.

In July 1755 the Chevalier, transmuted into Mlle Lia de Beaumont, went to St. Petersburg. She was accompanied by a Scot named Douglas, who belonged to the Stuart party and was secretly in the service of France. Douglas was Mlle Lia's uncle and chaperon.

Mlle Lia, using her beauty, charm and wit to best advantage, succeeded quickly in being presented at the not-too-exclusive Russian court. Being French, she easily attracted the Tsarina's attention. In due time she revealed "her" true identity to Elizabeth. Elizabeth, thrilled to the marrow by this adventure, was delighted with the idea of playing a trick on her Chancellor and agreed to correspond secretly with Louis XV. The correspondence was carried on in a code that Lia de Beaumont had brought with her, hidden in the binding of a book. This direct exchange of letters between the two sovereigns was the first step in a long series of secret negotiations that eventually culminated in the dismissal of Bestuzhev-Ryumin and the conclusion of a military alliance between Russia and France against England and Prussia.

On returning to France, Charles d'Eon resumed masculine garb. He received a commission in the army during the Seven Years' War and distinguished himself by his bravery as captain in a regiment of dragoons. When the war drew to an end and peace overtures were made by France to England in 1762, he again became an agent of Louis XV. He was sent to London, where he amazingly won the friendship and favor of George III.

The French government was most eager to know the utmost concessions the English were prepared to make in the negotiations for peace. The Chevalier went to work on a certain British official who carried a portfolio containing ultra-secret documents filled with the information the French needed. This official had a great weakness for the bottle. Chevalier d'Eon had brought a large stock of excellent wine from his family estate in Burgundy with him to England. One night, with the help of another French diplomatic agent, the Duc de Nivernais, he drank the Englishman under the table, abstracted the precious papers from the portfolio, copied them hastily, and sped away to Versailles.

In February 1763, when the terms of the treaty were finally agreed upon, George III selected the Chevalier d'Eon to convey the news to the French government that, as far as England was concerned, no obstacle now stood in the way of the formal signing of the peace. Louis XV then appointed the Chevalier Minister Plenipotentiary to London. In view of his signal services in the past and of his credit in England, he fully expected soon to be promoted to the rank of ambassador. But a court intrigue resulted in the appointment of the Comte de Guerchy instead. D'Eon was furious, and before long he and Guerchy daily had disgraceful rows at the embassy. Eventually the situation became unbearable for both.

Louis XV seems to have felt uneasy about the situation. Charles d'Eon had shown himself skillful and faithful and had been poorly rewarded, indeed. But it was the King's policy never overtly to oppose the decisions of his ministers. He offered to let d'Eon remain in England as his personal envoy with an annual salary of 12,000 livres. The Chevalier had no choice but to accept. For a decade he remained in London, officially a discontented French subject—which, indeed, he was—and at the same time the confidential agent of the French King.

In 1771, one of Bestuzhev-Ryumin's nieces, then traveling in England, met him by accident and recognized him as Mlle Lia de Beaumont. Soon the rumor spread in London that the Chevalier was not a man, but a woman in disguise. People who till then had paid scant attention to him began to notice his high-pitched voice, his clear complexion, and the feminine shape of his figure. D'Eon enjoyed the notoriety that now came to him. After years of eclipse, he was the center of interest once more.

Certain English lords made bets among themselves about the Chevalier's sex, and some of them even talked of using direct methods to ascertain whether this French freak was a he or a she. But the Chevalier declared that he would use his sword to punish any such indiscreet attempt. Since his fame as a fencer had crossed the Channel, this threat was enough to deter even the boldest, but it increased the general curiosity tenfold. At the time of Louis XV's death, d'Eon had become a European celebrity.

After his accession to the throne, Louis XVI decided to close this unsavory chapter of his grandfather's policy. The Chevalier d'Eon received orders from Versailles to leave London at once. He was willing enough to return to France, but he wanted a guarantee against possible persecution by the powerful Guerchy family. And, more than anything else, he wanted money. So he set conditions to his return; and in the bargaining game that followed, it soon appeared that the Chevalier held an unexpected trump card in his hand.

After the Treaty of Paris of 1763, Louis XV had been obsessed with the idea of wiping out the shame cast on French arms by the disasters of the Seven Years' War. This could be effected, he had believed, if a French army were to be landed by surprise in England. He therefore asked d'Eon to gather technical information about the possibility of launching such an operation in the near future. Letters, maps, and detailed plans had been exchanged between the King and the Chevalier for several years. The Chevalier had carefully kept all these documents. If they were made public now, a serious crisis would undoubtedly develop in France's relations with England.

D'Eon managed to let the London government know that he possessed certain interesting papers. At the same time he informed Versailles that he was quite ready, for a price, to surrender Louis XV's compromising letters, but hinted that the English were aware of their existence and would probably be willing to pay a goodly sum for them. He asked to be officially cleared of all accusations made against him by the Guerchy group. Moreover, he wanted to be paid the various indemnities, rewards, and bounties that, he said, the late King had promised him. According to his calculations, they amounted to 318,477 livres.

Versailles answered with an emphatic "No."

It is almost certain that d'Eon had no intention of becoming a traitor and actually delivering the highly confidential letters he had received from Louis XV into the hands of the English. Yet he wanted to get the highest possible price from the French for these letters. His salary of 12,000 livres had been stopped, and he soon found himself in almost desperate financial straits. He succeeded in borrowing £5000 from a certain Lord Ferrers, giving him as guarantee for his loan a sealed trunk filled, he said, with the invaluable papers coveted by both the French and English governments. A seal and a promise given by a "gentleman" to keep it intact were in those remote days considered sufficient protection against the inquisitiveness of the two most powerful kingdoms of Europe.

Versailles was puzzled and worried. Was the Chevalier at bottom a thoroughly crooked character? Or was he merely bluffing in the hope of getting an exorbitant sum? D'Eon realized that his contact with the English had made him highly suspect in the eyes of the French. Would he not be thrown in the Bastille for the rest of his life if he ever set foot on French soil? Reciprocal distrust and fear had brought about a complete and dangerous deadlock in the negotiations between the Chevalier and the Ministry of Foreign Affairs.

It was at this point that Sartines suggested to his embarrassed colleagues that Beaumarchais be given the mission of taking care of the Chevalier d'Eon, as he had taken care of Morande and Angelucci. Beaumarchais received this proposal with a mixture of annoyance and joy. It irked him to be associated once more with a shady blackmailing case. On the other hand, he felt a strong attraction to high politics. Perhaps this new assignment would be a springboard into truly worth-while political activity. Fairly rapidly he reached a practical understanding with the Ministry of Foreign Affairs. He would go to London to deal with the Chevalier d'Eon, but he would be authorized to send Vergennes confidential, documented reports on the political situation in England.

A serious political crisis had been brewing in England for several years over the American colonies. Part of public opinion, dissatisfied with George III's authoritarian rule, took the colonists' side. John Wilkes, Lord Mayor of London, led the most violent attacks on the King. Was England on the brink of a new revolution?

The French public and government were not particularly concerned at that time with the problems of the American colonies, but they followed with the keenest interest the events taking place in London. They realized that there was a connection between American affairs and English affairs, though they failed to understand the exact nature of it. If Beaumarchais could throw some light upon that aspect of the English difficulties, he knew that his reports would be read and appreciated in high places.

The negotiations between Beaumarchais and d'Eon lasted from April until December 1775. They were astoundingly complicated, and their intricacies have not yet been fully puzzled out. Two masters of intrigue now stood face to face, both pretending, feigning, feinting, each vying with the other in trickery and craftiness.

At first Beaumarchais, pretending to be in London for his own affairs, made no attempt to establish contact with the Chevalier. He wanted to compel his opponent to show his anxiety and weakness by making the first move. Indeed, d'Eon, having somehow heard that Beaumarchais was empowered to examine his claims, called on him one evening, and the two schemers started to talk.

The crux of their discussion was Beaumarchais' suggestion that d'Eon in the future wear only women's clothes. This would give the Chevalier the advantage of being automatically beyond the reach of the Guerchys, and would safeguard him from being incarcerated in the Bastille. In those days in France a woman was hardly ever openly censured for irregularities in her behavior. Her errors were by consensus attributed to feminine irresponsibility and accordingly overlooked or condoned. On the other hand, women were absolutely debarred from active participation in public life. Thus, if d'Eon became a woman, he would *ipso facto* cease to be a danger to the government.

It is still not known whether Beaumarchais thought d'Eon a

woman or a man. Equally convincing and authentic documents can be produced to "prove" either of these hypotheses. In fact, these two artists in deception covered their tracks so well that it is next to impossible to discern the unbelievably tortuous path they followed.

In any case, the Versailles government at once grasped the advantages offered by d'Eon's change of sex. On August 7, 1775, Vergennes wrote the King: "If M. d'Eon is willing to adopt the costume of his sex, there will be no objection to his return to France. But under any other circumstances, he should not even express that wish." And on August 26, he sent Beaumarchais the following instructions: "Whatever desire I may have to see, know, and hear M. d'Eon, I shall not conceal from you, Monsieur, the uneasiness that besets me on his account. His enemies are watchful, and they will not easily forget what he has said of them. . . . If M. d'Eon agreed to change his costume, every difficulty would be settled. You may use this remark in any way you see fit."

In October of the same year, Beaumarchais informed Vergennes that an agreement had been reached: "The definite statement of his [or her] sex, and the promise to live henceforth in the garb of a woman, is the only barrier that can be set to prevent scandal and avoid disaster. I have requested and obtained this." The Chevalier had signed a formal document pledging himself to deliver the compromising papers to Beaumarchais and to dress in the future as a woman. In return, he would receive a pension of 12,000 livres and be allowed to live unmolested in France.

It was also understood that d'Eon would receive a lump sum to enable him to pay off his debts before leaving England, but the exact amount was not stipulated. Each of the dissemblers evidently hoped to get the better of the other in the haggling they foresaw on that point.

Before any payment was made, Beaumarchais wanted to get hold of the famous dangerous documents. It turned out that the sealed trunk d'Eon had given Lord Ferrers was filled with trash. After some wrangling, d'Eon finally surrendered the actual letters written by Louis XV: they had been cleverly concealed in five small boxes under the flooring of his room. Then began the discussion about the lump sum to pay off his debts. He asked for 13,933. Beaumarchais acted as though he were absolutely amazed by such a fantastic request. D'Eon lowered his claim: he would settle for 8000. But Beaumarchais now had the papers he wanted; he did not mind keeping d'Eon in suspense a little longer.

At this stage the Chevalier, now officially a woman, pretended to fall in love with Beaumarchais. "Who the dickens," Beaumarchais wrote Vergennes, "would have fancied that to serve the King in this affair I would have to pay court to a captain of dragoons? The whole adventure seems so ludicrous to me that I have the utmost difficulty to keep from laughing so that I may properly finish the present report."

In the end, the Chevalier d'Eon had to take what Beaumarchais was willing to give: 5000. From that time on d'Eon, feeling cheated, was to pursue Beaumarchais with unrelenting hatred.

The French government was delighted with the way the matter had been handled. Beaumarchais had been discreet, efficient, and ingenious and he had not made the slightest attempt to derive any personal profit from the settlement. When he finally appeared at Versailles, in December 1775, with the long-expected papers,

Vergennes received him with genuine cordiality. The Minister of Foreign Affairs had a professional appreciation of the skillful negotiator and a personal esteem for a man who had been much maligned but had shown himself—at least in the present circumstances—honest, reliable, and trustworthy.

Upon his return home, Beaumarchais found himself confronted with a new and troublesome problem. On April 18, 1775, André Caron, taking advantage of his son's departure for England, had stealthily married his housekeeper. Beaumarchais had not concealed his displeasure this time. But when the health of the old man—for whom matrimony was too great a strain—alarmingly declined, father and son had again become reconciled. Caron had died on October 23 of the same year. A few days before his death, he had written Pierre-Augustin, then busy negotiating with the Chevalier d'Eon in London, "I pray the Lord every day to bless you, reward you, and keep you safe from accident. This will ever be the prayer of your good friend and affectionate father."

Then, after the Chevalier d'Eon's affair had been adjusted, the widow brought out a secret financial settlement she had induced the old man to sign at the time of their wedding. She now asked Beaumarchais to pay the sum allegedly due her.

The widow's claim would not have stood any legal test. In the last years of his life, Caron had been entirely dependent on his son for support and therefore had no right to give away money he did not possess. But she threatened to bring suit against Beaumarchais, knowing full well that he could not afford, under the existing circumstances, to appear in a public trial about such a sordid matter as a squabble over money with his father's widow. The cunning woman coldly put it up to him: face a scandal or pay and pay quickly. He paid—6000 livres.

Many years later, at the time of Beaumarchais' death, all the documents concerning this disgraceful affair were found tied in a bundle. On the cover of the bundle, Beaumarchais had written in his own hand: "*Infamie de la veuve de mon père pardonnée.*"

Chapter 7

MY FRIENDS, THE FREE MEN

---

1. *M. le Comte, Will You Do Nothing for the Americans?*

SHORTLY AFTER Beaumarchais' arrival in London, in April 1775, the news of the Concord-Lexington battle filled Great Britain with consternation and the French government with glee. Vergennes was delighted to be able to receive through Beaumarchais—then officially engaged in the Chevalier d'Eon case—reliable information about the attitude taken in high British political circles toward the American problem. Beaumarchais frequently saw Lord Rochford, who was still Minister of Foreign Affairs in Lord North's Cabinet. "If our impression of Lord Rochford's character is correct," Vergennes wrote at that time to Beaumarchais, "it will not be difficult to make him talk more than he intends to." Indeed, the English lord talked freely and volubly with his French friend about England's colonial difficulties, and his remarks were regularly relayed to Versailles.

Furthermore, Théveneau de Morande introduced Beaumarchais to John Wilkes. The Lord Mayor's colorful personality, violent, abusive language, and demagogic manners had endeared him to the London mob, and he had become the center of a political agitation bordering on open revolt. On September 21, 1775, Beaumarchais stated in one of his confidential reports that Wilkes, sitting near him at a large dinner party, had exclaimed: "The King of England has long done me the honor of hating me. For my part, I have always done him the justice of despising him. The time has come to decide which of the two has shown better judgment and on which side the wind will cause the heads to fall."

The people Beaumarchais met in Wilkes' house were a mixed crowd. Many of them were extremist Whigs—not always perfectly well-bred gentlemen, to be sure, but invariably forthright in their defense of liberal ideas and outspoken in their support of the American colonials' cause. A number of Americans also congregated there. Since the official break between England and the colonies had not yet taken place, they were still considered British subjects, and they could present the American point of view in a free and convincing manner.

For about a year, Beaumarchais was a constant visitor at the Lord Mayor's house. He had gone there at first mainly to get a clear picture of certain aspects of the English political scene. In time, however, the ideas that he heard forcibly expressed by Wilkes' friends wrought a fundamental change in his outlook on life.

Up to then his outlook had been shaped by his subconscious

recollection of his experiences as a youth. His unsuccessful revolt against parental power had left in him a strange mixture of resentment and respect for André Caron's superior strength. In the following years, his behavior revealed the same pattern of reaction toward society at large. He sneered at authority and yet obstinately tried to ingratiate himself with those who possessed it. He attacked socially prominent men and yet felt a certain uneasiness, almost a sense of guilt, in doing so. In recent years, the snubs he had suffered from supercilious noblemen and the flagrant iniquities of which he had been the victim had aroused intense bitterness and anger in him. But he still did not look much beyond his own problems, his own interests, his own grudges. Thoroughly dissatisfied with his social environment and none too pleased at heart with himself, he felt at loose ends spiritually.

At this juncture, the American and English liberals whom he met in London in 1775 opened for him vast new horizons. Their challenge of George III's absolutist rule was not a reprehensible rebellion against lawful authority. They were merely asking for their rights, and these rights were in their views founded upon a strong political tradition and a lofty idea of man's inherent dignity.

A moral justification for resistance to oppressive authority, in the name of principles standing above authority, was precisely what the French "philosophers" were trying to establish at the same time in France. But Beaumarchais had so far remained almost completely beyond the orbit of their influence. Their headquarters were the literary cafés, where his enemies had their stronghold. Of course, the theories of Voltaire, Diderot, and Rousseau were in the air, and he must have breathed them unconsciously, as everyone who lived in Paris during that period did. Yet his main personal contacts had been with courtiers at Versailles, with financiers of the Pâris-Duverney circle, and, more recently, with disreputable interlopers like Morande. He had not found a deep and genuine longing for moral and social reform in any of these groups.

The impact of "American principles" completely revolutionized Beaumarchais' ways of thinking. It brought to the surface of his mind ideas that must have lain dormant for a long time and gave them a compelling, motivating force. Thenceforward he was to be an impassioned advocate of universal human rights and a steadfast champion of freedom not for himself alone, but for every man on earth. This revelation of a superior life purpose, reaching far above and beyond the petty interests of the individual, did not come to him instantaneously, but grew slowly within him. This moral growth, which can be followed through his correspondence, went on from the second half of 1775 until the middle of 1776. At the end of that period, an almost entirely new element had entered his life: he possessed an Ideal.

That the "Ideal" should have entered Beaumarchais' life through the channel of America was not a matter of pure chance. America enjoyed immense popularity in France in those days. The Americans were usually described to the French public—by enthusiastic, though perhaps not always perfectly accurate, travelers—as models of frugality, decency and kindness. What with the romance of a young and "virtuous" people taking hold of a boundless and virgin continent, America appeared to the French as a dream country of freedom and hope. When Jean-Jacques Rousseau's ideas became widely accepted, the Americans were considered living examples of men who were happy and good because they had escaped the corrupting influence of an oversophisticated society and been regenerated through a wholesome, direct contact with nature.

To this must be added the fact that the French are by instinct always likely to take the side of the underdog. At first sight, the American Insurgents seemed hopelessly weak before the tremendous might of the British Army, the British Navy, and the British Exchequer. For that very reason the heart of the French went out to those brave people across the ocean who, in spite of appalling odds, stood up to fight for their rights. In the eyes of the French, American rights became the symbol of the rights of men everywhere. The Americans themselves became an inspiration for all the oppressed, who looked forward to the day when they also would find the courage to rise against the tyranny weighing upon their lives.

The man who more than anyone else contributed, though unwittingly, to this change in Beaumarchais' outlook was the Virginian Arthur Lee. Lee was then a dynamic man of thirty-five. He had been educated at Eton and had studied medicine at Edinburgh. After a halfhearted attempt at establishing a medical practice in Virginia, he had returned to England to become a lawyer. He had been accepted at the Temple in 1766, but for many years broad political issues had held infinitely more fascination for him than narrow legal problems had. When Franklin had left England in the spring of 1775, Lee had been appointed "Agent" of the Colony of Massachusetts in his stead, thanks mainly to the influence in the Massachusetts Assembly of the group led by John and Samuel Adams.

Arthur Lee was ambitious, impetuous, witty, talkative, and fond of scheming and intriguing. In short, he possessed all the good qualities and defects that would please a man like Beaumarchais. Beaumarchais had first met him at Wilkes' house; but soon the two men saw each other privately and held long, confidential conversations together. Almost from the start, Beaumarchais was amazed to find how deep the rift was between England and her American possessions. This was not merely a family quarrel. Here was an intelligent, honorable man, an accredited representative of the important Colony of Massachusetts, who sincerely, passionately, wanted the complete severance of political links between the Colonies and Britain.

Toward the middle of September 1775 Beaumarchais paid a flying visit to Versailles about the Chevalier d'Eon affair. He saw Vergennes and explained to him what he had learned through Lee about the situation in America. Vergennes was most eager to help the Americans, mainly to embarrass the English. But any action along that line was blocked by a major obstacle: the King. Nothing could be done without the King's consent, and the King wavered, hesitated, procrastinated.

Beaumarchais and Vergennes soon came to a perfect understanding: they both wanted to push the slow-witted Louis XVI toward a decision. Vergennes, who had held the portfolio of Foreign Affairs for only slightly more than a year, could not risk his position by speaking too bluntly to His Majesty. It was agreed that Beaumarchais would send in confidential reports addressed to Vergennes or Sartines, and Vergennes would see to it that they came under the King's eye. Beaumarchais would be free to say things that could not pass a dignified Foreign Minister's lips. Wasn't he, after all, the irrepressible, irresponsible Beaumarchais?

The first of these reports, dated September 21, 1775, shows

scarcely more than a cynical political opportunism. France should take advantage of every chance to weaken her old rival, England. The French government should give financial help to the Insurgents. A certain sum could be earmarked for their use. Part of it might be sent directly to America. The rest might serve to purchase guns, perhaps in Flanders, then the great center in Europe for contraband arms. These guns would later be conveyed through devious channels across the Atlantic. Yet, one can already perceive a throb of genuine, personal emotion in certain of Beaumarchais' sentences: "The Americans, resolved to suffer anything rather than yield, and filled with that enthusiasm for liberty which has so often made the little Corsican nation so dangerous to the Genoese, have 38,000 effective men under the walls of Boston. . . . I say, Sire, that such a nation must be invincible."

Nothing is known of the King's reaction to this report. But when Beaumarchais returned to Versailles in December 1775, he learned most disconcerting news from Vergennes. The King refused to take action in the Anglo-American conflict, on purely religious grounds. Louis XVI had been brought up a devout Christian. Was it not said in the Scriptures that a man should return good for evil? The English having done much harm to the French in the past, it was the duty of the French today to follow the evangelical admonition and to refrain from taking any step that might hurt them.

Beaumarchais was dumbfounded. Immediately, on December 7, 1775, he wrote the King a long letter, evidently with Vergennes' approval. He could not lightly dismiss His Most Christian Majesty's scruples of conscience—"your scruples . . . so delicate that you do not want to favor a measure that may injure your enemies." But the main argument he boldly put forward to overcome the

King's repugnance to follow Vergennes' advice rested upon the revolutionary idea that a sovereign is responsible not only to God, but also and mainly to the *people*. The will and welfare of the Nation now balanced, nay, superseded, the traditional theory of the divine right for him. "I entreat you, Sire," he said, "in the name of your subjects, to whom you owe the best of your endeavors . . . This lamentable excess of justice toward your enemies would be the most flagrant injustice toward your subjects, who would soon have to pay for scruples so out of place."

The King did not answer this daring missive. A few days later, under the pretext of submitting to him a questionnaire about the trousseau to be given Mlle d'Eon, Beaumarchais repeated his request about America in the most direct terms.

Soon afterward, Beaumarchais returned to London. Officially, he was engaged in liquidating the Chevalier d'Eon affair. For eighteen months d'Eon refused to wear feminine garments, as his contract had stipulated. During that time he remained in England, making himself as obnoxious as he could, to annoy the man who in his opinion had cheated him of his due. Thus he unwittingly provided Beaumarchais with a most convenient pretext for prolonging his sojourn in London.

Eventually, however, the English authorities became suspicious of Beaumarchais' activities, mainly because of his association with Wilkes. So, at Vergennes' request, the French government entrusted him with the official mission of purchasing on the London market Portuguese and Spanish coins then at a premium in the West Indian trade. But his true mission was to keep an eye, through Arthur Lee, upon the developments in America.

These developments had lately confirmed all the predictions

Lee had made to Beaumarchais. The Colonies were now engaged in an all-out struggle with England. Through a series of decisions, the last of which had been dated November 8, 1775, the Continental Congress had created a "Secret Committee" for the purchase of guns and supplies in Europe. On November 29, Congress had appointed a Committee of Five to correspond with friends of America abroad. In December 1775 this "Committee of Secret Correspondence" requested Arthur Lee to act secretly as its agent in London. From that time on, Lee became to Beaumarchais the authorized representative of the unrecognized but effective American government.

At that time the situation of the American government was truly critical. The English had contracted with the Landgrave of Hesse-Cassel and the Duke of Brunswick for the delivery of German mercenaries. Evidently, a large regular army, equipped and trained according to European methods, was soon to be sent across the Atlantic. Would the Americans, however brave individually, be able to offer strong, organized resistance to the professional soldiery? Even patriotic Americans had serious misgivings. The obvious solution for the Insurgents was to ask the help of a great European power against England.

Since France was known to be England's faithful enemy, it seemed a not-too-difficult job to persuade her to intervene on the American side. Being ignorant of the wave of emotional sympathy for the American cause then surging in the French people, Congress decided to try to convince the French government that it was to France's interest to provide America with military supplies. Congress offered a treaty of commerce as an inducement for such a move.

The American proposal was sent from Philadelphia to Lee in London and then relayed by Beaumarchais to Versailles. Versailles remained noncommittal and reticent. On February 29, 1776, Beaumarchais wrote the King: "The Sieur L. (M. de Vergennes will tell Your Majesty his name), the secret deputy of the Colonies in London, completely discouraged by the useless efforts he has made through me to obtain gunpowder and ammunition of war from the French Ministry, said to me today: 'For the last time, has France absolutely decided to refuse us all help and thus become the victim of England and the laughingstock of Europe because of this incredible torpor? Since I have to give a definite answer, I am waiting for your final reply before I send my own. We offer France, as a price for her secret assistance, a treaty of commerce that will secure for her for a certain number of years, after peace is signed, all the profits with which we have enriched England for a century—and, moreover, a guarantee of her possessions according to our power. . . .' "

At the same time, Lee begged Vergennes, also through Beaumarchais, to allow him to come to Versailles. He wanted to discuss with the French Foreign Minister the clauses of the contemplated treaty. Vergennes, however, steadfastly refused to grant him that permission. He had to tread slowly and carefully around innumerable political pitfalls. On the one hand, French public opinion was becoming more ardently pro-American every day. On the other hand, the deeply religious King still objected to any measure that he considered un-Christian. "Being faithful to his principles of justice, [the King] does not want to take advantage of the situation in which the English find themselves," Vergennes wrote Beaumarchais as late as April 26, 1776, "to increase their embarrassment."

Simultaneously, Vergennes had to watch the course that Prussia, long an ally of England, was about to follow. Furthermore, he was engaged in thorny negotiations with Spain. Spain was a friend of France, but she was also an American colonial power and looked askance at the revolt of the North Americans against their mother country. Wisely, cautiously, Vergennes temporized.

Beaumarchais had no use for wisdom, for caution, for temporizing. He was more and more devoted to the American cause for its own sake, and that cause now appeared in imminent danger. The British expeditionary force was ready to sail. The lack of trained officers, especially in technical arms, and the shortage of ammunition and guns on the American side were creating grave concern in Philadelphia. Lee was now sending out truly frantic appeals to France. He hoped that France would grant a large loan with which the Colonies could purchase gunpowder in Flanders and Holland. As for artillery officers and engineers, in which the American army was woefully deficient, the French Ministry of War alone in Europe seemed in a position to provide—secretly, of course—the indispensable qualified men.

Throughout the first months of 1776, Beaumarchais literally harried Vergennes with his pleadings on America's behalf. He definitely took his cue from Lee on the nature of the assistance to be given the Americans, but the passionate warmth of his tone proved that help to America was no longer a matter of political expediency to him.

"I had a long conference the day before yesterday, in the evening," he wrote Vergennes on April 26, 1776, "with the man you thought best not to allow to come to France . . . He asks me continually if we are going to do absolutely nothing for them.

. . . Without wasting his time repeating to me how important their success is to France, because he does us the honor of believing that we agree with him on that point, he simply tells me: 'We need arms, gunpowder, but, above all, we need engineers. You are the only people capable of helping us and whose interest is to do so.' . . . The Americans are in as good a situation as they can be. Army, fleet, food supplies, courage—everything is excellent. But without gunpowder and without engineers, how can they be victorious or even defend themselves? Are we going to let them perish rather than lend them one or two millions? . . . Monsieur le Comte, will you do nothing for the Americans?"

Then on May 3: "Ah, Monsieur le Comte, as a favor to me . . . some powder and a few engineers! It seems I have never wanted anything so much." And a few days later, on May 8: "I can pledge my sacred faith to make any sum reach them through intermediaries, by way of Holland, without any risk and without any other authorization than that which exists between us. . . . But engineers! Engineers and gunpowder!"

Meanwhile, diplomatic relations between France and England were rapidly deteriorating. In November 1775, the moderate Lord Rochford had been replaced as Foreign Minister by the more aggressive Lord Weymouth. Although Rochford retained great influence in the Tory party, the attitude of the British Foreign Office toward France stiffened markedly. There was no question of war between the two nations as yet, but by intimidation England wanted to prevent France's becoming the arsenal of American democracy.

In the spring of 1776 the English authorities seized an American merchant ship bound for Nantes. This was strictly their right according to international law. But they further demanded that the French merchant to whom the ship's cargo was consigned be punished by the French government.

Beaumarchais saw his chance to step in and tell Lord Rochford what had long lain on his heart. When he reported to Versailles in great detail his exchange of sharp remarks with the English lord about England's presumption of ruling the seven seas, he had the joy of hearing not only that Vergennes had endorsed his stand fully, but that the King himself, nettled by England's arrogant behavior, had at long last relinquished his attitude of meek, evangelical forbearance. "I take pleasure," Vergennes wrote him on that occasion, "in letting you know that His Majesty has very much approved the noble and frank manner with which you repelled the attack made on you by Lord Rochford about the American vessel, destined for Nantes, that was led to Bristol. You have said nothing that His Majesty would not have prescribed you to say if he had been able to foresee that you would have to explain a matter so far removed from the business entrusted to you. . . . Receive my own congratulations, Monsieur. After I have assured you of the King's approval, mine will not seem very interesting to you. Nevertheless, I cannot forbear applauding the wisdom and firmness of your conduct and reassuring you of my complete esteem."

Beaumarchais now stood in high favor in Versailles. How much his reports contributed toward persuading the well-meaning Louis XVI to adopt a realistic stand in political problems, and to what extent these reports helped Vergennes convince his colleagues in the ministry that effective aid should be given the Americans at once, will never be known. That the coolheaded and reserved

Vergennes should have expressed his satisfaction in such glowing terms goes far toward proving that Beaumarchais played more than a minor part in deciding the French government to intervene in the American conflict.

2. *Roderigue Hortalez & Cie*

AT THE beginning of May 1776 the French government had definitely, though secretly, decided to send supplies to America. Dr. Barbeu Dubourg had been selected to serve as intermediary with the Insurgents. Barbeu Dubourg, a botanist of some note, had lived several years in England and knew English well. He had occasionally dabbled in business, but his chief claim to the job for which he had been chosen was his close friendship with the most popular of all Americans, Benjamin Franklin.

Benjamin Franklin had been in France only twice, in 1767 and in 1769, and had stayed but a short time, yet he had succeeded in winning the love and admiration of the French. His reputation as a scientist had made him welcome among the learned, who wield an enormous influence on French public opinion. The striking simplicity of his clothes, the bonhomie of his manners, and the plain, homespun quality of his remarks, which revealed a great deal of common sense and shrewdness, made him appear the model American—natural, honest, kind, and wise.

Some of Franklin's writings had been translated into French by a Premonstrant named Lesqui; but Lesqui's literary style was poor. Barbeu Dubourg had offered to revise these translations, and

Franklin had gratefully accepted. He was so pleased with the result that he made Barbeu Dubourg general editor of all his books published in France. Henceforth the two men were united in affection and absolute trust. In the cafés of Paris, where he was a frequent guest, Barbeu Dubourg made much of his connection with Franklin. But when it came to outfitting vessels, recruiting sailors, and organizing shipments of guns across the ocean, it soon became evident that he had more literary skill than executive ability. He lacked youthful energy—he was over sixty-five—and his business methods smacked of academic fussiness. Moreover he tended to be garrulous, and Vergennes feared that some unguarded talking on his part might create serious difficulties with England.

Then Vergennes and Sartines thought of Beaumarchais. Beaumarchais had shown in the recent Chevalier d'Eon affair that he could be discreet and trustworthy. Furthermore, under the great Pâris-Duverney he had learned all the intricacies of the war-supply trade. A message was sent to him in London, instructing him to return to France at once. On May 24, 1776, he arrived in Paris. He was told the problems confronting the government and requested to submit a practical plan for the rapid dispatch of help to the Americans.

Beaumarchais, overjoyed, at once composed a memorial incorporating the ideas he had so often discussed with Lee in London. France should give the Americans an immediate subsidy of one million livres. Half of that sum would be sent directly to America to give a little life to the paper money issued by the Colonies, which showed alarming signs of weakness. Beaumarchais suggested that the Spanish and Portuguese coins he had bought in London be used for that purpose. The rest of the money would buy gunpowder and guns abroad. These purchases could be made by the French government under the cloak of a business firm for which Beaumarchais proposed the fictitious name, Roderigue Hortalez & Cie.

This program, however, was not accepted by the ministry. Versailles did not want to deal directly with the Insurgents: France was officially at peace with England and could not interfere in a struggle between the British Crown and its discontented subjects. Moreover, the French Cabinet had no intention of sending money to the Americans or buying anything for them in other countries. The French were themselves short of cash, and it happened that their own arsenals were filled with surplus of war matériel.

The Seven Years' War had made military experts realize that the equipment of the French army had to be renovated. In 1765, plans for a new artillery system, submitted by Jean-Baptiste Vaquette de Gribeauval, had been adopted, but little had been done to implement them until the end of Louis XV's reign. In October 1775, Maurepas appointed the energetic Comte de Saint-Germain Minister of War and he at once took steps to have guns of the Gribeauval model produced in large numbers. What was to be done with the older guns? They were much too good to be discarded and thrown away as junk. Why not send them to the Americans?

An artillery expert, Major Philippe Charles Tronson Du Coudray, was instructed to go through the French arsenals and sort out the matériel that could be spared without impairing the fighting strength of the French army. The French government also decided to let the Americans have good, standard-quality gunpowder, regulation muskets as well as shoes, clothing, and blankets, which they needed badly. These supplies were to be taken from French military stores, conveyed in deep secrecy to French harbors on the Atlantic coast, and then shipped to America.

Early in May, Barbeu Dubourg had been designated to direct shipping operations. Now, however, Beaumarchais was to take the whole affair practically into his own hands. He would organize an independent commercial firm under the name he had suggested, Roderigue Hortalez & Cie, for which he would receive a million-livre loan from the government. Another million would be forthcoming from Madrid. He was expected to raise at least an equal sum from his personal business acquaintances. He would send the Americans the supplies they needed: gunpowder, guns, muskets, blankets, shoes, and such. These supplies would be secretly put at his disposal by the French arsenals and military stores. He would pay for them or, if he preferred, replace them—in the case of blankets and shoes, for instance—with similar approved articles. He would charge the Americans a reasonable price, and take payment not in cash but in such products as tobacco and rice. The French government would help him sell these commodities in France. While providing him with the indispensable initial capital, the government wanted his firm to be self-supporting. He would run it freely and under his own responsibility. If he made a profit, well and good. If his books showed a deficit, he would somehow have to bear the loss.

As an inducement to accept these rather stringent terms, Beaumarchais was given verbal assurance that the sentence by which he was stripped of certain legal rights would be reversed as soon as possible. The period during which he could appeal the sentence had passed, but there was naturally a loophole: the Conseil d'Etat had the power to grant him "Letters of Relief," thanks to which he could appeal at any time. Before the end of May, 1776, Beaumarchais petitioned the Conseil d'Etat for Letters of Relief.

On June 5, 1776, Vergennes sent the Treasury an order to pay the Sieur de Beaumarchais one million livres. On June 10, Beaumarchais received payment in gold coin. The coins were put in canvas bags, the canvas bags were placed in his carriage, and, accompanied by Gudin, he drove to the Rue de Condé house. The bags were taken to the reception room, where he called together all the members of his family. Then, like a magician—and perhaps like a child—he poured, before their amazed eyes, all the glittering gold in a heap upon the floor.

Two months later, on August 11, 1776, Beaumarchais received another million from the Spanish Ambassador. Around the same time, he persuaded prominent French merchants to contribute a third million. His main partners in the enterprise were a ship charterer from Nantes, Jean-Joseph de Monthieu; a businessman from Le Havre, Pelletier Du Doyer; and a Jewish financier from Bordeaux, Joseph Peyrera.

The French government's decision meant the complete shelving of Arthur Lee's projects. Beaumarchais suspected that Lee would not be pleased to be left out of the Franco-American aid plan, but the main thing for him—and presumably for Lee—was that America should get what she needed. On June 12, 1776, he sent Lee in London a brief, cautiously worded note: "The difficulties I have found in my negotiations with the minister have determined me to form a company that will send your friend ammunition and powder as soon as possible to Cap Français, * against return cargoes of tobacco."

After a rapid survey trip to the Atlantic seaports from which the supplies could most conveniently be shipped overseas, Beaumarchais busied himself organizing the firm of Roderigue Hortalez in Paris. He established his headquarters on the Vieille Rue du Temple, in a huge building that had been occupied by the Dutch Embassy under Louis XIV and that had retained the name Hôtel de Hollande. The district had once had an aristocratic air but in the course of time it had been invaded by business and now looked drab. Nevertheless, Beaumarchais and all his family moved out of the comfortable Rue de Condé home and settled in the midst of the clerks, accountants, bookkeepers, and secretaries constituting his staff. He now waited only for Vergennes to put him in contact with a responsible American agent.

In March 1776, the Committee of Secret Correspondence had appointed Silas Deane American agent to Paris. This appointment had been made without the knowledge of Congress. Certain delegates at Congress were Tories, who communicated all matters of importance to the English, so, to prevent dangerous leakages of news, most of the decisions of the Committee of Secret Correspondence had to be kept confidential. Moreover, the choice of Silas Deane had been made under peculiar circumstances.

The son of a humble Connecticut blacksmith, Deane had been a brilliant student at Yale, but had encountered many difficulties in beginning his career. Eventually, however, his pleasant person-

* Cap Français was a district in the northern part of the island of Santo Domingo.

ality had enabled him to marry a rich widow, and, from then on, his affairs had taken a turn for the better. On becoming a widower himself he married, at the age of thirty, Elizabeth Saltonstall, who belonged to one of the most influential families in New England. This connection gave him an opportunity to take a prominent part in the political life of the Colony of Connecticut. He was elected to the First Continental Congress, then to the Second Continental Congress, but a cabal of his enemies prevented his re-election to Congress in October 1775. Meanwhile he had made good friends in Philadelphia, and they took care of him by having him sent to Paris as agent of the Committee of Secret Correspondence.

Deane had easy, winning manners oddly blended at times with a definite aloofness. He was warmhearted and generous toward his friends, but contemptuous, offensive, and haughty toward those he suspected of being hostile to him. Like many men of modest origin who advanced by an advantageous marriage, he had a feeling of self-diffidence and insecurity. He had to convince himself of his worth; hence his constant desire to occupy a position of social or official eminence; hence, also, his tendency to act beyond the instructions he received, merely to assert his power.

The written instructions Deane had received in March 1776 from the Committee of Secret Correspondence stated that he was to go to France in the guise of a merchant. He was not to claim the status of a diplomatic envoy. He was, nevertheless, authorized to offer France "the commercial advantages Britain had enjoyed with the Colonies," and was to try to obtain immediate help from the French in return. It was further specified "that the supply we at present want is clothing and arms for twenty five thousand men, with a suitable quantity of ammunition, and one hundred field pieces; that we mean to pay for the same by remittances to France or through Spain, Portugal, or the French Islands." Moreover, Franklin gave Deane a letter of introduction to Barbeu Dubourg: "You will find M. Dubourg a man prudent, faithful, secret, intelligent in affairs, and capable of giving you very sage advice."

Deane arrived in Paris on July 5. Franklin's letter secured him a hearty welcome by Barbeu Dubourg. But Barbeu Dubourg had already been superseded by Beaumarchais, and his efforts to help Deane failed dismally. This failure made him realize that Beaumarchais now had the ministry's confidence. Jealous and angry, he wrote, on July 13, a letter to Vergennes in which he accused Beaumarchais of "loving to gad about" and "loving splendor." He even added: "It is rumored that he is keeping girls." At the same time, he sent Beaumarchais a friendly letter inviting him to dinner. He evidently hoped to worm information out of him about his connection with the authorities.

Vergennes humorously communicated Barbeu Dubourg's letter to Beaumarchais. Beaumarchais no less humorously accepted Dubourg's invitation to dinner—with a few piquant remarks: "What has it to do with our business if I am a man who loves to gad about, loves splendor, and keeps girls in my home? The girls I have been keeping the last twenty years, Monsieur, are your very humble servants. There were five of them, four sisters and one niece. Three years ago, to my great sorrow, two of these kept girls died. I keep now only three, two sisters and my niece—which, however, is still extravagant for a private individual like myself. But what would you have thought if, knowing me better, you had heard that I had carried the scandal so far as to keep men also—two nephews, quite young and rather good-looking, and the unfortunate father who brought this shameless keeper of women into the world? As for my love of splendor, that is even worse. For the last three years, finding that laces and embroidered garments did not satisfy my vanity, I have affected plain, fine muslin around my wrists. The most superb black cloth is not too elegant for me, and I have been known to push my rascality so far as to wear silk in hot weather. But I beg you not to write these things to M. de Vergennes: you might ruin me in his opinion."

Seeing that Barbeu Dubourg's efforts were leading him nowhere, Silas Deane applied for an audience directly to the Ministry of Foreign Affairs. Vergennes granted it to him at once, and the interview took place on July 17, 1776. Vergennes knew little English, and Deane's French was poor, but Vergennes' chief assistant, Conrad Alexandre Gérard de Rayneval, served as interpreter. Their talk lasted two hours. At the end, Gérard mentioned Beaumarchais to Deane and, immediately afterward, let Beaumarchais know that a secret representative of the American government had come.

On July 18, Beaumarchais wrote Deane: "I have the honor of informing you that for a long time I have organized a scheme to help the brave Americans shake off the yoke of England. . . . I have already spoken of my plans to a gentleman in London * who says he is much attached to America. But our correspondence has been followed with difficulty and in cipher, and I have received no reply to my last letter. . . . Since you are clothed, Monsieur, with an authority that enables me to have full confidence in you, I shall be happy to resume, in a more certain and regular manner, a negotiation that, till now, had barely started."

* Arthur Lee.

The following day, Beaumarchais and Silas Deane met for the first time. Beaumarchais' English was hardly better than Deane's French, but his sincerity and enthusiasm were obvious. He was not simply eager to make a profitable deal; he was also and above all eager to help the Americans. He would be only too glad, he said, to extend credit to them. He would grant them exceptionally long delays for the expected payments in kind. He would not charge them any interest on the sums due if the remittances were, by accident, not made exactly at the agreed time. He did not want any special guarantee: the Americans were "virtuous people." He trusted them completely.

Deane was compelled to restrain Beaumarchais' ardor. He thought it best for all parties concerned to establish their relations on a regular commercial basis. To prevent misunderstanding, they decided to embody the substance of their agreement in a set of letters to be exchanged within a few days. Deane wrote on July 20, 1776: "With respect to the credit we ask for the supplies and munitions which I rely on obtaining from you, I trust that a long credit will not be necessary. One year's credit is the longest my countrymen are in the habit of taking, and as Congress has secured large quantities of tobacco in Virginia and Maryland, as well as other articles, which will be shipped as soon as vessels can be had, I have no doubts that ample returns in produce will reach you here in six months, and that the whole will be paid for within a year. . . . Should there be a balance in your favor after the expedition of the credit agreed upon, the usual rate of interest will be allowed you."

Beaumarchais replied on July 22: "As I believe that I am dealing with a virtuous people, it will be enough for me to keep an exact account of my advances. Congress will be free either to pay for the merchandise at its current value at the time of its arrival or to accept it at purchase price here, taking into account delays and insurance costs and adding a commission proportionate to the trouble and the care involved, which it is impossible to fix accurately today. I propose to serve your country as though it were my own, and I hope to find in the friendship of a generous people the true reward for the work I take pleasure in dedicating to them."

Soon afterward, Deane answered: "I think that your proposals for the settlement of the price of the merchandise and of the supplies are both just and equitable. The generous confidence which you place in the virtue and justice of my constituents fills me with the greatest joy, and gives me the most flattering hopes for the success of the enterprise, for their satisfaction as well as yours, and enables me to assure you again that the United Colonies will take the most effective measures to send you return cargoes and to justify in every way the feelings that you have for them."

On August 15, Deane explained to the Committee of Secret Correspondence why he had had to by-pass Franklin's protégé: "I find M. de Beaumarchais . . . possesses the entire confidence of the Ministry; he is a man of wit and genius, and a considerable writer on comic and political subjects; all my supplies are to come through his hands, which at first greatly discouraged my friends,* but had I been as doubtful as they, I could not have stepped aside from the path so cordially marked for me by those I depend on."

Perhaps out of consideration for Franklin, the French government gave Barbeu Dubourg a small, symbolical share of the supplies to be sent to America. He made a great ado about this

* Dr. Barbeu Dubourg.

minuscule task, trying to impress people around him with the idea that he was managing a most important affair. But in his heart he held a mortal hatred for the man who had robbed him of the glory of being the great provider of the Americans.

Arthur Lee was no less incensed at these developments. On hearing that definite arrangements were being made in Paris for sending equipment and arms across the Atlantic, he sailed for France and reached the capital on August 22, 1776. But he found himself before a wall, or rather a series of walls. Deane treated him with the distant coldness he used so well against possible rivals. Beaumarchais, pledged to secrecy by Vergennes, was cordial to him, but, at the same time, disconcertingly evasive. The Ministry of Foreign Affairs, which had previously refused to receive him as an unofficial envoy, persisted in ignoring him.

Furious, Lee returned to London. Perhaps moved by anger, perhaps sincerely suspicious of the queer Hortalez firm, he at once sent to Philadelphia, through Thomas Story—a secret agent of the Committee of Secret Correspondence, then passing through England—a verbal message that the supplies to be shipped to America by the French under the name of the firm Hortalez were a gift. The message was received by the Committee of Secret Correspondence on October 1, 1776, and duly recorded, but not communicated to Congress because "we find by fatal experience," it was stated in the record, "that Congress consists of too many members to keep secrets." At the same time, Arthur Lee, in his letters to personal friends in America and to his two brothers, Richard Henry Lee and Francis Lightfoot Lee, who were members of Congress, began to spread damaging rumors about Beaumarchais and Deane.

Deane and Beaumarchais, blissfully unaware of the storm that was brewing in Philadelphia, and utterly indifferent to Barbeu Dubourg's sour face, enthusiastically went ahead with their work. News of the Declaration of Independence, which reached Europe on August 17, 1776, caused an almost lyrical outburst in Beaumarchais. On August 18, he wrote for the first time directly to the Committee of Secret Correspondence. "The respectful esteem I have for the brave people who defend their liberty under your leadership," he said, "has induced me to form a plan concurring in this great task by establishing a large commercial firm for the sole purpose of serving you in Europe. . . . Your deputies, gentlemen, will find in me a sincere friend, in my house a shelter, in my coffers money; and I shall assist them by every possible means in their transactions, whether of an open or a secret nature. . . . You may be certain, gentlemen, that my indefatigable zeal will never fail to clear up difficulties, ease up prohibitions, and, in short, facilitate all the trade operations that I shall undertake much more to your advantage than to mine. . . . One thing can never change or decline: my avowed and ardent desire to serve you to the utmost of my power."

Until the end of the year 1776, Beaumarchais lived in a frenzy of activity. He constantly dashed back and forth from Paris to Bordeaux, Nantes, Le Hâvre, Marseille. He bought ships, had them outfitted, provisioned, loaded. He hired sea captains and crews. He corrected mistakes, adjusted differences, overcame obstacles. He seemed to be present simultaneously everywhere, and he enjoyed all the stir and bustle immensely. Yet there was not the slightest confusion or disorder in the firm of Roderigue Hortalez & Cie. Everything was run smoothly, swiftly, efficiently. On November 29, 1776, Silas Deane could truthfully report to the Committee of Secret Correspondence: "I should never have completed what I have, but for the generous, the indefatigable and spirited exertions of Monsieur Beaumarchais, to whom the United States are, on every account, greatly indebted, more so than to any other person on this side of the water. . . . I cannot in a letter do full justice to Monsieur Beaumarchais for his great address and assiduity in our cause; I can only say he appears to have undertaken it on great and liberal principles, and has, in the pursuit, made it his own. His interest and influence, which are great, have been exerted to the utmost in the cause of the United States."

Beaumarchais' influence was now great indeed. Vergennes trusted him completely. The two men exchanged confidential letters showing as much familiarity as the naturally reserved Vergennes could allow. Vergennes regularly sought Beaumarchais' opinion on important affairs of state, and, more often than not, his opinion was seriously taken into account by the ministry.

The eventual reversal of Beaumarchais' court sentence now seemed a matter of course. A few formalities, however, were still necessary. The Conseil d'Etat had first to grant him the Letters of Relief for which he had petitioned a few months earlier. He was in Bordeaux, on one of his trips connected with the sending of supplies to America, when he heard astounding news: his petition had been denied. This denial meant almost a confirmation of the original sentence. He rushed back to Versailles and found Maurepas very embarrassed, almost apologetic. The Keeper of the Great Seal, Hue de Miromesnil, who was supposed to look after the matter, had neglected to inform the Conseil d'Etat of the government's wishes in regard to Beaumarchais. Maurepas had upbraided him, but had to admit that he himself had far from given his full attention to

Beaumarchais' case. The whole thing could be fixed quickly, however. Indeed, only a few days later, on August 12, 1776, the Conseil d'Etat docilely reversed its decision.

Beaumarchais boldly declared that he would not leave Paris—even for the American cause—until the Parliament had granted him full redress. He now had so much power in high circles that the normal legal delays were cut short, and a retrial was arranged to take place within three weeks.

He engaged as his attorney Gui Target, who had never collaborated with the Maupeou Parliament. For having kept himself "undefiled" and "pure," Target had been nicknamed *la vierge* by the public, and Beaumarchais humorously called him "My dear virgin." Shortly before the case came to court, Beaumarchais circulated a pamphlet in which he summarized his grievances, which he wittily, though irreverently, entitled *Le Martyr Beaumarchais à la Vierge Target.*

On the day of the trial, Beaumarchais went to the Parliament attired in a dramatically plain black suit. His face had been made up to look strikingly pale. On his hand, which he nonchalantly kept well in view, shone the enormous diamond the Empress Maria Theresa had given him. He remained eloquently silent throughout the proceedings. Target, "the virgin," scarcely mentioned Beaumarchais at all in the presentation of his defense, but attacked the infamous Maupeou Parliament. The Attorney General, Antoine Séguier, who was supposed to conduct the case against Beaumarchais, concluded his own brief speech by asking the tribunal to quash the judgment passed in the Goëzman suit. The tribunal did not even withdraw for deliberation, but immediately declared that henceforth M. de Beaumarchais' status would be the same as it had been before February 1774. Thus, Beaumarchais automatically recovered his full civil rights. Incidentally, he was also reinstated as a judge once more. As soon as the verdict was proclaimed, shouts and cheers broke out in the courtroom. Beaumarchais was carried in triumph on the shoulders of his friends. He had nothing but friends now.

One of his friends, and a true one, was missing, however—the Prince de Conti. The Prince had died two weeks earlier, on August 22, 1776, after an illness of many months. Until the end, Beaumarchais visited him regularly, and was the only person Conti saw with genuine pleasure. The Prince was notoriously an agnostic. When he approached death, he smilingly declined to receive the sacraments of the Catholic Church. The members of his family were filled with horror. If he persisted in his attitude, he would be denied a Christian burial. The scandal would be appalling. But the Prince seemed to take a last malicious delight in annoying his relatives. Finally, the distracted family appealed to Beaumarchais, who coaxed his old friend into accepting the ministrations of the Church.

After his official rehabilitation, Beaumarchais threw himself into American aid with renewed energy and fervor. He needed both. In the previous months, he had encountered only a few small hindrances; now, grave difficulties appeared everywhere.

The English Ambassador in France, Lord Stormont, had been informed by spies that ships loaded with merchandise certainly not in great demand in the French West Indies were slipping quietly out of French harbors and sailing west. Whither? Vergennes, courteously queried on that subject by Stormont, professed complete ignorance, adding, in the course of their interview, that he did not approve of the American uprising: he believed that a revolution here inevitably begot a revolution there. Stormont, who was acquainted with the progressively deteriorating political situation in France, nodded approvingly, and went away more or less satisfied.

But soon his spies reported unusual movements of arms and ammunition on French roads at night and unexplainable concentrations of war supplies in French ports. At the same time, pro-American feelings were voiced by the French public more and more challengingly. Lord Stormont made several new and stronger representations to Vergennes, mentioning by name the Hortalez firm whose activities were most suspicious. Vergennes again gave lame excuses: it was impossible for him to control what the French people said—Lord Stormont knew that—or even, very often, what they did. Stormont snorted: the French government could at least, he said, take steps to prevent open contraband of arms on French territory. Vergennes assured Lord Stormont that the French government would do it presently.

The French government then issued several ordinances against the smuggling of war supplies, but it was known in high places that Beaumarchais would disregard these ordinances. Unfortunately, a few minor French officials insisted upon enforcing the law! Beaumarchais frequently protested to the Ministry of Foreign Affairs against these preposterous regulations, but was told that such hitches were regrettable, yet inevitable. He had to pursue his work with increased caution and, naturally, at his own risk.

Barbeu Dubourg was, under the circumstances, a painful thorn in Beaumarchais' flesh. Far from concealing his activities, Barbeu Dubourg boasted of them everywhere. But since the ways of eluding observation were not very numerous, he often put English spies on Beaumarchais' tracks as well as on his own. More than once, the carefully laid plans of Hortalez & Cie would fail at the last moment owing to some indiscretion traceable to the old man. Then Beaumarchais would write to Vergennes: "Dubourg must be made to keep silent and not compromise the Ministry." Or again: "If while we close the doors on one side, someone opens the windows on the other, it is impossible for the secret not to escape." Or even: "Is there, then, no means of stopping the mouth of that cruel gossiper?"

Another serious source of worry for Beaumarchais was the Congress' failure to send him a message either directly or through Deane, confirming or disavowing the contract he had made with the latter. American ships crossed the Atlantic, bringing cargoes consigned to French merchants and mail destined for private individuals, but never a letter from the Committee of Secret Correspondence to their agent in Paris. On October 1, 1776, Silas Deane, finding himself in an acutely embarrassing state of uncertainty, wrote to the Committee: "For heaven's sake, if you mean to have any connection with this Kingdom, be more assiduous in getting your letters here. I know not where the blame lies, but it must lie heavily somewhere, when vessels are suffered to sail from Philadelphia and other ports quite down the middle of August without a single line."

This silence was to a large extent due to the intense concern created at that time in Philadelphia by sudden military disaster. In July, 1776, the long-dreaded British expeditionary force, numbering over 30,000 men under Sir William Howe's command, had appeared before the city of New York. In August, Howe severely defeated George Washington on Long Island. In September, he occupied New York. From New York, the English could easily strike at Philadelphia, and, according to eighteenth-century ideas, taking an enemy capital meant that the issue of a war was decided.

Congress then made new efforts to enlist the active support of the French. On September 26, 1776, Benjamin Franklin, Thomas Jefferson, and Silas Deane were appointed American Commissioners to Paris. When Jefferson declined the post, he was replaced, on October 22, by Arthur Lee.

In the meantime, Washington's army had been reduced—by illness, desertion, and the legal return home of the soldiers once their short term of service was ended—to barely four thousand men, ill-fed, ill-clad, and in the lowest possible spirits. On December 18, 1776, Washington himself wrote to his brother: "If every nerve is not strained to recruit a new army, I think that the game is pretty nearly up."

These discouraging events became known in France in October, 1776. For the next three months, all the news from America told of American reverses. Beaumarchais, utterly distressed, tried desperately to send more and more supplies overseas. He violated the government ordinances against contraband of arms as best he could, but the ordinances markedly hampered his efforts. On November 12, 1776, he wrote to Vergennes: "Believe me, Monsieur le Comte, my heart is often oppressed with anguish when I see how things are going—or rather how they are not going."

The American defeats evoked diametrically opposite reactions from the French government and from the French people. The government had seen in the Anglo-American conflict mainly a providential opportunity to weaken England. But if England was to be rapidly and completely victorious in that conflict—as now looked probable—it was the French statesmen's strict duty to keep France free from too close an association with the Insurgents. The French people, on the contrary, saw only one thing: the Americans needed help, and help they must have at any cost. Two causes were given—rightly or wrongly—by the French public for the American retreat: the American army, it was said, lacked good equipment and qualified officers. Since Bunker Hill, the gallantry of the American fighting man had become axiomatic. But it was one thing to stand fast in trenches against a frontal attack and another thing to outmaneuver in the field trained troops using all the subtleties of the European war technique. Officers, good officers, were needed at once to prevent a complete American collapse.

The French people responded to the American need with a flood of volunteers. Hundreds and soon thousands of young Frenchmen declared themselves ready to go overseas. Practically all of them were officers on active duty with the French army. In theory, they had to ask the Ministry of War for regular leave, but, as a rule, the Ministry merely winked at their departure. There were a few adventurers among them, but not many. The American situation at that time looked too bleak to attract soldiers of fortune. Most of the volunteers, in the fall of 1776, were young men filled with enthusiasm for the idea of Liberty, and eager to fight for her cause.

Thus did La Fayette present himself, on November 6, 1776, to Silas Deane, asking the favor of serving in the American army. "I am well nigh harassed to death," Deane wrote to the Committee of Secret Correspondence, on November 28, 1776, "with applications of officers to get out to America." On December 3, 1776, he said to John Jay: "Had I ten ships here, I could fill them with passengers to America. I hope the officers sent will be agreeable; they were recommended by the Ministry here, and are at this instant really in their army, but this must be a secret."

Beaumarchais did his best to assist Deane in selecting the volunteers, particularly artillery experts. "It seems to me that the cause for their [the Americans'] falling back in such a manner," he wrote to Vergennes on November 9, 1776, "is that they do not know how to use their artillery. They have courage but no military science. It seems to me of utmost importance that nothing should stop our sending artillery officers and engineers, who will soon change the complexion of their way of establishing entrenchments and organizing defenses."

At the end of 1776, Beaumarchais had loaded two hundred field guns and a large quantity of war supplies on several ships at Le Hâvre. It was understood that a group of artillery officers would be sent along with the guns, to instruct the Americans in their use. Major Du Coudray, who had supervised the recruitment of these officers, had won both Beaumarchais' and Deane's high regard in the past months with the zeal, the competency, and the co-operative spirit he had shown in discharging his duties. At this juncture, however, the Major saw a unique chance to secure for himself a spectacular promotion. He was willing to go to America, he said, and he persuaded Silas Deane to give him a commission of Major General in the name of Congress. Beaumarchais and Deane sincerely believed at first that America was lucky to obtain the services of such a man. But as soon as Du Coudray had his commission in his pocket, he began to act in the most incredibly highhanded manner.

Three of Beaumarchais' vessels, *Le Romain*, *La Seine*, and *L'Amphitrite*, were to carry practically all the two hundred guns to America. Du Coudray and the artillery officers were scheduled to sail with these ships. But the officers, while waiting for the day of sailing, which naturally depended upon the direction of the wind, bragged openly in Le Hâvre's cafés about their going to America. Beaumarchais was on tenterhooks.

Suddenly Du Coudray left Le Hâvre and went to Versailles. He knew Comte de Saint-Germain personally and wanted to arrive in America with the added distinction of being under the direct orders of the French Minister of War. Beaumarchais complained vigorously to Vergennes. The wind at Le Hâvre might at any moment become favorable for sailing. Yet no sailing could take place while Du Coudray was absent, and postponing the departure of the convoy might prove catastrophic. If English spies discovered the true destination of his ships, they would almost certainly be intercepted. Vergennes relayed this complaint to Saint-Germain, who sent Du Coudray back to Le Hâvre at once.

Beaumarchais followed him there, to make sure that everything would proceed smoothly. But then he himself committed the worst blunder. *Le Barbier de Séville* was about to be performed at Le Hâvre. The playwright could not resist the temptation of attending dress rehearsal and giving directions to the actors. Though he had assumed the name of "Durand" to conceal his identity, English spies were not slow in discovering who he was. Lord Stormont, immediately informed of the whole affair, made bitter representations to Vergennes. Vergennes had no alternative but to issue an order forbidding the sailing of *La Seine*, *Le Romain*, and *L'Amphitrite*.

When Vergennes' order reached Le Hâvre, however, *La Seine* and *Le Romain* alone were still at anchor. *L'Amphitrite* had left, with Du Coudray on board. Beaumarchais rushed to Versailles, but when he got there he found the situation completely changed: Benjamin Franklin had arrived in France.

3. *First Clouds*

"The commotion caused by M. Franklin's arrival is inconceivable," Beaumarchais wrote to Vergennes on December 16, 1776. Franklin had crossed the Atlantic on a small armed sloop and had landed, on December 3, at Auray, on the coast of Brittany. On December 7, he was in Nantes and, on December 21, in Paris. Everywhere he was greeted with wild enthusiasm. His coming to France became a symbol to the French people: the symbol of the American will to go on fighting for justice and freedom in spite of disaster.

In contrast to the court of Versailles, whose attitude was calculating and guarded, the mass of the people openly showed their deep sympathy for the American cause. For the man in the street, precisely because the American armies were all but crushed by England's superior force, it was France's imperative duty to step in—even if a dangerous war with England would ensue. On January 4, 1777, Franklin wrote to the Committee of Secret Correspondence: "The cry of this nation is for us; but the court, it is thought, views an approaching war with reluctance." On January 17, Deane confirmed these views: "The hearts of the French people are universally for us," he said, "and the opinion for an immediate war with Great Britain is very strong; but the court has its reasons for postponing a little longer."

Shortly afterward, however, news of General Washington's extraordinary military recovery in the last days of 1776 and the beginning of 1777—notably at Trenton and Princeton—reached France. Once more the court earnestly considered the possibility of French intervention on the American side. But there were still great obstacles to such a move. French finances were in a precarious state, and the expenses of a war would probably mean France's financial ruin. Also, France could not act without her ally, Spain. Finally, in spite of Sartines' frantic efforts, the French fleet was not yet ready for a contest with the British Navy.

With a perfect understanding of these circumstances, Franklin refrained from causing the French court the slightest embarrassment by indulging in overt propaganda. He had informed Deane of his appointment as Commissioner and summoned Lee from London. On January 28, 1777, the three Commissioners presented themselves to Vergennes; then, modestly and discreetly, they established their headquarters in a remote suburb of the capital, Passy. Franklin scarcely ever went out, except to attend meetings of the Academy of Sciences, of which he was a corresponding member. But his house was constantly thronged by savants and writers of mark, by frivolous but influential society ladies eager to see the new social lion, and also by numerous important political personages. Soon he completely eclipsed his two colleagues and became a dominant power in Paris.

Franklin was far from kindly disposed toward Beaumarchais. The first letter he had written upon arriving in France, on December 4, 1776, had been to his "*cher bon ami*," Barbeu Dubourg.

Once in Paris, he renewed his affectionate intimacy with the old botanist. It may fairly be surmised that Barbeu Dubourg unburdened his heart to Franklin about the matter of the American supplies, and drew a none too flattering picture of the man who had supplanted and mocked him. From the beginning Franklin adopted a definite stand toward Beaumarchais: he completely ignored him. This attitude may be explained by Franklin's desire not to create difficulties for the French government by attracting attention to the supplies sent to America by the Hortalez firm. Yet there was certainly also an element of distrust and ill-concealed hostility in his frigid reserve toward Beaumarchais. Moreover, Beaumarchais had for many months worked harmoniously with Deane, and the two men had grown fond of each other. Franklin was always correct in his relations with his fellow Commissioner, yet he made it perfectly clear that Beaumarchais, being Deane's man, meant nothing at all to him.

Arthur Lee made Beaumarchais' position even more difficult. Believing himself double-crossed by Beaumarchais and Deane, Lee expressed, and perhaps sincerely entertained, the worst suspicions about their dealings. In his letters to Philadelphia, he never ceased to hint that Congress had been the victim of some dark machination of theirs. Thus, he wrote on January 3, 1777, to the Committee of Secret Correspondence: "The politics of this court [Versailles] are in a kind of trembling hesitation. It is in consequence of this that the promises, which were made to me by the French agent in London, and which I stated to you by Mr. Story and others, have not been entirely fulfilled. The changing of the mode of conveying what they had promised was settled with Mr. Deane, whom Mons. Hortalez, or Beaumarchais, found here upon his return from London, and with whom all the arrangements were afterwards made." Lee was also bitterly jealous of Franklin, and soon relations among the three Commissioners became acrimonious and tense. The calm and levelheaded Franklin himself was now often irritable; and on January 30, 1777, Beaumarchais complained in a letter to Vergennes that Deane had for a month shown "*une humeur empestée.*"

Lee had recently taken a strong dislike to France. Was it because he saw both Deane and Franklin warmly appreciated by the French, who had snubbed him? In fact, the French Ministry of Foreign Affairs suspected him of acting in collusion with the English. In any case, Lee now believed that America should seek other allies besides France. In February, 1777, he left Paris with the avowed purpose of securing those alliances. He had pinned great hopes on Prussia. But Frederick the Great was a realist. "I intend to draw out these negotiations," Frederick wrote to his brother, Prince Heinrich, on June 23, 1777, referring to Arthur Lee's proposals, "so that I may fall in with the side for which Fortune will declare herself." While Lee was thus kept dangling in Berlin by the wily Prussian King, Franklin, Deane, and Beaumarchais enjoyed about six months of comparative peace and quiet.

Nevertheless, even during that period, a series of unpleasant incidents showed clearly that Beaumarchais' position in 1777 was no longer what it had been in 1776. The first difficulty arose when it became known that Du Coudray had, through sheer bluff and bluster, taken command of the *Amphitrite* over the skipper's head. On his own authority and against the skipper's formal advice, he had brought the ship back to Lorient on pretext that some damages caused by a storm had rendered her unseaworthy. Beaumarchais immediately notified Du Coudray in stiff terms that, on board of any Hortalez ship, he would have to accept the status of a private passenger or find some other means of conveyance to America.

Deane then realized how wrong he had been in giving Du Coudray the Commission of Major General. In full agreement with Beaumarchais, he tried to correct his mistake. Accordingly, he wrote him a letter in which he said: "The strange, ungrateful, and perfidious conduct of this man mortifies me and embarrasses me strangely, and, as I wish with all my heart I had never seen him, I wish equally that he may never see America." Beaumarchais communicated this letter to Vergennes. Vergennes, naturally eager to prevent undesirable officers from leaving France, talked over the matter with Maurepas. Orders were given to Du Coudray to return immediately to his original garrison in Metz.

But Du Coudray disobeyed these orders and went to Versailles instead. He had good friends there, and they brought him to Franklin's house. On February 6, 1777, Franklin, perhaps to play a good trick on Beaumarchais and Deane, gave Du Coudray a warm recommendation to Congress and somehow prevailed upon Deane to sign the recommendation along with him. Deane was evidently no match for Franklin. Later, finding himself most embarrassed by his recantation, he told Beaumarchais rather lamely that the recommendation merely stated that Du Coudray was a good officer, which, from a technical standpoint, was true enough.

Du Coudray hastened to cross the Atlantic, though not on one of Beaumarchais' ships. Once in America, he found himself almost at once involved in sensational feuds. But even in the midst of his difficulties, he did not forget to avenge himself upon Beaumarchais and Deane. For several months he waged a violent campaign against them, openly charging them with conspiracy, greed, and fraud. Although he died shortly afterward, on September 16, 1777, accidentally drowned while crossing the Schuylkill, the slanders he had circulated lived on for many years. Indeed, his brutal accusations seemed to confirm the more insidious rumors about Deane and Beaumarchais that emanated from the circle of Arthur Lee's brothers and friends.

At Versailles, meanwhile, Maurepas and Vergennes had been very annoyed by the Du Coudray affair. They had had to swallow Franklin's implied censure because they did not want to quarrel with him over such a trifling matter as a recommendation given to an officer. But they blamed Beaumarchais for offering, if not the cause of, at least the occasion for, this mortifying experience. Beaumarchais tried to explain the network of circumstances in which he had been caught, then added: "I feel strong against everything except your displeasure. Never judge me without hearing me. This is the only favor I ask." Yet, from that time on, a definite cloud spread over their relations.

Vergennes now knew that there was little love lost between Beaumarchais and Franklin. Franklin was such an essential piece in the Franco-American game that Beaumarchais would have to be withdrawn into the background. Supplies would still secretly be sent to America, but other channels would have to be used. As early as February 1777 Beaumarchais became aware that certain other intermediaries had been called in by the government to fulfill—at least in part—the functions he had performed with such success and zeal. His letters to Vergennes took on a sad, melancholy tone. Although he was glad to hear that the Americans were receiving the supplies they needed, he could not help showing chagrin at being slowly set aside. On February 4, 1777, he wrote to Vergennes: "It is a pity that the Dutch should get the main profit from the transportation of these materials. It does not matter, however. The most important thing is not to let America come to grief through lack of good ammunition."

Vergennes and Maurepas still consulted Beaumarchais about important political problems, however. He now favored granting the American government official recognition, even if it meant war with England. But would it not be necessary, in case of war, to increase the already crushing taxes beyond all limits of endurance? Beaumarchais said that adequate resources could easily be found if French finances were reorganized. Since he had acquired through his association with Pâris-Duverney the reputation of being a financial wizard, Maurepas asked him to set down his suggestions in writing. Beaumarchais offered a plan, which he called the "Plan Sully."

The Duc de Sully had been, at the beginning of the seventeenth century, the most popular minister of the most popular of all French Kings, Henri IV. After the disastrous Religious Wars, Sully had succeeded, thanks to a program of equitable taxation and honest thrift, in putting the tottering French finances upon a sound and secure basis. The plan Beaumarchais advocated had little to do with the actual measures Sully had adopted in the past. It was, in fact, hardly more than a rehash of the ideas of reform spread by the most advanced "philosophers" of Beaumarchais' own time. It essentially called for a drastic curtailment of the aristocrats' financial privileges, and for the acceptance by the wealthy class of a fair, proportionate share in the nation's fiscal burden.

When the Comte de Maurepas and the Comte de Vergennes, both stanch conservatives, read this report, they were filled with suspicions and misgivings. No wonder Beaumarchais was such a zealous supporter of the American Revolution! He evidently favored all the "subversive" ideas which the American Insurgents had put forward, and which were arousing so much enthusiasm among the discontented subjects of the King of France. Vergennes had been right when he had remarked to Lord Stormont that a revolution here inevitably begot a revolution there.

Naturally, the "Plan Sully" was rejected. Henceforth, Vergennes and Maurepas looked upon Beaumarchais as a potentially dangerous man. Far more than his past irregularities and questionable adventures, his political ideas alienated their good will. From then on they were coldly courteous, though always commendably fair, in all their dealings with him, and they no longer took him into their confidence.

Beaumarchais undoubtedly sensed their suddenly altered attitude in his regard and probably guessed the cause for the change. Once more, his half-forgotten grievances rankled in his mind, and to them was added a concealed but bitter resentment at being slowly overshadowed and unjustly neglected. To allay his accumulated rancors, he composed, in the course of the year 1777, the first draft of a new play, *Le Mariage de Figaro*. Beaumarchais did not write his play all in one stretch, but by fits and starts, very much as inspiration or anger moved him. He incorporated into it most of the sarcasm about aristocracy and attacks on the social order of his time that he had been compelled to cut out of the second version of *Le Barbier de Séville*—hence the disconnected and complicated character of the new comedy. Yet he put into *Le Mariage de Figaro* the best that was in him: his mature philosophy of life, and an epitome of his whole existence.

Beaumarchais himself appeared once again in the guise of Figaro. But Figaro was no longer an irrepressible, happy-go-lucky, and somewhat shallow barber. He had retained most of his gaiety, but he had lost some of his youth, and had gained much earnestness and depth. He now stood as the symbol of all men of high merit and low birth who are thwarted in their legitimate hopes and efforts by an absurd, unfair, and oppressive society. Figaro had personal grievances, which were provided in the play by a rather thin plot: Count Almaviva, whom he has formerly helped win a wife, now tries to steal his own fiancée. But above and beyond these grievances, he seeks for the kind of injustice of which he is the victim, a general, rational, and broadly human redress.

Figaro's fiancée, Suzanne, is, in many respects, a stage counterpart of Beaumarchais' sister Julie. She has her sharp wit, her cheerful courage, and her teasing humor. It is noteworthy that, though Figaro's love for Suzanne is supposed to constitute the central theme of the play, no love scene ever takes place between these two protagonists.

All the real love element is concentrated in Countess Almaviva —the former Rosine of *Le Barbier*—and her godson, Chérubin. Godmother—godson. The godmother could be a mother. . . . "*Qu'elle est imposante!*" the youthful and adoring Chérubin says of her. There is a great deal of Beaumarchais' own personality in Chérubin, at least the adolescent part of his personality, a part that never completely disappeared within him. As for the Countess, she evidently embodies the mature and somewhat buxom type of woman toward whom Beaumarchais was always irresistibly drawn.

The character of Marceline—the middle-aged woman who wants to marry Figaro and is found to be Figaro's own mother—casts an even more revealing light upon Beaumarchais' subconscious emotional trends.

Bartholo has receded into the background. He is still reminiscent of André Caron, however. At long last, he is officially uncovered and openly recognized as Figaro's father. The last episode of his life brought out in the play is a love affair with his housekeeper.

A jolly, comical caricature of Judge Goëzman appears as Judge Guzman Brid'oison. Little bitterness is evident in the presentation of his character, only retrospective amusement and contempt.

Beaumarchais' whole anger was now concentrated on the *grands seigneurs*, the haughty-minded and empty-headed aristocrats who exploited, despised, cheated, and bullied the commoner. "Because you are a great lord, you believe you are a great genius! Nobility, fortune, rank, position, all that makes you so proud! What have you done to enjoy so many advantages? You have taken the trouble of being born—and nothing more. Your birth apart, you are a very ordinary man. While I . . . by Jove! Lost in obscurity, I needed more science and skill just to subsist than were needed to govern all Spain for a hundred years. And you want to fight with me!"

This thundering challenge was one day to awaken a tremendous echo in the hearts of millions of Frenchmen. For the time being, however, Beaumarchais kept unpublished the burning expression of his indignation and rage.

From a literary standpoint *Le Mariage de Figaro* towers far above *Le Barbier de Séville.* In *Le Barbier de Séville*, Beaumarchais had provided good-humored entertainment, offered good-natured satire, and created three unforgettable though somewhat superficial characters. In *Le Mariage de Figaro*, he presented a broad study of human nature and left an enduring message. Within one "mad day"—*La Folle Journée* was the play's apt subtitle—a bewildering medley of unexpected events tumble over one another, opening at each new turn of action far-reaching views into hidden aspects of human character, institutions and customs. Thus Beaumarchais' picture of the working of Justice, of which he had a first hand knowledge, and his remarks on diplomacy, of which he had caught more than a glimpse, have lost nothing today of their pungency and appropriateness. His analysis of love—showing the questing sentimentality of the adolescent Chérubin and the flirtatious curiosity of the gardener's daughter Fanchette (a replica of Beaumarchais' sister Fanchon when she was a girl), as well as the Count's sensuous, blasé cynicism, and the Countess' wistful, somewhat morbid fondness for a boy much younger than herself—runs through a gamut of perennial sentiments which are explored with consummate tact and yet penetrating insight.

The central theme of the play, the struggle between Figaro and his master, was for Beaumarchais' contemporaries a symbol of the struggle going on between commoners and aristocrats. This conflict is now for us a matter of past history; yet it gives the play a solid background of real feelings and problems, strongly situating the action at a definite place and at a definite time. Behind this historical interest, men of all times can perceive in *Le Mariage de Figaro* the ever-recurring revolt of the underdog, conscious of his rights, against unfair oppression, and the everlasting fight of sheer intelligence hopefully pitted against brutal force. The deep, genuine emotion ringing through this appeal for social and individual justice, oddly blended with a most brilliant, sparkling dialogue, goes far toward making *Le Mariage de Figaro* one of the French stage's greatest masterpieces.

4. *Sailing On*

THROUGHOUT the year 1777, Beaumarchais sent to America an enormous amount of vital supplies. Curiously enough, Roderigue Hortalez & Cie reached its maximum efficiency when its founder's personal credit with the authorities was ebbing. The firm now ran like clockwork. Beaumarchais had well-drilled agents in every important French port. He no longer had to dash wildly from one place to another. Practically everything could be controlled from headquarters at the Hôtel de Hollande.

Although Beaumarchais still remained very active, he could now spend many hours peacefully and happily at home. Indeed, his home life was peaceful and happy. On January 5, 1777, Mlle de Willermaulaz had brought a daughter into the world. She was christened Eugénie. The child's illegitimacy caused her father no concern whatever.

Beaumarchais' main concern in those days was for his ships plying between France and America. He now possessed a fleet of from twelve to fifteen vessels. It is impossible for the modern historian to keep track of them, because their names—*La Concorde, L'Amélie, Le Ferragus, Le Mercure, La Thérèse, La Seine, L'Heureux, La Marie-Catherine, Le Comte de Vergennes, L'Amphitrite, Le Flamand, Le Marquis de La Chalotais, Le Pérou, Le Romain, Le Zéphyr, Le Fier Roderigue*—were often changed or shifted around to confuse the English spies who haunted the French harbors. His ships sailed as a rule from Bordeaux, Nantes, Le Hâvre, or Marseille, all nominally bound for Martinique or Santo Domingo. But after touching these islands, and very often before then, they would swing sharply northward and gain an American port.

Portsmouth, in New Hampshire, was, throughout the war, the main landing point for Beaumarchais' supplies. Early in 1777, the first big Hortalez convoy brought in there at one time three million livres' worth of goods: two hundred field guns, thousands of muskets, kegs upon kegs of gunpowder, countless bundles of blankets, clothes, and shoes—enough to equip 25,000 men. The people of the town, lining the water front, could hardly believe their eyes. Then, after a while, when they realized that all that abundance pouring from the French ships was indeed for America, they broke into wild shouting, cheering, dancing, laughing, and crying, cold and hard-boiled Yankees though they were.

On their way back to France, Beaumarchais' ships usually called at Charleston in the hope of getting a return cargo of tobacco or rice. But practically always they had to sail back empty.

The area in which George Washington was personally in command received very little of the equipment sent by Beaumarchais in 1777, which may be one of the causes for Washington's comparatively poor showing in the second part of the 1777 campaign. During the same period, the northern region, which constituted General

Horatio Gates' sector, received by way of Portsmouth an uninterrupted flow of gunpowder, arms, and clothing from the Hortalez fleet. The remarkable fighting strength shown by General Gates' troops in 1777 was to a large extent due to the help coming from that source. An important number of men could be properly equipped; their morale rose; broad-scale operations could be easily undertaken—and these operations led, before the year ended, to the crucial victory of Saratoga.

Beaumarchais' activity in 1777 was not limited to sending ships to Portsmouth. He also gave considerable assistance to the American Commissioners in Paris in selecting the volunteers who wanted to go to America. The men who came forward for that purpose in the spring and summer of 1777 were, as a rule, somewhat different from those who had swamped Deane's office in the fall of 1776. In the fall of 1776, the war news from America had been exceedingly black. The volunteers then were mostly French army officers. The majority of them were, like La Fayette, eager above all to fight for ideals and glory. To them America was a symbol of freedom. They had been told that America was about to succumb for lack of trained officers. They came to save her.

These idealistic volunteers frequently became a source of serious difficulty to America. They were generally handicapped by their ignorance of the English language and of local conditions and customs. Moreover, the American officers already in command vehemently protested when foreigners were promoted over their heads. Countless painful conflicts followed. Even La Fayette had to offer to serve as a private and without pay to be accepted into the American army. Deane, who had given commissions to these volunteers in 1776, was held responsible for the whole trouble. In

1777, Congress sent the Commissioners strict orders to be extremely circumspect in choosing volunteers.

By that time, the war picture had completely changed. The American cause was no longer in immediate peril. The fact that Sir William Howe had not taken the capital, Philadelphia, after his early victories was interpreted as a sign that his superiority had been highly overrated. Furthermore, it was now felt that France would sooner or later enter the conflict on the American side. Whatever the final outcome, a protracted war was evidently in sight.

Europe had not had a "worth-while" war for nearly fifteen years. Everywhere, but particularly in Central Europe, unemployed professional soldiers could be found, waiting for a chance to ply their trade. They were adventurers often without ideals, but they were also often remarkably fine fighting men. Some of them were decent according to their own code, others were hardly better than bandits. In 1777 most of them turned their eyes toward America.

The American Commissioners in Paris realized that some of these new volunteers could be invaluable to the United States, but they were often at a loss to distinguish conscientious mercenaries from disreputable characters. Beaumarchais was more familiar than Deane or Franklin with European riffraff, and they were glad to profit from his experience.

Their most spectacular find was Baron Friedrich Wilhelm von Steuben. The son of a German officer who had sought his fortune successively in the Russian army and the Prussian army, Steuben had entered the Prussian service shortly before the outbreak of the Seven Years' War. He had attained the rank of Captain of

Infantry and had been for a while attached to the Prussian General Staff. At the end of the war, however, he had been discharged, more or less in disgrace, perhaps because of the personal enmity of the powerful Graf von Anhalt, perhaps because of the discovery that his claims to noble descent were spurious.

After this misadventure, Steuben led for fourteen years a most precarious existence. First he tried to go to Denmark, where Comte de Saint-Germain was then reorganizing the Danish army. Saint-Germain appreciated Steuben's value as an officer, yet could arrange nothing worth while for him in Denmark. Steuben then accepted the position of *Hofmarschall* to Prince Hohenzollern-Hechingen. The Prince gave Steuben the title of Baron, but very little money, for he himself was in almost desperate financial straits. He even went to live incognito in Montpellier for three years because the cost of living was low in Southern France. His *Hofmarschall* naturally followed him there; but when, more hard up than ever, the Prince returned to Germany, Baron von Steuben tried to join the French army. He failed. He tried to join the Austrian army. He failed. Then he started negotiations to enter the service of the Margrave of Baden, at the same time renewing his application to the French Ministry of War. The Minister of War was now Comte de Saint-Germain. He remembered Steuben very well, and recommended him warmly to Vergennes for the American war. Vergennes sent Steuben to Beaumarchais.

Beaumarchais, who immediately liked Steuben, gave him a room in his own house and introduced him to Franklin and Deane. But Franklin and Deane had just received stern instructions from Congress about volunteers. If Steuben wanted to serve in the American army as a private and without pay—as La Fayette had offered to do—he would be welcome. But Steuben was not interested in fighting under such conditions.

Franklin, however, being assured by the French Ministry of War that Steuben was truly an outstanding officer, tried to induce him to go to America by promising him a grant of forest land there. Steuben, of course, would have to pay his own passage across the Atlantic. Steuben did not hide his lack of enthusiasm for these proposals. Once more he asked to be admitted to the French army. Impossible. He asked to be admitted to the Spanish army. Impossible.

Nothing seemed left to him, in August 1777, but to return to Germany and somehow to reach an agreement with the Margrave of Baden. But when he arrived there, he found that his enemies had in his absence spread the rumor that he was guilty of gross, unnatural sexual practices. This accusation precluded his being accepted by the Margrave and even his resuming the miserably paid position of *Hofmarschall* to Prince Hohenzollern-Hechingen.

Despondent, almost desperate, he returned to Paris. Beaumarchais again hospitably gave him a lodging at the Hôtel de Hollande, and told him that going to America was now his only chance. Then a picturesque hoax was concocted. Captain von Steuben went about dressed in the uniform of a Prussian Lieutenant General. He was impressively followed by an aide-de-camp, Louis de Pontière, and a military secretary, Etienne Duponceau, both hired by Beaumarchais. Who first had the idea of the masquerade is not known, but it may be remembered that Steuben then lived at Beaumarchais' house, and that Beaumarchais always had a predilection for theatrical solutions to all problems. The United States had snubbed Captain von Steuben. Would they refuse the help of a Lieutenant General of Frederick the Great?

On September 4, 1777, Deane and Franklin jointly wrote General Washington: "The gentleman who will have the honor of waiting on you with this letter is the Baron Steuben, Lieut. Genl. in the King of Prussia's service." Steuben had never had the rank of Lieutenant General and had left the King of Prussia's service fourteen years ago. Both Deane and Franklin knew that, but, unlike their illustrious correspondent, they were not hampered by too many scruples about remodeling the truth.

Beaumarchais lent Steuben 3120 livres for the expenses of his journey. Steuben sailed from Marseille on one of Beaumarchais' ships, *Le Flamand*, which also carried Beaumarchais' nephew, Lépine's son, who was later to fall on an American battlefield. Beaumarchais also helped finance the overseas trip of two of Steuben's nephews who wanted to join him in America.

On December 6, 1778, Beaumarchais wrote to his correspondent in America, Francy: "Remember me often to my friend M. le Baron de Steuben. I congratulate myself, from what I hear about him, on having given so great an officer to my friends, the free men, and having forced him, in a way, to follow that noble career. I am not by any means uneasy about the money I lent him for his voyage. Never did I make an investment that gave me so much pleasure, for I put a man of honor in the right place. I hear that he is Inspector General of all American troops. Bravo! Tell him that his glory is the interest on my money and that I do not doubt that, on those terms, he will repay me with usury."

Beaumarchais expected only glory as payment for the interest on his loan to Steuben; he was certainly fully rewarded. But if he had hoped to receive a more tangible refund on the capital itself, he must have been sadly disappointed. Among the innumerable unpaid bills found in his files at the time of his death, the following document tells its own story: "*A Steuben, pour avances faites en particulier pour passer en Amérique, et à ses neveux pour aller le joindre, 5997 francs, 2 sols, 7 deniers.*"

5. *On the Brink of Bankruptcy*

STEUBEN'S was not the only bill for which Beaumarchais failed to collect the money owed to him, in connection with his American venture. From the middle of 1777, worries over unpaid bills became for some time the major problem of his life. The ships he sent regularly to America, filled with supplies, came back empty no less regularly. At first he blamed the failure of the Americans to deliver the promised return cargoes on the uncertainties of war. But trusting that the contract he had made with Deane in July 1776 would be honored, he went on sending his goods. From the beginning of his operations until September, 1777, he sent five million livres' worth of merchandise overseas.

Beaumarchais had received one million livres from Versailles and another million from Madrid. The rest he had obtained from French merchants whom he had persuaded to participate in his enterprise. These merchants were becoming restless. They demanded that Beaumarchais either pay dividends on their shares or refund their money. He could give them nothing but exhortations to believe in the good faith of the American Congress, for he had not received a single return cargo or even a letter from America.

America was then going through a grave financial crisis and had no money with which to pay outstanding debts. Moreover, the Beaumarchais business seemed far from clear to Congress. Lee's insinuations and Du Coudray's accusations had given many people in Philadelphia the impression that the Hortalez firm was a blind behind which all sorts of crooked transactions were taking place. Further, the committees that had been in charge of relations with foreign countries were then being reorganized. On April 7, 1777, the Committee of Secret Correspondence became the Committee of Foreign Affairs, and on July 5, the Committee of Commerce took over the functions of the Secret Committee. Lastly, the military situation had taken a turn for the worse in the summer of 1777. Howe had launched an offensive against Philadelphia, had pushed back Washington's troops, and had taken the city in September. Congress had hastily withdrawn to Lancaster, then to York. In October, it is true, Gates was victorious at Saratoga, but almost immediately the "Conway Cabal" tried to have Washington replaced by Gates as Commander in Chief. In the midst of the bitter wrangling that followed, Beaumarchais was naturally forgotten.

Beaumarchais now found himself gravely embarrassed in the management of Roderigue Hortalez & Cie. He had, not unreasonably, planned to discharge his firm's debts with the money he expected to realize from the sale of the promised return cargoes. But the return cargoes never came. Three times he had to appeal to the Ministry of Foreign Affairs to prevent the firm from completely collapsing. Three times Vergennes lent him important sums of money: 400,000 livres on May 31, 200,000 livres on June 16, and 474,496 livres on July 3, 1777. These loans kept him going, but added to his difficulties, for they were necessarily carried on the debit side of his ledger.

In the end, Beaumarchais decided to send a personal representative to America to investigate the situation and report directly to him. He selected for that job an active and intelligent young man, a nephew of Théveneau de Morande, Jean-Baptiste Théveneau de Francy. Francy sailed from Marseille on September 26, 1777.

Shortly before that time, however, Beaumarchais had to his great dismay come to realize that the work he was engaged in was no longer considered important by the ministry. The main cause for the sudden change in the ministry's attitude was that the government had secretly but definitely decided at the end of July, 1777 to intervene openly very soon in the Anglo-American conflict.

The French fleet now stood ready to measure its strength with the British fleet. On May 2, 1777, Vergennes had written to the French Ambassador in London, Marquis de Noailles: "We have taken advantage of the present circumstances to create anew a Navy that up to now existed only in name. Today, the King's Navy is in good condition." On the other hand, Necker, who had become Directeur Général des Finances in June 1777 now affirmed that, thanks to a loan system he had just contrived, France could wage a major war without increasing taxes. Lastly, Vergennes had succeeded in making the Madrid government agree to active intervention on the side of the Americans. The date for that intervention was tentatively set for the beginning of 1778, mainly to enable the French fishing fleet on the Banks of Newfoundland to return home safely before the outbreak of hostilities.

Vergennes summarized these developments in a long report, dated July 23, 1777, which was fully endorsed by the other Cabinet Ministers and approved by the King. "If it is proved," said Vergennes, "that they [France and Spain] ought to support the Colonies of America, and this in so effective a manner as to assure their complete separation from Great Britain . . . it remains only to determine the way this assistance can be given. Peace is incompatible with open assistance." He also declared that "it is indispensable to determine a fixed and precise time" for intervention. "January or February 1778 is the time past which the two Crowns [France and Spain] would have nothing left but to regret the opportunity missed." Then, on July 26, 1777, Vergennes communicated the government's decision to the French Ambassador in Madrid: "The two Crowns will be subjected next year to the expense and trouble of war."

This decision radically altered Beaumarchais' position. Up to that time, the bulk of French aid to America had crossed the Atlantic on the Hortalez ships. But these ships had never been very numerous. Soon scores and scores of French vessels, lavishly loaded with everything needed to conduct a large-scale war would sail away under the protection of the French Navy. After July 1777 Hortalez represented the tail end of a phase of Franco-American relations, and held only cursory and fading interest for Vergennes, Sartines, and Maurepas.

Beaumarchais felt very hurt by the ministers' indifference toward his firm, but he could not fathom its cause. He was no longer in the government's confidence and remained ignorant of the new plans.

These plans were not even communicated to the Americans. Vergennes had said in his report of July 23, 1777: "If the two Crowns have decided to make war . . . would it not be suitable that some [French] emissaries, who would not be accredited directly by us, but could be accredited through the deputies of Congress now residing in France, be authorized to talk confidentially with the main leaders of the said Congress who form the Secret Committee * and let them know about the resolution taken by the two Crowns?" But this recommendation was not acted upon, and the decision of the French ministry to side openly with the Americans early in 1778 remained a top secret until the very end. The reason for the secrecy was that the government feared leakages of news, which might enable the English to take steps disastrous to the French. English spies surrounded the Commissioners, and Vergennes particularly distrusted Lee. Several times he gave confidential information to Franklin on the express condition that nothing would be said to Lee.

Lee had returned from his European tour in June 1777. From that time on, for about eight months, low and undignified squabbles marred the atmosphere of the Commissioners' headquarters in Passy. Lee still hated Franklin, but he hated Silas Deane even more. As Beaumarchais was on the very best terms with Deane, he found himself constantly involved in the Commissioners' feuds.

Lee did everything in his power to prevent return cargoes from being sent to Beaumarchais. On October 6, 1777, he mendaciously wrote to the Committee of Foreign Affairs: "Upon this

* Vergennes undoubtedly meant the Committee of Secret Correspondence (or rather, since July 5, 1777, the Committee of Foreign Affairs), and not the Secret Committee.

subject of returns, I think it my duty to state to you some facts relative to the demands of this kind from Hortalez. . . . The Minister has repeatedly assured us, and in the most explicit terms, that no return is expected for these subsidies."

Even so, in December 1777 a small return cargo of indigo and rice arrived in Lorient, on the ship *L'Amphitrite.* It was the first return cargo sent to Beaumarchais. Its value was only 150,000 livres. Franklin and Lee at once declared that the cargo belonged to them. Beaumarchais protested. Lee was particularly offensive. Deane, on the other hand, took Beaumarchais' side. For some time a disgraceful tug of war took place between the two parties, but eventually Lee and Franklin let go.

On December 20, Beaumarchais wrote Francy: "Even the deputies of Passy claim the honor of annoying me—me, their country's best friend. They have probably mistaken my patience for weakness and my generosity for stupidity. As much as I am that friend so much am I offended by the dishonest liberties the deputies of Passy have tried to take with me. . . . I owe Mr. Deane the justice of saying that he is both ashamed and sorry for the behavior of his colleagues toward me—for which Mr. Lee is to blame."

Beaumarchais' antagonism to Lee and Franklin was increased by his belief that they were playing a most equivocal game between France and England. As a matter of fact, throughout the second part of 1777, Franklin was in constant contact with English secret agents, who visited him in Passy. It seems that Franklin—who did not know that the French government had already resolved, in July, 1777, to intervene openly in the Anglo-American conflict—tried to make Vergennes fear that the Americans and the

English would patch up their differences and unite again, unless France at once recognized and officially supported the United States.

In the last months of 1777, Beaumarchais organized on his own initiative a network of private spies who checked on all visitors received by Franklin, Lee, and even Deane. Visitors from England were shadowed and their intentions investigated; whenever possible, even their topic of conversation with the Commissioners was ascertained. Beaumarchais then sent his findings to Vergennes.

Nevertheless, Beaumarchais' love for America remained intact. After news of Saratoga reached Paris, on December 4, 1777, he wrote Francy, on December 20: "In spite of all these annoyances, the news from America overwhelms me with joy. Brave, brave people, whose warlike conduct justifies my esteem and the noble enthusiasm felt for them in France! In short, my friend, I want some return cargoes only to be able to serve them anew—to meet the engagements I have contracted and to contract fresh ones to their advantage." Then he gave his correspondent the following advice: "Do as I do myself: despise petty considerations, petty measures, petty resentments. I have affiliated you with a magnificent cause."

Although the magnificence of the American cause filled Beaumarchais' heart, the munificence of the American Congress did not fill his pocketbook. His position as a businessman became increasingly bad, and his credit fell very low. He had to contract short-term loans at extravagantly high rates of interest to keep going—hoping against hope that return cargoes would at long last arrive. He had to borrow to pay his clerks, to pay his crews, to pay the rent on his warehouses in the various ports from which his ships sailed. His balance sheet had become a nightmare to him, and he could see himself ruined, dishonored, bankrupt.

On January 22, 1778, he wrote Vergennes: "Thanks to a tour de force, I have put myself on my feet for twelve to fifteen more days. But, *grand Dieu!* is this living? The more I affect a tranquil air, the more my secret torment increases. I have examined myself thoroughly. I am not guilty of the slightest irregularity. . . . If I am to be helped, you cannot do it too quickly and too secretly, because bills of exchange are like death—they wait for no one. Ah! Monsieur le Comte, my balance sheet will show you what an active man you have let be ruined and dishonored, if you allow this horrible misfortune to happen to me. I have not the courage to speak about England because I am dying of sorrow."

Vergennes did rescue Beaumarchais, though only after he had gone through an agony of fear. "You have taken too kind an interest in my frightful situation," Beaumarchais then wrote him, "for me to let you remain ignorant of the unbounded joy I have felt since yesterday. Yesterday, with my teeth clenched in fury at having received no news, I was waiting for the time to close my cashier's wicket and refuse to make the heavy payment due on the fifteenth, which, since the fifteenth fell on a Sunday, was actually demandable yesterday, the fourteenth. . . . This morning, my joy is overflowing. I no longer face the dishonor of bankruptcy, which, despite all my efforts, I could not have justified without being—much against my will—disastrously indiscreet."

At the end of 1777, the French government had resolved secretly to give the Americans a subsidy of two million livres. The money was not delivered through Beaumarchais, but handed to Franklin, with bankers named Grand acting as go-between. Beaumarchais heard of the deal and on January 1, 1778, wistfully wrote Vergennes, expressing his grief that "Messrs. Grand should have gained a confidence I thought I had so well deserved."

Occasionally, the ministers still used Beaumarchais' cleverness. Thus, at the end of October, 1777, he had had a long conversation with Vergennes and Maurepas. Being ignorant of the decision the French Cabinet had taken four months earlier to intervene in the war, he clearly, urgently, and forcefully presented reasons for France's granting the United States government official recognition. In January 1778, when the time for that long-planned recognition came near, Maurepas and Vergennes, vividly remembering his argument, asked him to write a memorial on the subject. He immediately composed a *Mémoire particulier pour les Ministres du Roi.* When, on February 6, 1778, France officially recognized the new republic and signed a treaty of commerce and friendship with her, the French government reproduced passages of Beaumarchais' memorial almost verbatim in its declaration to justify the step taken, from the standpoint of international Law.

The secret of France's planned recognition of the United States had been so well kept that the news of the actual event struck even the English with surprise. It took England no less than four months to make final preparations for war.

Then, on July 17, 1778, the British frigate *Arethusa* attacked the French frigate *La Belle-Poule* off the coast of Brittany. The French frigate was victorious, and a wave of pride swept over France. The French saw in the outcome of that first combat, however unimportant in itself, a symbol of the rebirth of the French Navy, and an omen of future success. For some time French ladies of fashion in Versailles and Paris wore upon their heads, instead of the customary feathered hat, a small model of the frigate *La Belle-Poule.*

Chapter 8

WAR AND INTRIGUE

---

1. Politics

FRANCE'S OFFICIAL RECOGNITION of the United States and the outbreak of hostilities between France and England brought to a close an important historical chapter in Beaumarchais' life. From that time on the operations of the French and British royal Navies completely dwarfed the activities of the Hortalez firm.

At no time during the conflict could either the English or the French gain absolute control of the seas. Many battles were fought between French and British fleets. Sometimes one side, sometimes the other claimed a "great victory," but the naval struggle between the two powers actually ended with a draw. The essential fact, however, was that the English were never able to stop or even seriously hamper the crossing of the Atlantic by innumerable

French vessels carrying huge stores of arms and supplies, and finally a fully equipped French expeditionary corps, to America.

Under such circumstances, the goods that Beaumarchais went on sending overseas for three more years did not have the same value as at the end of 1776 or the beginning of 1777, when Hortalez was America's main source of help from abroad.

In March 1778 Beaumarchais received news that, in November 1777, Congress had decided to order Silas Deane back home. The discontent in the American army created by the commissions Deane had given foreign volunteers, the Beaumarchais-Hortalez imbroglio, and the intrigues fostered by Arthur Lee were the main causes for his recall. John Adams, who belonged to Lee's political group, had been designated to replace Deane as Commissioner in Paris. Adams, Deane said to Beaumarchais, was aggressive and rough. What with Franklin's persistent iciness, Lee's open hostility, Maurepas' flippant indifference, Vergennes' rapidly dwindling support, and Sartines' utter absorption in Navy problems, Beaumarchais felt that he would soon be completely isolated.

The French government was sorry to see Silas Deane go, for throughout his stay in Paris he had shown a spirit of loyal cooperation. Vergennes gave him both a letter highly praising his work in France and a portrait of the King, which was a mark of special distinction. It was also arranged that he would leave with the first large escorted convoy officially sent by the French government to America. Thus, on April 10, 1778, he sailed on the battleship *Languedoc,* which also carried the first French Minister Plenipotentiary to the United States, Gérard de Rayneval.

Shortly before his departure, Deane wrote Beaumarchais, on March 29, 1778: "After the perplexing and embarrassing scenes you have had to pass through, it must give you the greatest pleasure to see at last the object of your efforts fulfilled, and a large French fleet ready to sail, which will convince the whole world of the sincere friendship of France and of her absolute determination to protect America's freedom and independence. I once more congratulate you on that glorious event, to which you have contribtued more than anybody else."

Beaumarchais was naïve enough to take this letter to Vergennes, perhaps to bolster his flagging credit with the Foreign Minister, perhaps to show him that the Americans appreciated his work. He could hardly have committed a worse psychological blunder. However shrewd a diplomat, however high-minded a statesman, Vergennes was none the less subject to the petty but very human feeling of wounded vanity that can assail a man on seeing a mere subordinate praised above himself by a competent third party.

As soon as Beaumarchais saw Vergennes make a wry face, he tried to repair the damage by assuming an attitude of utmost modesty, but in vain. As he wrote several years later: "Alas, this was the last of my successes. A Minister of the State Department to whom I showed this letter—who had treated me until then with the greatest kindness—suddenly changed his tone and manner to me. Although I protested that I did not want to appropriate any of his glory, nevertheless the blow had been dealt. He had read the praise: I was ruined in his mind."

Important private affairs, however, soon took Beaumarchais' attention, at least temporarily, from his political troubles. In March, 1778, the Parliament of Aix had taken up his suit with La Blache. The proceedings lasted nearly five months, for the court cautiously investigated all aspects of the case and painstakingly examined all the litigants' contracts, letters, claims, and counter-claims.

At first, Beaumarchais, who had entrusted a good lawyer named Mathieu with his interests, remained in Paris. But La Blache quietly established himself in Aix. He cleverly made no attempt to influence the Parliament, but simply did his best to make himself agreeable to the local society. He succeeded admirably. The good women of Aix were soon captivated by the delightful manners of the distinguished, wealthy, and attractive young nobleman. La Blache met most of the judges in their salons, not as a plaintiff, but as a fellow guest, almost as a friend. Public opinion was unanimously in his favor.

Mathieu communicated this alarming news to Beaumarchais, who went to Aix at once, accompanied by Gudin. He could not compete with La Blache in social graces and aristocratic prestige, so he used brutal tactics. He shut himself up with Gudin in his attorney's house and refused to see anyone, thereby creating a flurry of curiosity and surprise. Then he composed a memorial. It was not a masterpiece—it offered only a rehash of old arguments and stale facts that everyone knew—but it was worded in violent, scorching, and indeed objectionable language. Beaumarchais evidently knew that moderation in expression was not highly appreciated in southern France. La Blache tried to answer him in similar terms. Beaumarchais replied to his reply. For a while the two men waged a war of abuse, with Beaumarchais clearly outdoing his foe. Within a few weeks, public opinion had veered. When time came for the final verdict, practically everybody in Aix was on Beaumarchais' side.

The verdict was announced on July 21, 1778. La Blache's and Beaumarchais' memorials were to be torn publicly, and Beaumarchais was fined a thousand livres for the particularly offensive character of his publications. But the rest of the judgment was beyond his wildest dreams. La Blache was ordered to pay him the 15,000 livres stipulated in the Pâris-Duverney settlement of accounts, plus 5625 livres interest, plus 12,000 livres as indemnity for slander, plus 8000 livres for court costs, plus 30,000 livres representing the interest on the 75,000 livres Pâris-Duverney had promised to lend Beaumarchais without interest, which, owing to La Blache's action, had not been lent at all—a grand total of 70,625 livres. La Blache paid the full amount ten days later, then slunk away. He had had enough.

Back in Paris, Beaumarchais found himself again enmeshed in complicated and mystifying American political intrigues. His agent, Théveneau de Francy, had arrived in America on December 1, 1777. He was told that the Committee of Commerce had charge of trade relations with foreign countries. He went straight to the Committee with copies of the documents Beaumarchais had given him, which proved his good faith. The documents were closely examined, and after some discussion the Committee offered Francy a clear-cut, regular contract.

The contract, which was signed on April 16, 1778, had an impressive preamble: "Whereas Roderigue Hortalez & Cie of Paris have shipped, or caused to be shipped, on board sundry ships or vessels considerable quantities of Cannon, Arms, Ammunition, Clothing and other stores, most of which have been safely landed in America, and delivered to the agents of the United States for the use and service thereof, and whereas said Roderigue Hortalez

& Cie are willing and desirous to continue supplying those States with Cannon, Mortars, Bombs, Arms, Ammunition, Clothing . . . provided satisfactory assumption be made and assurance given for the payment in France of the just cost, charges, freight of cargoes already shipped as well as those to be thereafter shipped. . . . Now know Ye that John Baptist Lazarus Theveneau de Francy, agent of Peter Augustin Caron de Beaumarchais, as representative of the house of said Roderigue Hortalez & Cie, by him specially appointed and empowered to act fully and effectually in all things on his behalf . . . doth . . . in virtue of the powers in him vested, contract, agree and engage to and with the Hon. William Ellery, James Forbes, William Henry Drayton and William Duer, Esquires, a Committee of Commerce, properly appointed and authorized by the Delegates of the United States of America in Congress assembled to enter into, execute, ratify and confirm this contract for and on Behalf of the said United States, as follows . . ." Then followed seven clauses stipulating in great detail how Hortalez was to deliver the goods, and seven other clauses defining the conditions of payment by the United States.

The document was signed by the above-named parties, then sealed in presence of Charles Thomson, Secretary of Congress. Francy wrote Beaumarchais that the time of misunderstanding was over and that return cargoes would soon be forthcoming.

But when it came to the execution of the contract, Francy met with imponderable, innumerable, and unaccountable difficulties. At first, rather rashly, he blamed these difficulties on the Americans. On July 11, 1778, he wrote Beaumarchais: "In spite of the most formal pledges, these people find ways of obstructing all business and pretexts for breaking the most solemn promises." Soon, however, he discerned an intricate pattern of internal dissension behind Congress' reluctance to deal with Hortalez on a commercial basis.

A young man from Maryland, William Carmichael, who had served for some time as secretary to the Commissioners in Paris and who had just returned to America, helped Francy understand the nature of these dissensions. The two men had known each other in France; now they confidentially exchanged information. Carmichael was pleased to learn from Francy the opinion the various leaders of Congress had of him. On the other hand, he had a better grasp than the Frenchman on America's problems and also on the intrigues then proliferating in the American political world. He wrote Beaumarchais, on September 3, 1778: "We have as many intrigues and cabals here as you and your friends suffer from on the Continent. And why not? Are we not sovereign States, and are we not friends and allies of Louis XVI?"

One party in Congress was led by a powerful coalition of the Adamses of Massachusetts and the Lees of Virginia. This party was later to be accused, in the correspondence between Vergennes and the French ministers plenipotentiary in America, of being pro-English. It was not. Yet many of its members undoubtedly revealed traits of character that the French considered as typically British: a certain narrow-mindedness, a definite abruptness of manner, and a dogged determination to fight for what they thought was right. It was their English love of liberty which had made them rise against the British Crown, and they carried that love of liberty so far that they opposed any attempt to establish a broad, compresensive authority on American soil—even if that authority was needed to co-ordinate the war effort against the enemy, even if that authority was to be vested mainly in George Washington.

They looked askance at France. They realized that the United States needed help from abroad, but they wanted that help from several European nations and frowned on the idea of the United States' being too closely linked with only one of them. The fact that America received no effective support, nor even much sympathy, from any country except France left them somewhat out on a limb. Very well, then; they would accept France's assistance. But they insisted on saying that France was strictly out for her own ends, that France was waging war against England solely because it was her interest to do so. Furthermore, they were ready to pay France for her intervention and constantly talked of granting her commercial advantages or special fishing rights. They entirely discounted the strong sentimental attachment of the French people to the American cause. Perhaps they were not aware of it or perhaps they preferred to ignore its existence, wanting to owe gratitude to no one.

The opposite party, which included, among others, Benjamin Franklin, Robert Morris, Alexander Hamilton, James Madison, Robert R. Livingston, William Livingston, John Jay, and Silas Deane, was no less attached to liberty. Yet its members as a rule recognized the necessity of establishing a strong common, superior organization over and above the governments of the individual States. Generally speaking, they looked beyond local interests, and many of them had been influenced by the liberal theories of the French philosophers.

In the field of foreign policy, they were friendly to France, and stood for loyal co-operation with her. Many of them understood the complex nature of the problems involved in the French people's attitude toward America. Often they protested against the oversimplification of these problems, which made their opponents believe that France's help to the United States was merely a matter of selfish interest or a question of rivalry with England. Thus Franklin wrote Robert R. Livingston on the subject of France: "This is really a generous nation, fond of glory, and particularly that of protecting the oppressed. Trade is not the admiration of their noblesse, which still governs here. Telling them that their *commerce* will be advantaged by our success, and that it is their interest to help us, seems as much as to say: help us, and we shall not be obliged to you. Such indiscreet and improper language has sometimes been held here by some of our people, and has produced no good effect."

An important number of delegates in Congress had no definite views and, according to circumstances, swung from one side to the other, thus causing the most contradictory decisions to be taken, sometimes only at a few days' interval, and giving outsiders a feeling of hopeless inconsistency and confusion.

Comparatively little is known in detail of these fluctuations of policy. Yet, it is certain that the Conway Cabal was, even though the Adamses and the Lees carefully remained in the background, an episode in the struggle between the two great factions. Silas Deane's recall was another episode in that struggle, but because George Washington was not implicated in the fight this time, nothing prevented the leaders of the two groups from aggressively voicing their opinions. Soon the quarrel gained unprecedented violence and bitterness.

The commissions Deane had granted French volunteers in the fall of 1776—without discrimination or discretion, said his adversaries—became the object of many reproaches. But the main point at issue was the Beaumarchais-Hortalez deal because it involved money and the future.

The party led by the Adamses and the Lees claimed that the goods shipped by Beaumarchais were gifts for which no payments were due. The French, they asserted, had sent these supplies because it was their interest to do so. They knew that such a public statement would greatly embarrass the French government. Throughout 1776 and 1777 Vergennes had repeatedly assured the English Ambassador, Lord Stormont, that France maintained a strictly neutral and correct attitude toward the Anglo-American conflict. Was he to be shown up a liar, and this by France's ally? The Adamses and the Lees did not care. Bluntness was their motto. Since France had acted, so they thought, only with selfish motives, she was not entitled to special consideration even by her "friends."

The opposite party put forward the contract Beaumarchais and Deane had made in July, 1776 and the contract the Committee of Commerce and Théveneau de Francy had signed on April 16, 1778. Moreover they were ready to take the word of the French officials that the merchandise shipped by Beaumarchais were articles of private trade and not supplies given by the government.

When Deane arrived in America in July 1778 the British had just been forced to evacuate Philadelphia, and Congress was able to meet there again. Deane's position in Congress was critical. He had to contend with a well-organized hostile group. Moreover, his personal integrity was seriously questioned by many. Arthur Lee's brothers and friends whispered that Deane was a grafter and an unscrupulous rascal who stood by Beaumarchais because the two had made huge war profits together. Deane replied to these rumors by saying that Lee's mind was deranged, but no one believed his contention.

Deane appeared before Congress in August 1778. From the very start he felt the atmosphere loaded with antagonism and distrust. He reacted by displaying the worst aspects of his character: haughtiness, aloofness, and disdain. He declared that he could not answer the charges made against him because he had left in Paris the papers that would explain and justify his conduct. All this sounded strange and merely increased Congress' animosity toward him.

This animosity was heartily reciprocated by Deane, and for months he brooded over his grievances. During that period he often saw Benedict Arnold, who had recently been appointed Military Commander in Philadelphia and who also considered himself unfairly treated by Congress. The two men privately exchanged bitter reflections about the American government and even about American Independence.

After much wrangling, Deane's friends won out on having the French government officially queried by the American Commissioners in Paris on the status of the Hortalez firm. Vergennes gave the Commissioners a categorical answer: the supplies shipped by Hortalez had been sent by a private firm on a purely commercial basis.

Vergennes knew through the French Minister Plenipotentiary in Philadelphia, Gérard de Rayneval, that the Beaumarchais-Deane affair had become a test case between pro-French and anti-French groups in Congress. Moreover, he knew that Franklin, Adams, and Lee were hostile to Deane and Beaumarchais. He feared that because of a personal grudge they might distort the meaning of his reply, so he immediately instructed Gérard to communicate the text of the answer he had given the Commissioners directly to Congress, if necessary. "M. Franklin and his colleagues would like to know which of the articles have been supplied by the King and which have been supplied by M. de Beaumarchais on his own account, and they insinuate that Congress is convinced that all, or at least a large portion of what has been sent came from His Majesty. I am about to reply that the King has not furnished anything; that he has merely allowed M. de Beaumarchais to take what he wanted in the arsenals, on condition that he replace what he took."

When this letter reached Philadelphia, the Deane-Beaumarchais problem had already become a public scandal. Convinced that Congress was dominated by his enemies, Deane decided to appeal to public opinion through the press. On December 5, 1778, he published in *The Pennsylvania Packet* an address "To the Free and Virtuous Citizens of America" in which he roundly denounced Arthur Lee's machinations. Further he accused Congress of neglecting its duties and of being appallingly ignorant of foreign affairs.

This address touched off an explosion of violent polemics. Congress split almost at once into Pro-Deanites and Anti-Deanites. Behind the person of Deane, not only the Beaumarchais contract but the very nature of the relations between France and America were at stake. Gérard de Rayneval watched the developments closely.

On December 8, Henry Laurens, an Anti-Deanite who was President of Congress, had to resign. He was replaced by John Jay, a friend of Deane. On December 14, Thomas Paine, Secretary of the Committee of Foreign Affairs, joined the fray as a supporter of Arthur Lee. On January 2, 1779, he wrote under his usual pen name, "Common Sense": "If Mr. Deane or any other gentleman will procure an order from Congress to inspect an account in my office . . . I will give him or them my attendance and show them in handwriting . . . that the supplies he so pompously plumes himself upon, were promised and engaged, and that, as a present, before he ever arrived in France."

Gérard de Rayneval then struck swiftly and hard. Armed with Vergennes' instructions, he stepped forward and, on January 4, let Congress officially know: "That all the supplies furnished by M. de Beaumarchais to the States . . . were furnished by way of trade, that the articles which came from the King's stores and arsenals were sold to M. de Beaumarchais by the Department of Artillery, and that he had given obligations for the price of these articles."

The following day, he sent a formal protest against the indiscretion of a public servant, Thomas Paine, and asked that "suitable measures" be taken. On January 9, 1779, Paine had to hand in his resignation as Secretary of the Committee of Foreign Affairs. The rout of the anti-French party was complete.

The large majority of Congress was convinced, at least for the time being, that Deane and Beaumarchais had been the victims of slander. John Jay was authorized to send the latter formal apologies for Congress' past remissness and the promise of prompt remittances in the future: "The Congress of the United States," he wrote on January 15, 1779, "recognizing the great efforts you have made in their favor, present to you their thanks, and assure you of their esteem. They lament the inconveniences you have suffered in the support of these States. Unfortunate circumstances have prevented them the fulfillment of their wishes; but they will take the most effective measures to acquit themselves of the debt they owe to you."

When Beaumarchais received Jay's letter, he believed that his woes were over. Here at long last was a formal acknowledgment of debt; here was a pledge to pay from the highest official authority in America. So he sent more supplies and still more supplies. But politics resumed their course in Congress, and the promised remittances were never made.

2. *Beaumarchais' Private Navy*

IN THE end, Beaumarchais understood that he had nothing to hope for in the way of payments, at least as long as the war lasted. After Silas Deane's departure he practically ceased to have anything to do with the Commissioners. Yet he had with them a short and sharp conflict about a small cargo of tobacco which Francy had somehow managed to load on *Le Fier Roderigue* in the summer of 1778. The Commissioners tried to appropriate the cargo for themselves upon its arrival in France, as they had previously done in the case of *L'Amphitrite*, but once again they had to give in to Beaumarchais.

In September 1778 Congress decided to appoint Franklin sole representative of the United States in France, and on March 23, 1779, he presented his credentials as Minister Plenipotentiary to the French court. John Adams left Paris almost at once. Arthur Lee remained there, though only in a private capacity, until the end of 1780. But these changes had little effect upon Beaumarchais' position or ideas. He had as warm feelings as ever for the American people, but his opinion of American politicians was now somewhat different. He wrote Francy, on March 18, 1779: "My zeal for America has remained what it was, in spite of the disgusting treatment I have received. But the guilty neglect to answer even a single one of my letters, and the strange absurdity of contesting my claim to payment for what I sent them so generously, have drawn ironical smiles from indifferent people and reproaches from my friends, whom my enthusiasm had dragged into my American speculations."

By that time, however, Beaumarchais had taken practical steps to compensate his associates for their losses, and to keep his concern going without subsidies from Vergennes and without return cargoes from Congress. The necessity of meeting his obligations as a businessman forced him, from the second part of 1778 onward, to engage in regular, profitable trade.

The fact that he possessed a number of good merchant ships and that war was in full swing between France and England gave him a golden opportunity in this regard. His ships still carried supplies to America, but on their return trip they called at La Martinique or Santo Domingo to pick up colonial products, mostly sugar. Because of the war, the price of these commodities had risen sky-high in France. With a queer mixture of political idealism and mercantile practicality, Beaumarchais sent guns for love to the Americans, and made huge profits on the sugar his vessels brought back from the islands.

From its foundation in 1776 until its dissolution in 1783, the Hortalez firm engaged in business transactions involving over forty-two million livres, a truly enormous sum in those days. A close study of the balance sheets shows a total of 21,095,515 livres received, while in the same period the general outlay was 21,044,191 livres. Thus the profit amounted to 51,324 livres—or only slightly more than two tenths of one per cent. In other words, Beaumarchais just managed to keep his enterprise on an even keel. His gains and losses, however, were very unevenly distributed. While the firm's private trade account showed an extremely favorable balance, the account with the United States was deeply in the red. Would the United States ever pay their debt? If they did, Beaumarchais would be a very rich man. If they did not, he would just about break even.

In spite of his misgivings about American politicians, Beaumarchais went on sending supplies to America because he was more than ever attached to the ideas represented by the American cause. Moreover, now that his financial problems had been solved, he thoroughly enjoyed the war. He talked importantly of his "Navy," and his almost childish pride in it often drew smiles from Sartines and the French admirals. He had bought an old and rather dilapidated warship, *L'Hippopotame*, from the government Navy yards. *L'Hippopotame* was completely overhauled, splendidly outfitted, armed with sixty guns, and renamed *Le Fier Roderigue. Le Fier Roderigue* was the Hortalez flagship. It carried some cargo, but served mainly as an escort for the firm's unarmed vessels. Since the English did not have the mastery of the sea, *Le Fier Roderigue* was adequate protection against the English raiders occasionally encountered. Much to Beaumarchais' joy, his "Navy" even captured an English ship, the *Marlborough*, and brought her as a prize to a French port.

Beaumarchais' joy knew no bounds, though it was mixed with dismay and sorrow when he heard what had happened to *Le Fier Roderigue* on July 12, 1779. *Le Fier Roderigue* was escorting a convoy of eleven Hortalez ships, when, not far from the island of Grenada, the convoy came within sight of a French fleet led by Admiral d'Estaing. Admiral d'Estaing was about to engage a British fleet under Admiral Biron. He signaled *Le Fier Roderigue* to let the convoy proceed alone, and to join the French line of battle. During the battle that soon took place, Captain Montaut, in command of *Le Fier Roderigue*, was cut in two by chain shot, a third of the crew was killed, and the ship was so badly riddled with cannon balls that she had to be towed for repairs to Fort-Royal in Grenada, after the fight. But the French had won the battle.

That evening, Admiral d'Estaing sent Beaumarchais a message: "I have only time, Monsieur, to write you that *Le Fier Roderigue* held fast to her post in the line of battle and contributed to the success of the King's arms. You will forgive me for making such good use of her—all the more easily, since your interests will not suffer from it. Brave M. de Montaut, unfortunately, was killed. I shall soon send the Minister a statement of the privileges and favors I ask, and I hope you will let me have the necessary information to help me solicit those *your Navy* so justly deserves."

Alas, Beaumarchais' Navy had been all but wiped out. His unprotected convoy had been found by an English raider, and ten of the eleven ships had been either destroyed or captured. It meant a loss of two million livres for Hortalez. Yet when he received through Sartines the letter addressed to him by d'Estaing, he thought mainly of the fact that his ship had shared in a French victory. On September 17, 1779, he wrote Sartines: "Whatever may happen to my business, and even though my poor friend Montaut died . . . I feel as happy as a child . . . and my heart is bouncing for joy."

Shortly afterward, Beaumarchais applied for a loan of 400,000 livres from the government. He wanted to reconstitute his Navy. Thanks to Sartines, the loan was granted. Using this comparatively small sum as initial capital, he bought new ships, engaged new crews, and started his politico-commercial operations all over again.

3. *The Playwrights' Rights*

In spite of these absorbing tasks, Beaumarchais found time and energy to wage another campaign of liberation. The administration of theatrical affairs was completely in the hands of four *Gentilshommes de la Chambre*, the Duc d'Aumont, the Duc de Fleury, the Duc de Richelieu, and the Duc de Duras. The first two dukes considered their office merely a sinecure. But Richelieu and Duras, being both advanced in age and persistent admirers of the fair sex, paid some attention to their duties because they gave them the opportunity of enjoying the company of broad-minded young actresses.

The statute regulating the obligations and rights of actors and playwrights dated back to 1697. When it was promulgated the statute was a fair attempt to give a measure of protection to the playwrights, who till then had been absolutely at the actors' mercy. Yet it gave the largest part of the receipts to the actors. Indeed the actors had at that time been struggling for their very existence. Moreover, in the seventeenth century, authors frequently received an appreciable income from the great lords who loved to appear as patrons of letters. But this practice had almost disappeared in the eighteenth century. On the other hand, the theater was so in vogue in France that the actors' situation could no longer be considered precarious.

According to the 1697 statute, the actors kept for themselves nine tenths of the receipts of the five-act plays they presented. If the receipts for a play fell below five hundred livres twice in succession in winter time, or below three hundred livres in summer time, the actors could withdraw the play without asking the author's permission. But if the same play was subsequently revived by the actors, they were entitled to the full amount of the receipts.

A new statute in 1757 had left these terms substantially intact, but, because of the lower purchasing power of the French currency, had fixed twelve hundred livres in winter time and eight hundred livres in summer time as the amounts below which a play would become the actors' property, or—according to the expression used in those days—would "fall within the rules."

The actors used all sorts of tricks to cheat the playwrights of even their slight legal share. Thus, when a play seemed likely to be successful, the actors would present it twice in succession when they knew that some important function was taking place at court. The courtiers, who always bought the most expensive seats, naturally stayed away from the theaters on those days. The receipts would be low, the play would fall "within the rules," and the actors would present it again and again without having to pay the author a single sou. Furthermore, in calculating the receipts, the actors regularly left out important items—for instance, the price of loges rented by the year—so the unfortunate authors were lucky if they received one twentieth of the money the actors pocketed. Finally, to avoid unpleasant discussions, the actors never offered a playwright a detailed statement of accounts, but gave him a lump sum that they said was his share. If he was so ill-advised as to protest, some actress particularly well acquainted with Richelieu or Duras would see to it that the man was promptly put in his place.

The authors grumbled and raged privately, but were not bold enough to rise against a tradition established by the great Louis XIV, enforced by four dukes, and defended by cunning, greedy women with all the secret weapons at their disposal. Most of the playwrights thought it wiser to bend than to resist and be crushed.

Beaumarchais, however, was no longer in a mood to bend. When the actors of the Comédie Française announced that *Le Barbier de Séville* would be performed on December 23, 1775, he at once objected: an important social event was scheduled at Versailles that evening. Was the actors' move, he asked, purposely made to cause *Le Barbier* to "fall within the rules"? The actors did not answer. They canceled the announced performance, but, by way of reprisal, did not present the play again.

This was only a trifling matter to Beaumarchais, for he was then engrossed, body and soul, in the American-supply scheme. In May 1776, however, he wrote the actors, asking them to settle accounts with him. He received no answer. Months passed. Then, one day, Beaumarchais meeting Richelieu by chance, expressed his annoyance at this delay, though his attitude toward the Duke was most deferential. Richelieu knew that he stood high at that time with the Ministry, so he listened to him. But Richelieu was eighty-three and really did not understand what his complaint was about, so he had all the regulations and statutes on the administration of the French theaters sent to Beaumarchais. Beaumarchais would doubtless find in them a satisfactory explanation for his difficulties, whatever they were.

The actors were very alarmed by this unexpected turn of events. They did not want a conflict with a man who, since the Goëzman affair, had the reputation of being a dangerous antagonist. In November 1776 they asked him to come to one of their general meetings. He went. They offered him an advantageous compromise, but he explained that he was not seeking personal advantages. He had studied the problem of the author-actor relations and now wanted a fundamental and thoroughgoing reform of the system. This, the actors declared, was an altogether different matter. This was revolutionary! The meeting ended without any result in spite of a great show of cordial feelings on both sides.

The actors were now very eager to end this bothersome affair. On January 3, 1777, one of their delegates, Desessarts, went to the Hôtel de Hollande with 4505 livres—Beaumarchais' share for the thirty-two performances of *Le Barbier de Séville* which had been given so far. Beaumarchais asked for an itemized account that would explain how the actors had arrived at that particular sum. Impossible! What if all the authors were to ask for itemized accounts? Desessarts took back the 4505 livres.

Once more, several months passed without anything happening. Then, in June 1777, Beaumarchais tersely wrote the actors that if he did not receive the itemized account within a week, he would put the whole matter into the hands of an attorney.

The actors then appealed to the younger of their two protectors, Duras. From what the actors told him, Duras believed that Beaumarchais was up to some serious mischief, and therefore requested him to come and state his grievances. When he heard that Beaumarchais merely wanted a statement of accounts, he was amazed at the commotion that had been created. He felt that Beaumarchais' claims were neither subversive nor absurd. Seeing Duras now favorably disposed toward him, Beaumarchais warmed to his subject and drew a complete picture—and a somber one—of the way actors treated playwrights. Duras, who had formerly looked upon these problems only through the eyes of pretty actresses, seemed shocked by these revelations. He asked Beaumarchais to submit a program of reforms that would seem fair to him and his confrères.

Beaumarchais thereupon undertook the task of uniting the leading French playwrights for concerted action. He sent a dinner invitation to all the authors who had had at least one play performed at the Comédie Française, and found himself suddenly in a hornets' nest of petty jealousies, rivalries, and squabbles. Some dramatists refused to come if their enemies were also invited. Some wanted to be the leaders of the movement or take no part in it at all. Some were skeptical about the outcome of the struggle. Some were afraid. Some doubted Beaumarchais' good faith. In spite of these difficulties, which had to be ironed out one by one, twenty-three authors met at the Hôtel de Hollande on July 3, 1777. That date is usually considered today as marking the birth of the all-powerful Société des Auteurs Dramatiques of France.

The food was sumptuous. The wines were abundant, varied, and rich. After a while the company became amenable and mellow. In the end, four Commissioners were appointed to represent the authors: Bernard Saurin, Michel Sedaine, Jean-François Marmontel, and Beaumarchais. But because neither Saurin nor Sedaine nor Marmontel ever did any work in connection with his new functions, and because Beaumarchais was constantly busy throughout the second part of 1777 sending supplies to America and composing *Le Mariage de Figaro*, things remained at a standstill until the end of the year.

Then, in 1778, Beaumarchais resumed the struggle for the authors' rights—a struggle that lasted more than two years. The weakest points in Beaumarchais' position were his fellow authors' timidity, their unwillingness to take risks, and above all their spirit of discord.

The most dramatic episode in this miniature war occurred when the actors, aware of the dissensions in their opponents' camp, attempted to break up and scatter Beaumarchais' following. An author named Paul Dubuisson had written a play entitled *Nadir*, which he hoped to have performed at the Comédie Française. Though the play was exceedingly poor, the actors offered to present it—on condition that Dubuisson would start a secession movement among the playwrights. Dubuisson accepted the bargain and succeeded in detaching six members from the original group of twenty-three. Then, in his preface to *Nadir*, he wrote a glaringly libelous attack upon those who had remained faithful to Beaumarchais. The government censor, Jean-Baptiste Suard, who was probably a party to the plot, approved the publication of the preface, even though his job was to prevent the issuance of such lampoons.

Beaumarchais, up in arms, boldly demanded that the Minister of the Royal Household, Amelot, publicly disavow Suard, and said that otherwise he, Beaumarchais, would appeal to the public.

The French public, always passionately interested in literary quarrels, would certainly respond to the call. At the same time, he coaxed the playwrights who had remained faithful to him into signing a memorandum that was sent to Richelieu, Duras, and the King. Was another Goëzman affair in the offing?

Beaumarchais was then privately assured that if he dropped his threat of a public scandal he would receive satisfaction on the main issue—as much satisfaction as tradition and the influence of fair actresses on French politics allowed. Beaumarchais agreed to negotiate, and the negotiations lasted until 1780. Three decrees of the Conseil d'Etat dated March 17, May 12, and December 9 of that year embodied the concessions Beaumarchais obtained.

Thenceforth playwrights would receive one seventh instead of one tenth of the receipts, and all money paid by the spectators, including rentals of loges, would be counted in the receipts. On the other hand, the minimum amount of receipts under which a play would fall within the rules was raised from 1200 to 2300 livres in the winter and from 800 to 1800 livres in the summer. This was only half a victory for Beaumarchais. He had won some advantages for the playwrights, but the roots of the abuses he had fought against remained intact. He did not give up hope of wiping out those abuses, however, but he was not to attain his goal until well after the outbreak of the Revolution.

4. Beaumarchais, Publisher

Beaumarchais' next large undertaking was the publication of Voltaire's works. He and Voltaire had never had close personal contacts, yet when Voltaire came for his last visit to Paris, from February to May, 1778, the two men had at least one long and intimate talk. Voltaire, who knew he was about to die, is reported to have said: "All my hopes are centered on Beaumarchais." The final months of his life culminated in a sort of apotheosis. Benjamin Franklin brought him his grandson to be blessed; and Voltaire, placing his hand upon the child's forehead, whispered the famous formula: "*Dieu et Liberté.*"

After Voltaire's death, his fame soared to new heights. Everyone wanted to read the works of the writer who, along with Jean-Jacques Rousseau, had more than any other man shaped the ways of thinking of his century. But Voltaire's books—most of which had been banned by the various governments of Europe—were extremely difficult to procure. A Parisian publisher, Charles Panckoucke, with a flair for business had the idea of bringing out an edition of the celebrated man's complete works. He quietly bought up all the Voltaire manuscripts he could find and was lucky enough to purchase in one lot, from Voltaire's niece, Mme Denis, all the letters he had exchanged with Frederick the Great. Their publication would be one of the juiciest scandals to appear in print in years. What could be better for sales? Yet when Panckoucke had gathered together practically all the available material, his optimism turned into gloom. Voltaire had been such a prolific writer that the publication of his complete works would be ruinously expensive.

When Catherine the Great heard of Panckoucke's predicament, she made him an unexpected and startling proposal: she would gladly subsidize the publication, provided it were done in Russia. Evidently the works of the French philosopher would not have any deleterious effect on her ignorant muzhiks, and everywhere in Europe cultured people would sing the praises of the enlightened Tsarina. Comparisons would also undoubtedly be made between the breadth of views of St. Petersburg and the bigotry of Versailles.

Beaumarchais then suggested to Maurepas that, for the sake of French prestige, Voltaire's complete works be published by a Frenchman—by Beaumarchais. Maurepas, a Voltairean at heart, readily assented. How the pious Louis XVI was induced to approve the scheme still remains a mystery, but royal permission was unofficially granted. For Beaumarchais it meant above all spreading the advanced ideas which, since his contact with the American Revolution, had become the pivot of his life.

Soon Beaumarchais evolved a plan that was submitted to and accepted by the authorities. The works would not be printed in French territory, but the French police would receive orders to wink at the smuggling into France of the "forbidden" books. No government subsidy would be needed. Beaumarchais, who had just accomplished the miracle of balancing the Hortalez accounts without receiving practically any payment from America, could make a success of the venture.

Panckoucke was ready to sell Voltaire's manuscripts almost at cost. Beaumarchais went to his house, dramatically bringing 160,000 livres in gold with him. Their interview did not last long. When Beaumarchais returned to the Hôtel de Hollande, the manuscripts had replaced the gold in his carriage.

Beaumarchais founded a publishing firm, which he named the "Société Philosophique, Littéraire et Typographique." Beaumarchais himself *was* the Société, but he assumed only the modest title of "Correspondant Général." He bought three paper factories in Lorraine—at Arches, Archette, and Plombières. He sent one agent to Holland to inquire into the best methods of paper manufacturing, and another agent to England, to buy 150,000 livres' worth of Baskerville type. He rented from the Margrave Karl Friedrich of Baden an old, abandoned fortress at Kehl and set up his printing press there. At the beginning of 1780, everything seemed ready for a good start, so he wrote and distributed his prospectus: two editions of Voltaire's works would appear simultaneously, one in seventy volumes octavo, the other, and cheaper one, in ninety-two volumes duodecimo; fifteen thousand copies of each would be printed and sold by private subscription.

Almost at once, Beaumarchais was confronted with a series of unexpected problems. The Margrave objected to the printing of *Candide* because of the devastating picture of German nobility Voltaire had drawn in the character of Baron Thunder-ten-Tronck. Beaumarchais settled that difficulty by informing the Margrave that another German sovereign, Prince von Neuwied, who was short of funds, had offered to rent the Société Philosophique, Littéraire et Typographique convenient quarters on his own estates. The Margrave, who also needed cash, withdrew his objections as quickly and gracefully as he could.

For advance publicity, Beaumarchais read titbits from Frederick II's correspondence with Voltaire to the Paris salons. But Frederick II sent diplomatic representations to Vergennes. Vergennes, who did not want any friction with Prussia, told Beaumarchais that he would have to leave out of his edition the most "interesting" passages in the letters exchanged between Voltaire and the King. Beaumarchais had to bow to superior orders. Then Catherine

II promptly made a similar request on her own account, and again a few gems of Voltaire's correspondence had to go.

Beaumarchais also had to overcome endless material obstacles. He had appointed as general manager at Kehl a certain Le Tellier. Le Tellier was intelligent and industrious, but overbearing and harsh with his subordinates. The workers, however well paid, soon became restive and discontented. Time and again, Beaumarchais had to rush from Paris to Kehl, to settle some minor labor dispute that threatened to develop into paralyzing strife.

But the most exhausting task that Beaumarchais had to perform was the collation of the text to be printed. Within about a year, he read, corrected, and revised the enormous bulk of Voltaire's writings. Miron served as a proof-reader. Many passages in Voltaire's works were unintelligible without knowledge of the contemporary facts to which they referred; Condorcet composed the indispensable commentaries.

Now and then Beaumarchais inserted a few remarks of his own, though with a discretion one would hardly have expected of him. For example, Voltaire had mentioned in a letter to d'Argental the rumors accusing Beaumarchais of having murdered his two wives. "A man who is as lively, impassioned, and impetuous as Beaumarchais," Voltaire said, "may have given a slap to his wife, or even two slaps to his two wives, but he would not poison them." Beaumarchais added a footnote to this: "I can testify that Beaumarchais has sometimes been slapped by women, like most men who have loved them a great deal, but he has never committed the shameful act of striking any of them."

In the meantime, the Anglo-Franco-American war went on, but Beaumarchais' share in sending supplies overseas was now very small. After the loss of ten of his ships in July 1779 he had bought a few vessels—*L'Anna, La Ménagère, L'Alexandre, L'Aimable Eugénie*—but he concentrated his attention more and more upon the remunerative West Indian trade. The military operations in America were proceeding satisfactorily, and soon the Americans would not need help of any kind.

In June 1780 Silas Deane had returned to France in order to get the records of the deals he had made when he was America's sole representative in Paris. These records, he hoped, would enable him to clear himself before Congress. He still felt very bitter about the way he had been treated in Philadelphia and seemed in no hurry to return to the United States. After going over the accounts of Hortalez & Cie he came to the conclusion that Congress owed Beaumarchais 3,600,000 livres. He embodied his findings in an official document dated April 6, 1781. But soon afterward a scandal wrecked his authority and career.

Early in the summer of 1781, Deane wrote trusted American friends personal letters in which he denounced the leading politicians in Congress, calling them "unprincipled" and "vicious." At the same time, he expressed regret that America should have become independent of England. These letters were intercepted by the British. Realizing the propaganda value of such statements from one of the best-known protagonists of the American Revolution, the British published them in New York's Tory newspaper, *The Royal Gazette*.

Their publication spelled the end of Deane's political life in America. All his American friends hastily severed their connection with him. In despondency, almost in despair, he went to England, where he lived a few more years. He died in 1789 on his way to Canada.

The collapse of Deane's influence caused new headaches for Beaumarchais. Indeed, his financial accounts, endorsed as they were by an utterly discredited man, were bound to appear more suspicious than ever to Congress. At the same time, he was losing his main supporters in France. In 1780, Sartines had to withdraw from the Cabinet: Necker had discovered that the Minister of the Navy, without even informing the Finance Department, had spent for his dear ships twenty million livres more than had been agreed upon. Then, Maurepas died in 1781, and from that time on Vergennes never consulted Beaumarchais about anything.

Yet, however cold he may have been to Beaumarchais, Vergennes was always perfectly correct and fair to him. For instance, in 1778 the Chevalier d'Eon—who now lived in France as a woman—having heard of Beaumarchais' semi-disgrace, launched a last fierce attack against him. Vergennes immediately stepped forward and issued an official statement testifying to Beaumarchais' absolute integrity in the Chevalier d'Eon affair.

The Chevalier returned to England in 1783 and died there in 1810. A post-mortem examination performed before several witnesses ended the doubts about his sex. According to the report of the operating surgeon, Thomas Copeland, he possessed "male organs of generation perfectly formed in every respect."

News of the capitulation of Yorktown reached Paris on November 20, 1781, and caused there a delirium of joy. For Beaumarchais, as for most Frenchmen, the war was over. Naval operations continued for nearly two more years, until the signing of the peace at Versailles, on September 3, 1783. But by that time Hortalez had wound up its affairs.

In 1782 Francy returned to France. During his journey to America he had contracted tuberculosis of the lungs and he was to die less than a year after his return. Beaumarchais took him into his own home and looked after him until the end. Francy had always hoped to become a nobleman one day, so Beaumarchais sold him before his death his own office of Secrétaire du Roi.

Chapter 9

PRELUDE TO REVOLUTION

1. "The King does not want Le Mariage de Figaro *to be played—therefore, it shall be played."*

AFTER THE CAPITULATION of Yorktown, Beaumarchais was able to devote most of his time to the works of Voltaire. The first volumes appeared early in 1783, and Beaumarchais then realized that his publishing venture would in the end mean a huge financial loss to him. Yet he persisted in his undertaking, partly because he wanted to keep his pledge to the subscribers and partly because he was now ready to spend a fortune to spread the ideas of tolerance and freedom which, since the American Revolution, had given his own life a meaning and a purpose.

At Kehl, Beaumarchais still ran into grave difficulties. He had to replace the troublesome Le Tellier by Jacques Guilbert de la

Hogue, who was compliant and docile. But then a few workmen, who had taken Le Tellier's side, wilfully damaged the printing machinery in revenge for his dismissal. This sabotage had probably taken place with Le Tellier's knowledge, and a long, confused lawsuit between Beaumarchais and Le Tellier ensued.

Soon afterward, Beaumarchais' cashier, Cantini, absconded with a large sum of money. Beaumarchais then appointed as cashier Paul Gudin's elder brother, Philippe Gudin de La Ferlière—a thoroughly honest and reliable man who had been with the Hortalez firm for many years. But the money stolen by Cantini was never recovered.

The main cause, however, of the financial difficulties that beset the Société Philosophique, Littéraire et Typographique was the disappointingly small volume of sales. Only a limited number of wealthy people could afford the necessarily high subscription rates. Beaumarchais tried every method of sales promotion practiced in his time, including payment of premiums and drawing of lotteries, but all in vain. He had counted upon thirty thousand subscribers; he never had more than two thousand.

When the last volumes were printed in 1788, Beaumarchais could proudly say that he had fulfilled all his promises. The "Kehl edition" of Voltaire's writings was acknowledged by all to be a truly monumental work. But the monument had cost Beaumarchais about one million livres.

Beaumarchais could bear such a tremendous deficit because, during the same period, he had engaged in a number of other business transactions, none of them spectacular, but most of them handsomely remunerative. Yet, despite his activity and acumen, he never reached the summit of opulence Pâris-Duverney had attained in his time.

One reason for Beaumarchais' inability to accumulate great riches was his well-known and well-exploited openhandedness. He could never resist an appeal by a man or a woman in sore financial straits—and there was no dearth of such people in Paris. Paul Gudin, his intimate confidant, often said that Beaumarchais received more than twenty requests for help daily; and Philippe Gudin, his cautious cashier, constantly grumbled at the drain put on Beaumarchais' resources by his impulsive generosity.

This impulsive generosity was undoubtedly one of the most engaging traits of Beaumarchais' character. Thus, he himself recorded the feeling of anguish and horror that gripped him when he heard one day that his former business partner, Joseph Peyrera, who had been imprudent enough to take a trip to Spain, had been caught in Cadiz by the Inquisition and was about to be burned alive because of his Jewish faith.

Peyrera somehow managed to send Beaumarchais a short note from jail. "When I received it," Beaumarchais wrote a long time afterward, "my hair stood on end. I ran to Versailles and went down on my knees, crying, before M. le Comte de Vergennes. I tormented him so much that I obtained from him that he claim you from Spain as 'belonging to France.' Thus I saved you from being burned at the stake, and I sent you all the money needed for your trip back to France. You are one of the most grateful men I have ever found. All the members of your large family have written me to express their thanks."

Beaumarchais' liberality toward the distressed and sympathy

for the oppressed were responsible for one of the most delightful friendships of his middle age and one of the most harrowing trials of his later years. His friendship with the young German Prince of Nassau-Siegen began under the most bizarre circumstances. Because the legitimacy of his birth had been openly challenged in his native land, the Prince had established himself in Paris. Soon he became known to all Europe as a charming but mad knight-errant perpetually eager to fight wherever there was hard fighting to be done and also eager to enjoy the delicate refinements then the privilege of the most elegant aristocratic circles. Having absolutely no conception of financial orderliness and thrift, he spent half his time putting Europe's stoutest warriors to flight, and the other half timidly running away from his creditors in the French capital. In 1779, Sartines had compelled him to take a financial adviser: Beaumarchais. Beaumarchais was rapidly won over by the Prince's easy gracious manners, and the two became friends.

The Prince had married a Polish woman of incandescent beauty, Princess Sanguska. But the Princess was a divorcée, and her marriage with the Prince had naturally not been recognized by the Catholic Church—hence countless humiliations for both of them in France. Beaumarchais boldly decided to settle the matter with the Archbishop of Paris, Monseigneur Christophe de Beaumont. It goes without saying that his request to have the two young people's matrimonial status regularized ended in failure. But this very failure brought him still closer to the Prince and the Princess. They were grateful to him for his efforts, and fond of him for his unfaltering kindness. Soon they adored him—and borrowed from him endlessly. How could Beaumarchais refuse them anything when the Princess gazed at him with her large, appealing eyes and declared that his name should not be Beaumarchais but "Bonmarchais"?

One evening in October 1781 Beaumarchais was having dinner with the Prince. A judge of the Parliament happened to be among the guests, and through him the company learned the details of a scandal that was then the talk of Paris. Guillaume Kornman, cashier of the Quinze-Vingts—a celebrated Institution for the Blind dating back to the thirteenth century—had had his pretty wife locked up in the Château de Charollais, on the Rue de Bellefond, a place of detention for low-class prostitutes. Mme Kornman was a Protestant of Swiss origin. She belonged to a wealthy family. At the age of eleven she had become an orphan. At fifteen she had been married off by her guardians to Guillaume Kornman, an Alsatian from Strasbourg. Kornman was much older than the girl, and had evidently been interested mainly in her money. He was also a Protestant, and the wedding had taken place in Switzerland. In spite of the birth of two children, their union had never been a happy one.

In 1779, the Kornmans had become acquainted with the Royal Syndic of Strasbourg, Daudet de Jossan. Daudet de Jossan was a personal friend of the Prince de Montbarey, who had replaced the Comte de Saint-Germain as Minister of War in 1777. Montbarey belonged to the small, exclusive, and powerful clique around Queen Marie-Antoinette. At the beginning of Louis XVI's reign, Marie-Antoinette had had practically no influence on French politics. But in 1777 normal marital relations were established between her and her husband, and from then on she completely dominated the King and the kingdom. Then all sorts of pensions, positions, and privileges literally poured upon the members of her coterie.

Kornman pondered over the possibility of his getting a share of the favors. Aware that Daudet de Jossan and Mme Kornman were strongly attracted to each other, he subtly contrived to leave them alone together as often as possible. He would plan a trip to the country with them; then, at the last moment, some urgent and unexpected business would force him to remain in town. But he would not want to spoil the pleasure of the trip for his trusted wife and his best friend: let them go ahead without him. Thus, he felt he would soon have an irresistible power over Daudet de Jossan. Then he would ask him to speak to Montbarey, who would speak to the Queen, who would speak to the King about Monsieur Kornman's outstanding, though still unrecognized, abilities.

Daudet de Jossan was in love and thoughtless. Mme Kornman was thoughtless and in love. Kornman could already gloat over the success of the first part of his plan when he heard, in December, 1780, that Montbarey had been quietly eased out of office by a court intrigue. Overnight Daudet de Jossan found himself stripped of all power to help or hurt anyone. Overnight Kornman's temper soured, and he quarreled violently with his "best friend."

At the same time his attitude toward his wife became so unpleasant that she decided to ask for a divorce. Both she and her husband were Protestants and had been married in a part of Switzerland where divorce was legal; there was no reason, she thought, why she should not be free again. Kornman seemed willing to give her her freedom, but he wanted to keep the money she had brought him as dowry. She refused to agree to this, however. Then, on August 3, 1781, Kornman somehow managed to obtain a "Lettre de Cachet" ordering his unfaithful spouse incarcerated in the Château de Charollais. Mme Kornman was just at that time expecting another child. Was the child to be born in a jail for prostitutes?

The would-be divorcée's plight drew pity from everyone in the Prince of Nassau-Siegen's house, but particularly from the Princess. She begged and begged Beaumarchais to help Mme Kornman. At first he refused to have anything to do with a sordid affair that did not concern him. Then he was shown letters from Kornman to Daudet de Jossan which proved beyond doubt that the husband had deliberately thrown his wife into his friend's arms. Finally, he acceded to the Princess' wishes and agreed to present Mme Kornman's case to the King. The only favor he would ask, however, was that Mme Kornman, whose time was nearly at hand, be taken immediately to a surgeon's home so that her child would not be born at the notorious Château de Charollais. This favor was granted by Louis XVI on December 27, 1781.

Kornman was furious. A meddlesome stranger had robbed him of his best weapon against his wife, and he swore that he would one day make him pay dearly for his meddling. In the meantime, however, since Beaumarchais was known as a redoubtable fighter, Kornman held his peace, and Beaumarchais did not give the matter another thought.

Beaumarchais now faced another and more important problem. He had just delivered the manuscript of *Le Mariage de Figaro* to the actors of the Comédie Française, who had accepted the play on the condition that the government authorize the performance. No serious difficulties were expected from that quarter. Lieutenant General of Police Le Noir's relations with Beaumarchais were most cordial. He gave the play his full approval, and the official censor, Coquely, did the same. Everything seemed settled, and Beaumarchais now read excerpts from the best scenes in the literary salons. The pages read seemed extremely bold, but everyone agreed that *Le Mariage de Figaro* promised to be one of the most entertaining comedies ever produced on the French stage.

Marie-Antoinette expressed the wish to have the whole play read privately before the members of her circle. Beaumarchais gave a copy of his manuscript to the writer Chamfort, who delivered it to the Comte de Vaudreuil, Her Majesty's *Maître des Plaisirs.* Marie-Antoinette and her friends, particularly the Princesse de Lamballe and the Comtesse de Polignac, were delighted with the amusing, saucy and witty dialogue. Why could not this charming play be presented at the Royal Theater of Versailles? The King, of course, would have to give his consent, but he was no connoisseur of literature, and would doubtless follow his wife's opinion in this matter as in everything else.

A reading of *Le Mariage de Figaro* by Mme de Campan was arranged for the King. Then, much to everyone's amazement, he exploded. Mme de Campan has left in her *Mémoires* a record of his furibund utterances: "It is detestable! It will never be played! Why, if this play were to be performed, the Bastille would have to be pulled down! . . . That man mocks everything that ought to be respected in government. . . ."

Shortly afterward, Beaumarchais was curtly notified by Hue de Miromesnil that the King objected to his comedy; consequently it could not be presented. Miromesnil evidently felt a malicious joy in informing the playwright of the King's displeasure. He remembered how he, the Keeper of the Great Seal, had once been reprimanded by Maurepas for carelessness in connection with the Conseil d'Etat's granting Beaumarchais Letters of Relief. Even though Beaumarchais had only indirectly caused this reprimand, Miromesnil had kept a grudge against him. Under a mask of disinterestedness and integrity, he was coldly calculating and vindictive. Here at last was a chance for him to show that upstart Beaumarchais that there was a supreme authority in the kingdom to which even clever writers had to bow.

But Beaumarchais at present refused to bow even to the supreme authority. He did not hesitate to challenge the King himself, and went about openly repeating: "The King does not want *Le Mariage de Figaro* to be played—therefore, it shall be played." This was indeed, as has often been said, the true prelude to the Revolution.

Arrayed against Beaumarchais, besides the King, were such powers as the King's first brother, the Comte de Provence; the Keeper of the Great Seal, Miromesnil; the Archbishop of Paris, Monseigneur Christophe de Beaumont; and most of the Catholic clergy. Taking his part were the Queen and her friends; the King's second brother, the Comte d'Artois; and the majority of the French people. Beaumarchais enlisted the support of the influential literary salons through private readings of the play, but he reached the man in the street by a more curious method.

About three quarters of a century earlier, during the War of the Spanish Succession in Louis XIV's time, the rumor had spread that France's arch-enemy, Lord Marlborough, had been killed in the battle of Malplaquet, in 1707. An unknown rhymester at once composed a scurrilous song on Marlborough's reported death and supposed funeral, "*Malbrough s'en va-t-en guerre.*" For a while the song enjoyed a certain vogue mainly because its author had used for his tune a charming old melody dating back, perhaps, to the time of the Crusades. Soon, however, Marlborough proved very much alive. In fact, during the subsequent years, he defeated the French armies time and again. Fairly quickly "*Malbrough s'en va-t-en guerre*" ceased to be a popular song in France, yet it was long remembered—essentially as a joke on the English, though a joke which, owing to circumstances, had fallen lamentably flat.

"*Malbrough s'en va-t-en guerre*" was brought back to Beaumarchais' mind when his private Navy captured the British ship *Marlborough*. The war against England was then proceeding successfully for France, so the French could at long last poke fun at the English and, without feeling self-conscious, again hum the tune of "*Malbrough.*" Beaumarchais hummed the tune and, apparently struck by its intrinsic loveliness, undertook to restore the poetic feeling it had been robbed of by the anonymous song writer's incongruous and grotesque words. Thus he composed, to fit the ancient melody, new lyrics expressing the tender sorrow of a young page in love with a chatelaine, and incorporated them into *Le Mariage de Figaro*. This love ditty, sung by Chérubin to the Countess, is not without charm. It is a prefiguration of the "troubadour" poems that were soon to flourish in France at the dawn of the Romantic era.

At the same time, odd and unexpected events in entirely different quarters contributed to the tune's renewed popularity. In October, 1781, Marie-Antoinette had had her first son. The birth of an heir to the throne was a triumph for the young Queen and a cause of wild rejoicing throughout the country. The infant was entrusted to the care of a buxom wet nurse who was promptly nicknamed Mme Poitrine by the courtiers. Mme Poitrine often sang the old air of "*Malbrough*" to herself, and the courtiers, particularly those belonging to the Queen's party, sang it after her.

Suddenly, at the end of 1782 and in the first months of 1783, "*Malbrough*" became the rage of Paris. Not only could the song be heard everywhere, in the cafés and in the streets, but all sorts of objects, from fancy pastries to women's hats, were dubbed *à la Malbrough.* A bizarre blend of unrelated elements caused the "*Malbrough*" vogue, the most conspicuous of which was patriotism. The main goal of the Franco-British war, America's freedom, was now assured. Moreover, the French fleet under Admiral Pierre de Suffren had, from February to September 1782, won a series of victories over the English Admiral, Sir Edward Hughes, in the Indian Ocean. When, in October 1782, England officially sued for peace, the exultation in Paris had no bounds. The "*Malbrough*" song, which had not lost its early anti-English connotation, was soon adopted as a chant of triumph.

This expression of patriotic joy was, however, queerly though clearly joined with the national French sport of annoying the government. Everyone knew that the government had forbidden the presentation of *Le Mariage de Figaro* because of its "revolutionary" utterances. But the government could not forbid any Frenchman to sing a love song, even if the song was included in a forbidden play. Besides, it was an open secret that Marie-Antoinette had taken Beaumarchais' side, and the courtiers of the Queen's party, who had contributed to popularizing the tune, now used it as a challenge to their foes. Thus, for about two years "*Mal-*

brough" became the war song of the French crowds fighting along with Beaumarchais in his "war of nerves" against the King.

At one time, this war of nerves threatened to become an international affair. In 1782 Catherine II of Russia attempted to take advantage of the temporary eclipse of England's power and prestige in Europe by grabbing a goodly portion of Turkey's territory for herself. She approached France cautiously on the subject, but Vergennes pretended not to understand the Russian Ambassador's necessarily veiled words. So Catherine II decided to send her son and heir, the Grand Duke Paul, to France to explore the possibilities of an understanding.

The Grand Duke and his wife arrived in Paris incognito as the Comte and Comtesse du Nord. After hearing a private reading of *Le Mariage de Figaro*, they suggested to Beaumarchais that the world *première* of his comedy be presented in St. Petersburg. He politely declined this flattering offer, but let the court of Versailles know that he had rejected it for the honor of France. This clever move spurred the Queen's party to action. The Comtesse de Polignac, evidently with Marie-Antoinette's approval, took it upon herself to have the play performed in Paris, regardless of official objection, at a hall called "Salle des Menus Plaisirs" by the actors of the Comédie Française. She counted upon the King's natural inertia and his well-known reluctance to take any stand against his wife.

The King did nothing when the actors began their rehearsals openly; nothing when the day of the performance, June 13, 1783, was publicly announced; nothing throughout the afternoon of that day, when the streets in the vicinity of the hall were filled with huge crowds defiantly singing "*Malbrough.*" Then, in the evening, barely half an hour before curtain time, the Duc de Villequier, expressly sent by Louis XVI, asked the actors to desist "under pain of incurring His Majesty's indignation." The actors had no choice but to obey. The disappointed audience shouted "oppression" and "tyranny," and tumultuous, riotous scenes lasted throughout the night.

Then the Comte de Vaudreuil took up Mme de Polignac's project, though on a less spectacular scale: in September 1783, he had *Le Mariage de Figaro* privately performed at his own Château de Gennevilliers. The audience was small and composed only of invited guests. At the end, Beaumarchais, who was present, received a wild ovation.

The King shook his head. "You will see," he said, "that Beaumarchais will have more influence than the Keeper of the Great Seal." He resisted the pressure of public opinion a few more months and then gave in. To help the King save face, Beaumarchais agreed to alter the "unsuitable" passages of his play, but actually made only insignificant changes.

The rehearsals of *Le Mariage de Figaro ou La Folle Journée* at the Comédie Française began in February 1784, and the first public presentation took place on April 27. It was enthusiastically received. Night after night, the theater was filled to overflowing. The triumphant tune of "*Malbrough*" resounded throughout Paris. The King had lost his war against Beaumarchais, and everyone felt that, along with Beaumarchais, "the people" had won.

After some of Beaumarchais' enemies maliciously remarked that he would make a pretty penny out of his "forbidden" play, he quickly countered with a master stroke of publicity. Several years before, Jean-Jacques Rousseau had, in his book *Emile*, made an impassioned plea that French mothers nurse their babies themselves. Since that time "nursing mothers" had become the fashion in France. On August 12, 1784, Beaumarchais announced the creation of the "Institut de Bienfaisance Maternelle," intended to help the *pauvres mères nourrices*. All the proceeds of *Le Mariage de Figaro* would go to that institution.

Since the Catholic Church was, before the Revolution, in charge of practically all charity work in France, Beaumarchais asked the Archbishop of Paris to sponsor the Institut. The Archbishop, however, refused to give his patronage to Beaumarchais' plan, and his refusal drew comments that were not unfavorable to Beaumarchais. Beaumarchais then turned to the Archbishop of Lyons, Monseigneur de Montazet, who accepted his offer.

About the same time, Beaumarchais completed the libretto of *Tarare*, the philosophical opera on which he had been working intermittently since 1775. In its final form, this bizarre play contained transparent allusions to recent well-known events. The central theme of the opera was a struggle between an omnipotent Oriental despot and one of his subjects, a modest and honest commoner. Atar, the sovereign of the imaginary kingdom of Ormuz, was stupid, malevolent, and tyrannical. His subject, Tarare, despite his low birth, had the greatest talents and virtues. In his fight against the King, Tarare had to overcome countless obstacles thrown across his path by superstition, tradition or ill-fortune. In the end, he was triumphant, however, and by his own merit reached the pinnacle of honor and fame: Beaumarchais as he saw himself in the year 1784.

2. *From Prison to Propriety*

The success of *Le Mariage de Figaro* soon awoke old, latent enmities and jealousies. Vicious attacks were launched from all sides against Beaumarchais and his work. Most of these attacks remained anonymous, for he was so feared as an antagonist that few dared to fight him openly. Among those few, Jean-Baptiste Suard was outstanding. He loudly criticized *Le Mariage de Figaro* as subversive and immoral. His signed articles were always decorously written, but it was rumored, and not without cause, that he was also the author of other unsigned articles that were infinitely less conventional in tone.

In February, 1785, such an aggressive unsigned article appeared in *Le Journal de Paris.* Beaumarchais thought he could recognize in it Suard's pedantic style and immediately sent the periodical a scathing reply. Suard was dark-complexioned and puny; moreover, he was fidgety, restless, and always seemed to be hopping about. Beaumarchais compared him to a flea—an annoying vermin, perhaps, but utterly insignificant and, in fact, beneath contempt. "After I have conquered lions and tigers to get a comedy performed," he added, "do you think you will compel me to sink to the level of a Dutch housemaid hunting every morning the vile insect of the night?"

Actually the King's own brother, the Comte de Provence, not Suard, had written the incriminating article. After reading Beaumarchais' retort, the Comte de Provence went to complain to Louis XVI. Louis XVI was then playing whist and interrupted his game to listen to his brother. He did not relish the idea of any member of the royal family being compared to a flea, even by mistake. Moreover, he himself had evidently been likened to another animal, a lion—or was he perhaps a tiger? Impulsively, Louis XVI took one of his playing cards—it was a seven of spades—and wrote on it an order to put Beaumarchais in jail.

On that same day, March 7, 1785, Beaumarchais was having dinner at the Hôtel de Hollande with the Prince of Nassau-Siegen and another friend. Suddenly a knock was heard at the door, and a servant let in Police Commissioner Chenu. Chenu explained the cause of his intrusion, and showed Beaumarchais his unusual warrant of arrest. The Bastille, no doubt, thought Beaumarchais. He had expected such a thing for a long time, and remained perfectly calm. Incarceration in the Bastille was not a very cruel fate during Louis XVI's reign. In any case, he would probably not remain there very long: after a few months, he would be set free and would enjoy the prestige that came to a "martyr" of despotism.

He bade his guests proceed with their dinner and then followed Chenu to the carriage waiting for them outside. On his way to jail, he talked pleasantly with Chenu, whom he remembered from the good old days of his fight with the Duc de Chaulnes, but when the carriage reached its destination, he turned pale. He was not to be imprisoned in the Bastille; he had been taken to Saint-Lazare.

Saint-Lazare was mainly a prison for children, where the police brought juvenile delinquents or naughty boys who had indulged in pranks. The latter were usually given a good whipping or a plain spanking according to their misdeed and age. They were kept alone in a cell for a night, perhaps for a day or two. Then more often than not, they were released with the stern warning to behave themselves in the future.

Beaumarchais was treated like a naughty boy. Though he did not receive a whipping or a spanking, he was locked in a cell for one night. When Chenu arrived the following morning to give Beaumarchais his freedom again, he found the prisoner almost hysterical. Beaumarchais obstinately refused to leave jail. Chenu had not been instructed to remove him by force, so he let him have his way and, very much puzzled, reported the case to his superiors.

Soon all Paris knew that Beaumarchais had been locked up in Saint-Lazare. The capital fairly rocked with laughter. People who would have boiled with indignation if he had been put in the Bastille considered his spending a night in a prison for bad children merely a practical joke. Many inquired if he had received the customary spanking. Quite a few wished he had—he had always been so cocky, so sure of himself.

After brooding for six days in his cell, Beaumarchais decided to go home. But he was a completely changed man, for his imagination had magnified this minor incident into a major tragedy. He shut himself up in his house, and refused to see anyone. On March 22, 1785, he wrote to the Duc de Coigny, who had succeeded the Duc de La Vallière as Master of the Royal Hunt: "The insult I have received, Monsieur le Duc, having struck me from the society of men, I have imposed perpetual imprisonment upon myself in my own home. Since M. le Duc de Coigny ought not to be ever so slightly touched by anything concerning such a strange event, I beg you to accept my resignation as your Lieutenant General."

Up to that time Beaumarchais had been consistently bold and brave; he had always shown himself ready to trade blow for blow with his enemies; he had faced crushing disaster with indomitable fortitude. But now he was afraid, ashamed, whining. He wrote a long-winded memorial to explain that he never had any intention of offending the King. Night after night, he was haunted by the same nightmare: he saw himself being whipped in public, while the ladies and gentlemen watching the show clapped, laughed, and cheered.

After a few months, he began taking long solitary walks in the streets. Later, he mingled with people again; but he looked strangely subdued and sad. Then, when he occasionally ran into new conflicts, the public discovered with amazement that he was no longer the stout fighter of old.

Beaumarchais' incarceration in Saint-Lazare had been neither dangerous nor painful, but it had vividly brought back to his mind, at the age of fifty-three, a stage of his adolescence he had never altogether outgrown. Being treated like a naughty boy by superior authority had revived the feelings of unworthiness and guilt he had experienced during his great conflict with his father in the Rue Saint-Denis shop. The subconscious fears resulting from that long-past episode had remained buried in him for nearly thirty years. During that period, they had been overlaid with a crust of artificial self-confidence. The shock of his being suddenly identified with the "bad children" of Saint-Lazare had shattered that crust. The old hidden terrors had spurted out, and now flooded the surface of his psychological life. Once again he made a firm resolution "to be good." If people attacked him, he would henceforth run to the authorities, as a child to his parents, and ask for protection against the big, brutal bullies.

The King was flabbergasted when he heard of the change in

Beaumarchais' attitude that was evident to everyone. Was he up to one of his old tricks? No, indeed; Beaumarchais was now truly a reformed character. Louis XVI, who had not a drop of venom in his make-up, felt sorry for his "victim." He had been annoyed at him because of *Le Mariage de Figaro*. But this was now past, and everybody said that *Le Mariage* was a masterpiece that did great honor to France. It might well be so. To show Beaumarchais kindness—and to please his wife—Louis XVI readily gave his consent when it was suggested that *Le Barbier de Séville* be staged at the royal palace of Trianon by amateur actors and actresses drawn from the highest court circles. The Comte d'Artois took the part of Almaviva, and Marie-Antoinette herself the part of Rosine. Beaumarchais, who was invited to the performance, was graciously received by all, and heartily congratulated by the King. He was in favor once more.

Soon afterward, Louis XVI showed him favor still more tangibly. After the naval battle of Grenada, in which *Le Fier Rodrigue* had taken a glorious part, Beaumarchais had sent a petition to the government. Ten of his ships had been destroyed or captured by the enemy because they had been deprived of their escort by Admiral d'Estaing's orders. Beaumarchais expressed no regret that these orders had been given; but was he not entitled to some indemnity for his staggering losses? His claim had been recognized as legitimate, and partial payments had already been made to him. He had received 905,000 livres one time, and 570,626 livres another time. Louis XVI now decided to conclude this affair with spectacular generosity. On February 12, 1786, he granted him an additional sum of 800,000 livres, making a grand total of 2,275,626 livres. This largesse not only wiped out Beaumarchais' losses; it made him a wealthy man again.

The royal largesse did not, however, wipe out Beaumarchais' complex remorse and fear. He was now passing through a phase of intense moralism. For twelve years he had lived "in sin" with Mlle de Willermaulaz. There is not the slightest evidence that during these years he was ever disturbed by his moral irregularity. His little daughter, whom he dearly loved, was a natural child. If he had pangs of conscience on that score, certainly no sign of them appeared in the open—not until he was sent to Saint-Lazare.

But after his return from Saint-Lazare, while he remained under self-imposed imprisonment in his own house, he spent most of his time writing a play about the illegitimate child. In fact, he put two illegitimate children into his new comedy. This comedy, entitled *La Mère coupable*, was not comic at all. There is not a trace in it of the light, frivolous, roguish vein that ran through *Le Barbier de Séville* and *Le Mariage de Figaro*. Beaumarchais was now earnest, honest, moral, and boring.

La Mère coupable was a sequel to *Le Mariage de Figaro*, but the famous characters of the old play had been completely metamorphosed. Figaro now receded into the background, a mere shadow of his former engaging and disreputable self. He was no longer Beaumarchais' revolutionary mouthpiece. Strangely enough Beaumarchais was now embodied in Count Almaviva—a very altered Count Almaviva. The Count at present stood for the *grand seigneur* as he ought to be, and as Beaumarchais would have been —at least he thought so—if he had been a *grand seigneur:* generous, magnanimous, quick-tempered, perhaps, but liberal-minded and open to modern, advanced ideas.

In the play, Count Almaviva had—as Beaumarchais in actual life—an illegitimate daughter of whom he was intensely fond. Because of her illegitimacy, the Count found himself embroiled in emotional complications from which he could scarcely extricate himself. In Beaumarchais' case, however, he could easily extricate himself from the emotional complications arising from little Eugénie's status. All he had to do was to marry her mother—which he promptly did. On March 8, 1786, M. de Beaumarchais and Mlle de Willermaulaz were solemnly wedded in the Church of St. Paul.

Around the same time, Beaumarchais revised the manuscript of *Le Mariage de Figaro* for publication in book form. He composed a preface for the book in which he tried to prove, though not very successfully, that his comedy was a school for virtue. He also announced the forthcoming *La Mère coupable* and outlined his intentions for the new play: "I shall be lavish," he said, "with the attributes of the most austere morality, and I shall thunder against the vices I have treated with too much considerateness in the past."

Beaumarchais' legitimate spouse fitted perfectly into this new pattern of respectability. Mlle de Willermaulaz, who had always looked dignified, was now matronly and fat. There was not much romance left in her relations with Beaumarchais; but she was an excellent wife, and she ran the huge Hôtel de Hollande with perfect Swiss orderliness, cleanliness, and efficiency.

Julie had completely withdrawn from housekeeping. She was now a thin, spare old maid, often beset with melancholy. From time to time she had spells of gaiety, but she turned more and more to religion and poetry for inspiration. Her favorite reading was Edward Young's *Night Thoughts*, and, in 1784, she had published a gloomy little volume entitled *L'Existence réflèchie, ou Coup d'œil moral sur le prix de la vie.*

Beaumarchais had in recent years grown stout and stately. There was something slightly self-important yet genuinely kind in his demeanor that fully justified the name everyone gave him at home: "*Bon Papa.*" He was also becoming hard of hearing and had to use regularly a funny-looking ear trumpet. He now avoided the company of strangers, and felt truly at ease only when surrounded by his family and friends.

At the end of 1786 Beaumarchais half retired from business, for he was quite well off. He looked after his investments closely, and occasionally engaged in profitable, though limited, financial speculations; but he was convinced that his days of trial and effort were over.

Beaumarchais' desire to settle down to a life of solid comfort made him long for a commodious and substantial residence. He then sold the house on the Rue de Condé in which he had not lived for almost ten years. As for the Hôtel de Hollande, that enormous caravanserai he had rented essentially for business purposes, he would leave it without regret.

In June 1787 he bought a vacant lot of almost two acres in an east-side suburb of Paris, at the corner of the Boulevard Saint-Antoine and the Rue Amelot. His choice of location is a psychological enigma. There was no lack of available space in those days in the capital's best residential districts. Yet the ground he purchased was situated in one of the city's poorest, dirtiest, dingiest sections. It was almost completely surrounded by slums, and a few hundred yards away loomed the dark, forbidding silhouette of the Bastille. Perhaps his decision was subconsciously prompted by his recent change of political outlook, which, since the American Revolution, had made him turn toward the people. In any case, his decision was soon to become an unending source of trouble to him.

A well-known architect named Lemoyne helped Beaumarchais build his dream house. The first project he submitted called for a total expenditure of 300,000 livres. But soon Beaumarchais and Lemoyne vied with each other in adding splendid and costly features to the initial plan: marble columns, balustrades, statues, a lofty dome, and a large, artificial pond. Eventually, after two years of work, the price of construction rose to about three times the original estimate.

If that elaborate building had been erected in an elegant quarter of Paris, it would have looked pretentious enough but not aggressively out of place. But built as it was in the heart of the poverty-stricken Faubourg Saint-Antoine, it seemed to its neighbors an insult to their misery and a challenge to their hunger. Yet nothing was farther from Beaumarchais' mind than flinging an insult or hurling a challenge at anyone. Although he made an indiscreet display of his prosperity, he wanted to be liked and esteemed by his fellow citizens and, above all, to be left in peace.

3. *A Fighter's Decline*

UNEXPECTED circumstances soon shattered Beaumarchais' quiet bourgeois hopes. The first incident to reveal his hitherto hidden weakness was a struggle with Mirabeau. Two engineers, the brothers Jacques and Auguste Périer, who were experts on machines but knew little about business, had obtained the concession of supplying filtered water to the city of Paris. They began building a large reservoir on the hill of Chaillot, and installing a giant pump powered by steam, but they ran short of funds before they could complete these works. They then called on Beaumarchais for help. He advised them to form a stock company, the Compagnie des Eaux de Paris, and he naturally became one of its main stockholders.

But a group of financiers, the best known of whom was Etienne Clavière, took a bearish attitude toward the stock of the new company and succeeded in bringing about a rapid drop in the price of the shares. Beaumarchais tried counter measures, and soon the value of the stock began to rise again. Clavière and his associates, now threatened with heavy losses, appealed to Mirabeau.

Mirabeau, who later became an outstanding leader in the revolutionary movement, was at that time hardly more than an adventurer. Aggressive, pugnacious, and reckless, he had already attracted popular attention by his bitter attacks upon the government. But oddly blended in his make-up were a genuine devotion to the cause of justice and an unashamed venality that allowed him to sell his influence and talent to the highest bidder. Recently he had borrowed large sums from Clavière.

Mirabeau wrote a pamphlet against La Compagnie des Eaux de Paris. Beaumarchais replied, but his reply was quite unlike his former memorials. It was moderate in tone, courteous, and reasonable. Only one small evidence of Beaumarchais' old flippancy and irony could be found in it: he called Mirabeau's accusations *des mirabelles*, after the French name for a rather commonplace and insipid variety of plum—meaning that Mirabeau's argument should be dismissed as being of trifling importance.

Mirabeau at once wrote a new pamphlet filled this time with brutal invective against Beaumarchais. The public took notice: Mirabeau against Beaumarchais—an entertaining dogfight was in the offing, no doubt. Then nothing happened, nothing at all. Beaumarchais did not answer. Had the old gladiator lost his mettle?

This was the signal for Beaumarchais' old enemies to creep out of their holes one by one. Kornman, who had kept out of sight for five years, now lifted his head again. After Mme Kornman's release from the prostitutes' jail, she had again tried to obtain a divorce. Kornman's main weakness in his struggle with his wife was his reputation of being a contemptible scoundrel. Beaumarchais' intervention in 1781 had shown beyond doubt that Kornman had tolerated and even encouraged his wife's misconduct in the hope of deriving material advantages for himself. Whatever wrongs she might have committed, almost everyone felt inclined to sympathize with her and to take sides against her husband.

Kornman engaged the services of a penniless, fearless, and publicity-seeking young attorney named Nicolas Bergasse. Bergasse decided to discredit the unsavory facts about his client brought to light through Beaumarchais' action by discrediting Beaumarchais himself. Yet he hesitated for quite a while before launching his attack: all Beaumarchais' adversaries had so far come out badly battered from their encounters with the champion. But when Beaumarchais unaccountably failed to answer Mirabeau's challenge, Bergasse hesitated no longer and decided to strike.

Early in 1786, a large number of short pamphlets were distributed in the streets of Paris. Some of them were signed Bergasse, others were anonymous, but all contained vicious accusations against Beaumarchais. The old familiar slanders—from the alleged murder of Francquet down to the Chevalier d'Eon affair—were recalled, and a few new ones added for good measure. This time, Beaumarchais could not possibly afford to remain silent.

At first, since Bergasse was attacking him on Kornman's behalf, Beaumarchais raked up all the muck he could find in Kornman's past life and spread it thickly. But Kornman's personality soon dwindled into insignificance. The Kornman conflict turned into a private war between Beaumarchais and Bergasse. Almost daily Bergasse and Beaumarchais exchanged vile insinuations and vitriolic insults in their pamphlets. As a rule, Beaumarchais' pamphlets showed better literary style than those of his opponent, but Bergasse's pamphlets offered more dirt. Bergasse won. He accused Beaumarchais, the Prince of Nassau-Siegen, and Lieutenant of Police Le Noir of having enjoyed Mme Kornman's intimate favors. There was not a shred of truth in the charge. But how could such an accusation be technically disproved? The Parisian public was jubilant.

Most of Beaumarchais' former antagonists joined the fray. Mirabeau, the Comte de Provence, and Suard wrote anonymously against him. The habitués of the literary cafés followed; then the noblemen who had been flayed in *Le Mariage de Figaro;* then the supporters of the Catholic Church who had been incensed by Beaumarchais' publication of Voltaire's work. Not since the Goëzman case had Beaumarchais found such a formidable coalition lined up against him.

Whereas at the time of the Goëzman case he had faced the storm unflinchingly, Beaumarchais now cringed. Much to the public's surprise, he begged the authorities to protect him from his aggressors, and sued Bergasse and Kornman for libel before the

Parliament of Paris. Complacently and condescendingly, the authorities gave him the protection he had requested. At the government's frown, the campaign of pamphlets against him abated. When the libel suits were heard by the Parliament, the public at first followed the legal proceedings with curiosity, but soon turned away in disgust. Beaumarchais, the challenger of the Maupeou Parliament, Beaumarchais the old rebel, the old rascal, was now on the side of the law! Things dragged until April 1789, when the Parliament finally passed sentences on the cases. Kornman and Bergasse were ordered to pay Beaumarchais damages. But when the verdict was announced, the crowd booed Beaumarchais and cheered Bergasse.

Shortly before then, Beaumarchais had taken up his manuscript of *La Mère coupable*, and introduced in it a character whom he named Bégearss. Bégearss was the epitome of perfidy, depravity and wickedness, a villain for a melodrama. Beaumarchais felt that if *La Mère coupable* one day attained a success in any way comparable to that of *Le Mariage de Figaro*, Bergasse would be dishonored forever. Yet this was at best an indirect and delayed riposte. The former lightning speed and force of his strokes were gone.

Beaumarchais did not fare any better in his efforts to obtain payment of the money the American Congress owed him. In 1783 Congress had instructed the American Consul General in Paris, Barclay, to look into the Beaumarchais problem. Barclay examined the contracts and the records of the deliveries. In the end he declared that the statement of accounts Silas Deane had given out two years before was substantially correct. He cut down a few minor items here and there, such as commissions and traveling expenses, but on the whole endorsed Beaumarchais' claims.

At that time, America opened negotiations with France to borrow six million livres. The loan was granted by the French, and the two governments then decided to review and clarify their past financial agreements. It was found that since 1778 France had directly lent America about eighteen million livres, part of which had been sent as military supplies. Furthermore, France had indirectly lent Congress ten million livres. This ten-million-livre loan had nominally been secured in Holland but actually France had had to guarantee the loan and was currently paying the Dutch the interest on the full amount. With the new loan of six million livres, the total indebtedness of the United States to France would be thirty-four million livres.

A separate statement of accounts was drawn up for the "gifts" the French gave America during the same period. Six million livres' worth of "free" supplies had been sent across the Atlantic. Moreover, before her recognition of the American government, France had given America three million livres in cash. For these nine million livres, France expected no refund.

Benjamin Franklin, who had been in charge of most of the financial transactions between the two countries during the war period, read over these accounts, approved them, signed them, and sent them to Congress without special comment. Some time later, however, a mystifying irregularity was uncovered in the accounts. In the statement of gifts made, it was said that the French government had given America three million livres in cash before recognizing the United States. But Franklin had acknowledged receipt of only two million livres, which had been handed him through the bankers Grand. To whom had the third million been paid?

The French government, queried on that subject, was very

embarrassed. The third million was the million that had been loaned to Beaumarchais on June 10, 1776, as initial capital for the Hortalez firm. The French government had never intended to include it in the list of "gifts." It had been mentioned only through a blunder of the Royal Treasury. The fact that money had been provided by the French government to promote the contraband of arms to America in 1776 and 1777 was still considered "top secret" in 1786, so the government simply refused to give the Americans any explanation of the matter.

The attitude of the French Ministry toward the American authorities on this problem was thoroughly friendly and courteous. The French pointed out that the million in question was an absolutely free gift and that no difficulty between the two nations could possibly arise on that score. The Americans realized that a slip had been made somewhere and took no exception to the French reticence, but they remained puzzled.

For years the affair of the "lost million" taxed the ingenuity and imagination of American financial experts. Naturally, it occurred to them that Beaumarchais had probably received the million, but since his name was never mentioned by the French officials, the members of Congress were reduced to suspicion and surmise. It was enough, however, to make them indefinitely postpone payment of all sums due him.

Beaumarchais, who had not been in the confidence of the French Ministry for many years, was not informed of these new complications. He knew only that the United States were putting their house in order financially. He asked Congress once more to liquidate his account, but received no answer.

Thoroughly exasperated, he wrote on June 12, 1787, a letter

to Congress which was worded in the stiffest terms: "A people that has become sovereign and powerful," he said, "may perhaps be allowed to consider gratitude a virtue good for individuals but beneath the realm of politics. But nothing dispenses a state from being fair and particularly from paying its debts."

This time Congress responded to Beaumarchais' taunt: Arthur Lee was appointed to examine his accounts. Lee went gloatingly to work, and obtained startling results. According to his report, Congress did not owe Beaumarchais anything at all; Beaumarchais, on the contrary, owed Congress 1,800,000 livres.

Beaumarchais tried to forget his disappointment by contemplating a poetic future. After he had finished his libretto for *Tarare*, he had resumed negotiations with Gluck. Gluck, however, had politely declared that he was much too old to compose the musical score of so important a work, but that one of his best pupils, Antonio Salieri, an Italian living in Vienna, would no doubt gladly undertake the task.

Salieri and Beaumarchais reached an agreement soon. Salieri came to Paris and received a comfortable lodging at the Hôtel de Hollande. Beaumarchais overwhelmed his guest with kind attentions, but left the composer no independence whatever. He wanted the music completely subservient to the "philosophical" text he had written. Salieri, by nature compliant and weak, gave in without a struggle. The result was an extremely banal and flat musical score. Since the text itself was far from a masterpiece, the total effect was definitely feeble.

When *Tarare* was presented at the Paris Opéra, however, this fundamental weakness was completely masked by the gorgeousness of the show. All the tinsel picturesqueness of an artificial, theatrical

East had been lavishly used to create a gaudy, glittering pageant, and the maudlin plot unfolded smoothly before the eyes of an enraptured audience.

The first performance had been scheduled for June 8, 1787. Beaumarchais feared that the animosity created against him by the Kornman-Bergasse campaign would have unfavorable repercussions on his play, and begged the administration of the Opéra to postpone the *première*. In view of the huge expenses already laid out for the staging of *Tarare*, however, the administration of the Opéra decided to proceed with the original plans.

Beaumarchais' fears proved utterly unfounded. The public basked in *Tarare*'s easy, optimistic, and sentimental "philosophy." Indeed, everyone in France at that time felt that great changes were forthcoming. Most people, including Beaumarchais, wanted to believe that these changes would take place in an atmosphere of justice and brotherly love. "Tyranny" would be abolished, and "merit" would be given its due. A new Golden Age was about to appear on earth. It would rise, they hoped, suddenly and spectacularly, as in an opera, like a pure and resplendent dawn.

Chapter 10

REVOLUTION

1. *Storm and Stress*

THE EXPECTED great change did not begin as a resplendent and golden dawn. It came rumbling as a dark crepuscular storm. Beaumarchais watched its first fulgurations from an attic window of his unfinished house in the Faubourg Saint-Antoine as the people of Paris attacked the old fortress of the Bastille. He could see long, sulphurous flames darting from the guns at the top of the crenelated towers, while down below masses of men and women hurled themselves heroically and fanatically against the stone symbol of a detested past.

Beaumarchais was filled with both elation and alarm. For him, as for everyone in Europe, the fall of the Bastille marked the beginning of a new era. He did not regret the collapse of what the

Bastille had stood for. He wholeheartedly welcomed the triumph in France of the ideas of justice and freedom he had already hailed in the American Revolution. A bourgeois revolution, however, would have fully satisfied him. He hated the sight of the howling mobs carrying the heads of aristocrats at the ends of their blood-stained pikes. At the same time, he felt an immense enthusiasm surging all over France, and, in the French people, a deep and genuine desire to sweep the whole world clean of prejudice and oppression.

In the meantime, Paris needed bread. In September 1789 the rumor spread that Beaumarchais had huge stores of wheat hidden in his new house. To scotch the rumor, he asked the officials of his district to search the building from roof to cellar. Although no wheat was found in it, suspicions against its owner lingered on. Beaumarchais blamed his old foes for his new troubles, whereas the opulence of his mansion was enough to arouse the envy and distrust of his hungry and angry neighbors.

Beaumarchais now had two residences. Did he belong to the Blancs-Manteaux district, where the Hôtel de Hollande was situated, or was he a member of the Sainte-Marguerite district, where his Faubourg Saint-Antoine house stood? Both districts claimed him because he gave large sums of money to the poor. It must be said that his charitable gifts were not prompted by kindness of heart: they were propitiatory offerings to the starving and wrathful mobs.

When it became known that he had decided to give up the Hôtel de Hollande and to settle in the Faubourg Saint-Antoine, some people in the Blancs-Manteaux district, resenting his departure, accused him of having been expelled by the local authorities.

This was a grave accusation, for it placed him automatically among the "suspects." He had to go through long and tedious formalities to have it officially established that he had never been expelled, and had left the Blancs-Manteaux district on his own accord. He had the compensation—and it was an expensive one—of being welcomed with open arms by all the famished *citoyens* of the Sainte-Marguerite district, and their name was legion.

After the hectic final months of 1789, France went through a phase of comparative calm that lasted about two years. The crops of 1790 and 1791 were good, and there was no more talk of famine. The Constituent Assembly was working steadily and hopefully to build a new France. Confidence and optimism prevailed throughout the country.

Beaumarchais was now contentedly settled in his big house, the showplace of the Faubourg Saint-Antoine. People wrote to him for permission to visit his abode of luxury and wealth. Tickled with pride, he granted permission liberally, and visitors gazed with naïve wonder at the building's two hundred windows, and admired the sumptuous magnificence of the garden—a private garden with a pond!

Although Paul Gudin remained his best friend, a *bon bourgeois* named Gomel, who lived near by on the Rue des Trois Pavillons, became increasingly important in Beaumarchais' circle. The banker Alphonse Perregaux was also counted among Beaumarchais' intimates. More than once, the two put their heads together to execute an advantageous financial coup.

As a rule, Beaumarchais no longer launched large-scale enterprises. His only ambitious undertaking during this period was the clearing up of the remains of the Bastille. The bulk of the huge fortress had been pulled down by a contractor named Pierre-François Palloy, but a mass of rubble had been left lying about. As the debris was washed away by the rains, it threatened to clog the sewers and cause a disastrous flooding of the whole district. Thanks to Beaumarchais' skillful, practical measures, everything was disposed of without mishap.

Beaumarchais was now strongly handicapped in any type of work by his deafness. Often he pretended to hear what was said to him when, in fact, even with his ear trumpet he could perceive only a faint and indistinct murmur. Comical misunderstanding inevitably resulted, but his appreciation of the comic stopped at his own deficiency, and he would fly into a rage when his replies caused amazement or amusement in his interlocutors.

Nevertheless, even under those circumstances, he retained a certain amount of personal charm. In 1790, at the age of fifty-eight, he had a new affair with a young woman in her twenties, Amélie Houret de La Marinière. Amélie Houret had a pretty, saucy face, large brown eyes, a luscious mouth, and a knowledge of the ways and byways of love that soon completely turned her poor beau's graying head. That she was something of an adventuress is, of course, obvious; yet she was not mercenary, and she seems to have been genuinely fond of her oldish and foolish admirer. They were both so careful to keep their liaison a secret that it never disturbed Mme Beaumarchais' peace of mind or Beaumarchais' own domestic happiness.

Beaumarchais' only causes for worry were the vague fears he still had of his political enemies. Bergasse had been elected a member of the Constituent Assembly and was not without influence in high places; yet he made no attempt, at least openly, to harm his former antagonist. But around that time Beaumarchais clashed with another powerful man, Jacques Manuel, the Procurator of the Commune of Paris. Beaumarchais had been asked by mistake to pay the municipal taxes on his house, which he had already paid. He sarcastically pointed out the error to Manuel, who was nominally responsible for the blunder, and added offensive comments on the way municipal affairs in general were handled. Later he heard that Manuel had taken these strictures very badly indeed. As the political influence of the Commune of Paris grew by leaps and bounds, he realized that, for a trifling matter, he had brought upon himself an enmity that might one day prove disastrous.

For the time being, however, tranquillity reigned, and the mood of the country was hopeful. To fit that mood, the Opéra decided to revive *Tarare*. Beaumarchais hurriedly altered a number of passages in his libretto to include allusions to contemporary problems, generally in a bourgeois spirit of moderation and compromise. Thus, at the end of the play, the hero Tarare was made a Constitutional King, and received about the same powers the Constituent Assembly then gave Louis XVI. It goes without saying that the kindly Salieri made all the changes in the music that the changes in the text required.

The revised opera was presented on August 3, 1790. A few extremists on the left as well as on the right were displeased and hissed; but the middle-of-the-road program advocated in the new version of *Tarare* was favorably received by the majority of the audience.

Soon afterward, Beaumarchais became fully reconciled with Mirabeau. For months Mirabeau had fought in the Constituent Assembly to establish precisely the type of liberal bourgeois régime that Beaumarchais thought ideal. But exhausted by the thousand excesses he had indulged in during his tempestuous life, Mirabeau now longed for a rest. It happened that the monastery near Vincennes where Beaumarchais used to stop on his way home from school, when he was a young boy, was then up for sale. Its rural setting and quiet, serene atmosphere made it a perfect haven for the weary and worn-out tribune; but he learned that Beaumarchais intended to buy the old place for himself.

In September 1790 Mirabeau wrote to his former enemy. Admitting that he could not compete with Beaumarchais financially, he told him that the monastery would be an ideal retreat in which to spend his last days. With utmost courtesy, Beaumarchais replied that, under such circumstances, he would give up the idea of acquiring the property; moreover, he offered to help Mirabeau if he needed money for the purchase. He added only one small request: if Mirabeau became the owner of the monastery, he would be very grateful to receive from him the painting representing the Last Judgment, to which he had been so attached in his early boyhood. In this Mirabeau cordially acquiesced. Their correspondence had now taken a truly friendly tone. But Mirabeau died six months later, and Beaumarchais soon had to attend to other and more important cares.

The problem of actor-playwright relations, which had been left untouched since the compromise of 1780, was taken up again by the Constituent Assembly at the end of 1790, and Beaumarchais was naturally consulted. Complicated discussions and negotiations followed. Finally, Beaumarchais, Sedaine, and La Harpe were invited to submit a report to the Assembly. The conclusion of their report was that the actors' special privileges should be purely and simply abolished. These views were accepted and made into law by the Constituent Assembly in January, 1791. Beaumarchais seemed to have won one more of his innumerable fights. Yet it soon appeared that there were more angles to the question than Beaumarchais or the Assembly had been able to foresee. Serious difficulties cropped up almost at once in the application of the new law, and they were not to be solved until years later, by Napoleon.

In February 1791 Beaumarchais offered *La Mère coupable* to the actors of the Comédie Française. They did not dare reject the work of the famous and powerful playwright, but Beaumarchais sensed their animosity against him so strongly that he soon requested them to return his manuscript. Eventually he reached an agreement with the Théâtre du Marais, which was very accommodating, but also definitely second-rate. *La Mère coupable* was presented on June 6, 1792, and fell flat. The mediocre performance given by the inexperienced actors was partly responsible for the failure; but, above all, the public was no longer in the mood to wallow in the sentimentality of a cheap and lachrymose drama.

Indeed, after a lull of two years, violent revolutionary agitation had broken out once more in Paris. The Constitution of 1791 elaborated by the Constituent Assembly, while introducing many fair and sound reforms, had added to the country's old difficulties several new and almost insoluble problems. The Legislative Assembly, which had met for the first time on October 1, 1791, was now struggling helplessly with two of these problems.

The Constitution of 1791 had given the King the right of Veto. Through his Veto, he could block any decision taken by the Legislative Assembly, and so practically paralyze the whole machinery of the government. But Louis XVI was known to be good-natured and weak. When he made use of the Veto, Marie-Antoinette, who now had her husband completely under her thumb, was blamed for all the mischief. Eventually, as "Madame Veto," she became the object of fierce, blind hatred.

The second problem concerned religious differences. The Constitution Civile du Clergé, which had been appended to the Constitution of 1791, was splitting the nation and the Church itself into two hostile camps. Feelings ran high on both sides, and it was obvious that any fiery incident might cause a disastrous conflagration.

For several years, Beaumarchais' young daughter Eugénie had attended the fashionable school of the Couvent du Bon Secours. At the end of the 1791 school year, he withdrew her from the convent, for he was anxious to take her away from a probable center of conflict. But as he did not want to take sides in the conflict, he declared that his move had been prompted by the fact that the girl was now approaching marriageable age. So great was his reputation for wealth that he was immediately swamped with requests for her hand. Eugénie was only thirteen years old.

Clashes between opposing factions were now spreading throughout France. A large number of aristocrats, feeling threatened, decided to go abroad. Many of these *émigrés* were able military men, and the fighting strength of the French army was gravely impaired by their departure. Soon the governments in Vienna and Berlin felt that these circumstances provided them with a golden opportunity to "re-establish order" in France and also, by the way, to take one or two French provinces. At the same time, the French were carried away by a wave of mystic revolutionary exaltation. If war broke out, they would call all the oppressed people in the world to arms. On December 18, 1791, Representative Isnard prophesied at the Club des Jacobins: "The people of France will utter a great cry, and all the other people will respond. Fighters will cover the earth, and the enemies of freedom will be wiped out."

In Paris, riots had become daily occurrences. The Faubourg Saint-Antoine was a hotbed of extremists, and a center of tumult. Beaumarchais therefore decided to send his family to Le Hâvre. Compared to Paris, Le Hâvre was almost quiet, and, if worst came to worst, the women could easily leave from there for England. England was almost the only European country where a large part of public opinion openly and heartily supported the revolutionary movement in France. On the other hand, England was thought to be exhausted by her recent struggle with America. Even in case of war on the Continent, England, Beaumarchais believed, would certainly remain neutral and safe.

Beaumarchais himself remained tied to Paris by a most hazardous affair. The French arsenals were hopelessly short of muskets, enormous quantities of which had been sent a few years earlier to America. Owing to the plight of the French treasury, and also because war had then seemed unlikely, they had been replaced only in woefully inadequate numbers. Now, suddenly, the Ministry of War found itself confronted with the prospect of general hostilities starting almost any moment. The French artillery was, thanks to Gribeauval, the best in Eurpoe, and there was no dearth of man power in France. But muskets had to be procured at any cost and quickly.

It happened at this time that old but serviceable muskets were for sale in Holland. About two years earlier, at the end of

1789, a serious uprising had taken place in the Province of Brabant and in the Bishopric of Liége, which were then, like the rest of Belgium, under Austrian rule. The revolt had been crushed by the Austrian troops, however, and all weapons taken away from the insurgents.

A Brussels bookseller named Delahaye, who belonged to the pro-Austrian party, had had some of his property burned by the rioters. After the rebellion was quelled, he asked the Vienna government to grant him an indemnity for his losses. The government was most willing to give him an indemnity, but most unwilling to untie the strings of the imperial purse. Then an official in Vienna hit upon a clever scheme: Delahaye would be given all the arms taken from the rebels in the Province of Brabant; he would be allowed to sell them at his own profit, provided the sale took place outside Belgium. The Vienna administration would thus not only reward a faithful subject without spending a single thaler, but also get rid of all the weapons that had caused so much trouble recently.

But the Vienna government had already sold on credit about 50,000 guns to a Dutch merchant from Rotterdam named Ozy van Zequewart. He had transported the guns to Terweren,* a small Dutch seaport in Zeeland, but he had encountered so many difficulties in trying to dispose of them that he was only too glad to cancel the deal in favor of Delahaye. So Delahaye found himself the owner of about 200,000 muskets. Of that number, 50,000 were in Terweren, still nominally in Ozy van Zequewart's possession. The others were in various Austrian arsenals throughout Belgium.

Hearing that France was short of guns, Delahaye naturally

* Terweren or Tervere—called today Veere or Vere—is situated in Walcheren island.

thought of her as a prospective customer. He realized, however, that in view of the impending war between Austria and France, it might not be easy to transfer to French territory the muskets stored in Austrian arsenals. But the muskets in Zeeland could be shipped to France at once. Delahaye was a friend of Jacques Guilbert de La Hogue, Beaumarchais' former general manager at Kehl. Moreover, he knew that Beaumarchais had dealt in contraband arms on a huge scale to the time of the American war. Early in March 1792 he went to Paris and offered him his Terweren guns.

At first Beaumarchais emphatically declined the offer: he had lost too much money on American supplies. But Delahaye shrewdly applied moral pressure. France needed the guns. What would the people say if it became known that Beaumarchais had refused to get them? There were exactly 52,345 guns, all in good condition, complete with bayonets, packed in 922 crates and 25 barrels. They were cheap: only five florins apiece. Without further ado, they could be put aboard any ship calling at Terweren.

Patriotism? Fear of public opinion? Beaumarchais gave in. He went to see the Minister of War, Pierre de Grave, who jumped at the opportunity of acquiring muskets. The banker Perregaux agreed to finance the deal. Beaumarchais received 500,000 francs in assignats and gave as guarantee 750,000 francs' worth of securities, which were deposited in Switzerland. The formal contract between the various interested parties was signed on March 16, 1792.

The expected war between France on one side and Austria and Prussia on the other broke out on April 20, 1792. Holland was not directly involved in the conflict, but if the guns were made available to the French, Vienna and Berlin would undoubtedly say that the Dutch were helping France. On the other hand, if shipment of the muskets was forbidden, Paris would protest, and declare that the Dutch were siding with Prussia and Austria. After a certain amount of cogitation, the Dutch government decided to fall back on red tape. When the agent Beaumarchais had sent to Terweren asked for delivery of the arms, he was told that all sorts of formalities had to be gone through first. Time dragged and dragged, the phlegmatic Dutch being more than ever averse to hustle and hurry.

Beaumarchais' agent in Holland appealed to the French Minister at the Hague, Emmanuel de Maulde, for help. The French Minister asked Paris to send him definite instructions about the guns, but in vain. The Paris government was now in a state of hysteria. Pierre de Grave had fallen from office in April,1792. After him, Joseph Servan, then Charles Dumouriez, then Pierre Lajard then Charles d'Abancourt, then Servan again were, within only four months, successively Minister of War.

Each time there was a change Beaumarchais had to go to the Ministry of War, the Ministry of Finances, and the Ministry of Foreign Affairs, to explain anew the circumstances and conditions of the gun deal. But, on March 23, his old enemy, Etienne Clavière, became Finance Minister, and slyly contrived to put as many spokes in Beaumarchais' wheels as he could. Beaumarchais also had to contend with the ill-will of Clavière's close friend, Pierre Lebrun, who held an important position at the Ministry of Foreign Affairs.

In the end, Beaumarchais obtained a passport to Holland for La Hogue. The Dutch government then suggested that the guns be sold to a neutral country. Beaumarchais refused. He now wanted a passport to Holland for himself. He felt sure that if he could only get to Terweren, he would somehow be able to secure the delivery of the guns. Everyone in the Ministries of War, Finances, and Foreign Affairs had heard—and heard many times—the story of the Terweren guns, and looked upon Beaumarchais as a nuisance and a pest.

Indeed, for everyone, except for Beaumarchais, the portentous political and military events then taking place completely overshadowed the fate of a few old muskets. The Prussian and Austrian armies were pouring across the borders of France, and the French troops, utterly demoralized, were falling back. In most encounters so far, the French soldiers had fled after a few shots, shouting: "Treason! Treason!"

It is known today that Louis XVI and Marie-Antoinette had secretly communicated the French plan of campaign to the Austrians. In the spring of 1792 the collusion between the King and the enemies of France was only a matter of conjecture, though Louis XVI's systematic use of the Veto to prevent the Legislative Assembly's emergency measures of national defense from being put into effect seemed to corroborate the worst suspicions in this regard. Extremely violent and frequent demonstrations against the Veto and the King were staged in Paris throughout June and July 1792.

Then, on August 1, news came that the Duke of Brunswick, commanding the victorious Prussian army, had issued a Manifesto threatening Paris with "military execution and total subversion" if Louis XVI and his family were "insulted" again by the French crowds. This Manifesto was interpreted as blatant, irrefutable proof of the King's connivance with the enemy.

was at the time. They had received word that some weapons might be found in the Gomels' house on the Rue des Trois Pavillons.

Gudin knew that Beaumarchais was hiding there. Although the men of the patrol were not trying to arrest Beaumarchais, Gudin nevertheless went along with them to forestall any misunderstanding or accident. After the Gomel house was cleared of suspicion, he rescued Beaumarchais from his cupboard and reassured him. "Upon my word," Beaumarchais wrote, "I pressed my forehead in my hands to be certain I was not asleep and dreaming."

On the following day Beaumarchais returned home. The whole city had now fallen prey to mass hysteria. The King, the Queen, and their friends had been in league with the enemy. Treason was everywhere. All aristocrats were suspect. They were plotting, it was said, to strike the patriots in the back while the Prussians and Austrians were attacking in front. There was neither means nor time to find out who was guilty and who was not among their number. The plot had to be nipped in the bud. Arrests upon arrests were ordered by the panicky officials, and hundreds of noblemen were imprisoned. When the regular prisons were filled, the suspects were herded into monasteries, such as Les Carmes and L'Abbaye Saint-Germain, which were turned into emergency jails.

On August 23, 1792, Beaumarchais was arrested for having concealed muskets somewhere. He was first taken to the City Hall for preliminary questioning by the delegates of the Commune. Almost completely deaf now, he understood nothing of the charges made against him and replied at cross-purposes. The audience began to laugh, and Beaumarchais was about to be released, when the sanguinary extremist, Marat, jumped to his feet. In a harsh, croaking voice, he reminded the delegates that leniency under the present circumstances was a crime against the country. A dead silence fell on the room, and Beaumarchais was sent to L'Abbaye.

He was placed in a small cell crowded with a dozen other suspects, all of whom were noblemen. They showed him complete, though well-bred contempt. For a week they utterly ignored the presence in their midst of the man who had contributed more than his share to the rise of the revolutionary spirit.

On August 30, late in the afternoon, a guard came to fetch Beaumarchais. The Procurator of the Commune, Manuel, wished to see him—Manuel, the man he had mocked, taunted, and ridiculed two years earlier. Beaumarchais stepped out of his cell with as much calm as he could muster, but he was ready for death.

Manuel told Beaumarchais that he was free. Free? Yes, free. Manuel had come to free him. Beaumarchais could hardly believe what he heard. When he was sure he understood rightly, he was overwhelmed with emotion, confusion, and gratitude. Here was Manuel, his personal enemy, bringing him freedom, bringing him life. Mankind was indeed better than Beaumarchais had ever dared hope if it could produce such a magnanimous and noble soul. Manuel accepted these effusive, tearful thanks with becoming modesty and casualness: Beaumarchais' arrest had been a mistake, and it was only natural that the mistake should be corrected.

Beaumarchais did not know that his mistress, Amélie Houret, was also Manuel's mistress. Amélie had naturally let each of her admirers believe that he was the only one. Yet, despite her unconventional views on life and love, she was certainly a kindhearted woman. When she had heard that Beaumarchais' life was in danger, she had at once contrived means—known only to herself—to *make* Manuel save the old man.

Beaumarchais had been badly shaken by his jail experience. For some time his thoughts had been concentrated on the Terweren guns. Now the idea that he had to get these guns at all costs became an obsession. No sooner was he liberated from L'Abbaye than he rushed to the Ministry of War, where he was told that the Minister Servan was away. He then dashed to the Ministry of Foreign Affairs. Since August 11, Pierre Lebrun had been Minister of Foreign Affairs. Beaumarchais somehow managed to be received by him immediately. Once admitted into Lebrun's presence, he began to shout, as excited deaf men often do, and to gesticulate wildly. Lebrun was kind enough to the poor fellow, who looked utterly distraught, with his clothing rumpled and dirty, and with a week-old gray beard. But being busy, he mumbled a few vague courteous words, and in a friendly but firm manner pushed Beaumarchais out of the room.

Next, Beaumarchais ran to the City Hall. He wanted to be exculpated from all possible accusations. But he found an atmosphere of tenseness and dread. What could be done with that ludicrous fool and his ear trumpet? The clerks used the time-honored administrative trick of sending him from one office to another. When the City Hall closed its doors, Beaumarchais was forced to leave. For hours, all alone, he roamed the narrow, dark streets. At two o'clock in the morning, he turned up at his own house. Philippe Gudin had moved in temporarily, to keep an eye on the premises. He was frightened by Beaumarchais' appearance, for his eyes had a fixed and vacant stare like those of a sleepwalker. Mechanically, as though in a trance, Beaumarchais washed his hands and face, shaved, changed clothes, then went out again before daybreak.

Beaumarchais walked all the way to Versailles, where he had friends who would give him shelter. Indeed, his friends welcomed him as best they could. For three days he remained in a little lodge on their estate, worn out with emotion and fatigue.

Then he heard of the frightful September Massacres. On September 2, news reached Paris that Verdun had been surrounded by the Prussians. A wave of panic and madness swept over the city. Mobs broke into the prisons and monasteries where the suspects were detained and, under the pretext of disposing of the would-be traitors, indiscriminately slaughtered, after a mere pretense of judgment, about eleven hundred aristocrats.

At this juncture, Beaumarchais' reason snapped. "In my brains," he later stated, "I felt a hammering as in a glowing forge. I thought I was becoming insane." He fancied that murderers were on his tracks. In the evening of September 4, he stealthily left his friends' lodge. For hours he trod through plowed fields and country lanes, until, exhausted, covered with mud, haggard, and disheveled, he came to a farmhouse. The farmers had in the last few days seen a number of poor devils fleeing for their lives. They asked Beaumarchais no questions, but gave him a bowl of warm soup, and let him spend the night in their barn.

The following morning, the farmers, with their stolid indifference to the ebb and flow of French politics, prepared to take their vegetables to the Paris markets as usual. Beaumarchais entrusted them with a message for Lebrun, asking the Minister to grant him a new interview about the Terweren guns. The farmers faithfully delivered the message at the Ministry of War. Perhaps out of pity, Lebrun let Gudin know that he would receive Beaumarchais in the afternoon. But Gudin was unable to establish contact with Beaumarchais in time that day.

The day after, Beaumarchais set out for Paris on foot. Once more he walked across fields, for he was afraid of being assassinated if he followed the highway. He reached Lebrun's residence in the evening and knocked at the door. A servant came, and told him that the Minister was busy. Couldn't Beaumarchais postpone his visit until later, much later? Beaumarchais returned at half-past eleven, only to be informed that Lebrun had gone to bed and could see no one.

Torn between fear and anger, Beaumarchais gained his own lodging. Gudin assured him that order and calm had been restored in Paris, and it would be perfectly safe for him to remain there. But he stayed there only two more weeks.

For two weeks, he almost daily pestered Servan, Lebrun, Clavière, and even Danton, who was Minister of Justice and the dominant figure in the recently formed Conseil Exécutif Provisoire. Danton could not help laughing at the sight of a man like Beaumarchais who, having had such a narrow escape from death, was insistently drawing attention upon himself instead of holding his peace and trying to be forgotten. But Danton seems to have believed, and to have convinced his colleagues that Beaumarchais' naïve and untimely zeal was proof of his good faith. Perhaps they all merely wanted to get the old bore out of the way. In any case, on September 18, 1792, Beaumarchais was given an official order of mission to Holland. The order was signed Lebrun, Servan, Danton, Clavière.

2. Wild Wanderings

ON SEPTEMBER 22, 1792, Beaumarchais left Paris for Le Hâvre. On arriving there, he learned that, two days before, the French army under Dumouriez and Kellermann had won a decisive battle over the Prussians at Valmy. The casualties on both sides had not been large, but the Prussian officers had been able to judge the value of the Gribeauval guns. Moreover, when they saw the fanatical *élan* of the French revolutionary troops, they realized that a new and irresistible force had appeared on the battlefields of Europe. The Duke of Brunswick beat a hasty retreat.

Mme Beaumarchais then decided to return to Paris. The victory of Valmy had ended the truly critical phase of the war—so, at least, it was thought. The struggle would go on, with many vicissitudes, but no panic such as the one that had caused the tragic events of early September was to be feared in the future. The Convention, which had succeeded the Legislative Assembly on September 21, was taking matters capably and firmly in hand. Beaumarchais agreed with his wife that the capital would be as safe as Le Hâvre for herself, and probably much safer for their daughter.

Their daughter had fallen in love at Le Hâvre. Eugénie was sixteen years old, and her admirer, André de La Rue, was a young officer of twenty-five. André de La Rue, who had prudently spelled his name Delarue since the Revolution, had never been opposed to moderate and fair reforms in the social and political organization of France. He was the brother-in-law of General Mathieu Dumas,*

* Not related to the father of the famous novelist bearing the same name, who was also a general in the French revolutionary army.

who had been a member of the French expeditionary force under Rochambeau's command, and a personal friend of La Fayette. Partly through his family connections, he himself belonged to a group of military men who had been strongly influenced by liberal American ideas and, like most of them, had a decided distaste for insubordination, illegality, and violence. When, in 1792, bitter internecine conflicts and savage street riots had plunged the country into a state of near anarchy, he had made up his mind to leave for England. He had been waiting at Le Hâvre for an opportunity to sail away when he had met Mlle Eugénie Beaumarchais. Youth and springtime had done the rest.

Beaumarchais did not disapprove of André Delarue as a person, but he was aware that Delarue intended to become an *émigré*. Everyone knew that the fate of an *émigré*'s wife was not an enviable one. Mme Beaumarchais and her husband agreed that the best was to separate Eugénie and André at least temporarily. Eugénie had a difficult temper. She could be as impulsive and highly emotional as her father, and as mulishly stubborn as her mother. Yet she could not rebel against her parents' natural and sensible decision to return home to Paris. She said good-by to André Delarue with a heavy heart; and, before parting, the lovers swore eternal fidelity to each other.

After settling this awkward family problem for the time being, Beaumarchais sailed for England on September 28. He remained in London only a few days and, while there, he borrowed £1200—about 30,000 francs at the prevailing rate of exchange—from an English merchant who knew and trusted him. The discreet Englishman did not ask any questions about the way he intended to use this considerable sum.

Beaumarchais reached Amsterdam on October 7, 1792. He encountered there the same difficulties that his agent had. He could achieve nothing without the assistance of the French Minister in Holland, who had still not received orders from Paris concerning the Terweren guns. Beaumarchais waited in Holland for approximately six weeks. Then, early in December, letters from Paul Gudin and Manuel brought him alarming news.

After Louis XVI's downfall, his private papers had been seized and searched. Written proof of his long-suspected collusion with France's enemies had been found, and it had been decided that he would be tried for treason. Among the documents uncovered by the investigation were the letters Beaumarchais had sent the King in 1775 to exhort him to intervene in the Anglo-American conflict. Although the letters contained nothing that was reprehensible, one fact was taken in consideration: Beaumarchais had had a regular and secret correspondence with the King.

On November 28, 1792, one of the Representatives of the Convention, Laurent Lecointre, publicly denounced Beaumarchais as a suspect. Beaumarchais' letters to Louis XVI were not used as grounds of accusation, though they certainly prejudiced the Convention against him. But the affair of the Terweren guns, which Beaumarchais had for months been dinning into everybody's ears, now seemed extremely suspicious. Without further investigation, he was arraigned for "collusion and fraud." Pending regular trial, official seals were placed on his private papers in his house.

Through the same mail, Paul Gudin let him know that a still more confidential message was awaiting him in London, where he was urged to go immediately. In London, Beaumarchais learned from a letter written by Manuel that a secret agent had been dispatched by the police to Holland to lure him back to France. On the way to Paris, at Lille, the agent was to stir up a riot in which Beaumarchais would be "accidentally" killed.

Beaumarchais' first impulse was to rush to Paris to clear himself and confound his attackers; but the English merchant who had lent him £1200 three months before stepped in. The Englishman felt certain that Beaumarchais was honest, but felt no less certain that if he returned to France now, he would be a dead man. The Englishman liked Beaumarchais and was sorry for him. Yet if Beaumarchais chose to cross the Channel, that was strictly his own affair. But what about the £1200?

The Englishman then decided to take a step that would both satisfy his friendship and protect his pocketbook: he had Beaumarchais arrested and locked up at King's Bench for debt. He had only kind feelings toward Beaumarchais. He pointed out to him that by preventing him from leaving England he was probably saving his life—though, of course, if Beaumarchais paid the £1200, he would be free to go wherever he pleased.

From jail Beaumarchais wrote his wife and Paul Gudin frantic letters: he had to have £1200 at once. Gudin and Mme Beaumarchais set about collecting that sum, but it took them some time before they could scrape together 30,000 francs. Meanwhile Beaumarchais wrote a long memorial in which he explained in great detail all his actions during what he called "the nine most painful months in my life."

In Paris, Mme Beaumarchais not only did her best to procure the money her husband needed; she also harassed the authorities to have Beaumarchais' name stricken from the list of suspects until he had a chance to present his defense. Mme Beaumarchais, who had appeared somewhat insignificant and dull before the revolutionary crisis, now revealed herself consistently resourceful and stanch. Her request was granted, and on February 10, 1793, Beaumarchais was given a two-month delay within which he would have to come to Paris and justify himself. At the same time, the official seals were removed from his house.

When, at long last, Beaumarchais received the 30,000 francs from Paris, paid his debt, and was set free, the English merchant, feeling remorse for the trouble he had caused his friend, asked Beaumarchais if he could help him in any way. The political outlook in Europe was rapidly darkening. After Valmy, the victorious French armies had driven the Prussians and Austrians out of France, and had entered Austrian territory in Belgium. It was probable that Holland would soon be involved in the war. What would happen in that case to the guns stored at Terweren? Would the English merchant agree to become—for a consideration, of course, and for a limited time only—the nominal owner of the guns? If the guns were the property of a "neutral" businessman, they would be safe from possible confiscation by the Dutch.

To oblige Beaumarchais, the Englishman accepted this proposal, though very reluctantly. In any case, he did not want to assume the responsibility of keeping the guns for a long time. It was stipulated in their contract that if after two months Beaumarchais had not taken the muskets, he would have to pay the Englishman an extremely heavy penalty proportionate to the delay involved.

Upon his return to Paris, Beaumarchais completed and published the memorial he had composed in London. The memorial, which was addressed to Lecointre, did not show Beaumarchais the writer at his best. It was dull, meticulous, and technical; yet it was convincing. Lecointre, realizing that he had made a mistake, withdrew his charge. When Beaumarchais appeared before the Convention, he was immediately exonerated.

Once more Beaumarchais turned his attention to his muskets. Within the last weeks, the international situation had changed dramatically. Louis XVI had been tried, condemned to death, and, on January 21, 1793, guillotined. According to Danton, France had "thrown the head of a King as a challenge to Europe." Europe—particularly the Kings of Europe—took up the challenge, and formed a powerful coalition to crush the French Republic. Britain and Holland, among other nations, were now at war with France.

Both the British and the Dutch, aware of the existence of the guns at Terweren, were ready to buy them for their own use. But the English merchant, faithful to his pledge to Beaumarchais, came forward: these guns belonged to him, and he did not want to sell them to anybody. Such was the respect for private property in those days that no attempt was made to requisition the arms against the owner's will. Nevertheless, the English sent a warship to Terweren, and for a year and a half the ship remained at anchor there, keeping watch on the guns.

The French now needed guns more than ever. To fight against the allied armies once more invading France from all sides, men and still more men were called to the colors, but they lacked clothing and arms. A gigantic effort was made to procure muskets, bayonets, gunpowder, and cannon as speedily as possible. On March 25, 1793, the Convention created the Committee of Public Safety to co-ordinate and enforce all measures of national defense. In April, the Committee was reorganized under Danton's leadership.

Danton called Beaumarchais before the Committee, and on May 10, 1793, Beaumarchais received a new order of mission: he was to bring the Terweren guns to France. Holland and England were enemy countries. He would have to snatch the arms from the Dutch under the nose of the English—not an easy matter, to be sure. But Beaumarchais had the reputation of being a clever man, and he said he was a patriot. Here was a chance for him to prove both. Certain material difficulties, however, could not be overlooked by the Committee of Public Safety. The sum that had been earmarked in March 1792 for the purchase of the guns was no longer adequate: French paper money was depreciating rapidly. Perregaux came to the rescue, and promised to place 104,000 Dutch florins at Beaumarchais' disposal in Basel.

When everything seemed ready, Beaumarchais suddenly became ill. The intense nervous strain to which he had been subjected for a year began to tell on his health, and he went to Orléans for a rest. His niece, Tonton's daughter, was now married and lived there. After three weeks of quiet, he felt strong enough to sail for England. He carried a passport bearing the name Pierre Charron.

Beaumarchais arrived in London on June 28, 1793. London was filled with French refugees. Almost every day, men and women crossed the Channel, usually by stealth and in small groups, often under the most unexpected disguises. They were allowed to land in Britain without difficulty. The British knew that spies were entering the country at the same time, but it was not easy for the police to tell a skilled secret agent from a bona fide fugitive. Beaumarchais easily eluded all awkward inquiries and communicated with the English merchant who nominally owned his guns.

The merchant was glad to be relieved of his responsibility

and no less glad, it seems, to relieve Beaumarchais of his money. They had agreed that he would be entitled to a large indemnity if the guns were not taken off his hands within two months, and more than six months had elapsed. Beaumarchais naturally paid the stipulated sum.

Beaumarchais then went to Terweren. The guns were still there, and so was the British warship. After probing the situation, he decided upon the following stratagem: he would again make a fictitious sale. For a handsome commission, he found an American willing to fall in with his scheme. Since America was neutral, neither the English nor the Dutch could object if arms belonging to an American citizen were transported to America on an American ship. But Beaumarchais had a secret understanding with his confederate: something would happen to the American ship somewhere in the Channel, and it would have to enter a French port. The guns would be landed stealthily, and both the English and the Dutch would be outwitted.

The Dutch, however, were suspicious. They did not want to interfere with legitimate American trade; they merely asked the American "businessman" to leave a substantial deposit as guarantee that the guns would actually be taken across the Atlantic. As soon as the guns were unloaded on American soil, the money would be refunded. If, on the other hand, they failed to reach their official destination, the deposit would be forfeited. Though this made the total cost of the guns prohibitively high for the French, Beaumarchais decided to meet the conditions imposed. Since he had not enough cash to pay the sum requested as security, he asked his American partner to keep an eye on the guns while he went to Basel, by way of Germany, to obtain the necessary funds.

While this dickering was taking place, a tremendous moral and social upheaval began to shake the continent of Europe. Contrary to general expectations, the French had not been overwhelmed by the seemingly crushing superiority of the coalition formed against them in the first months of 1793. The Convention had raised fourteen armies, and fierce fighting raged on all the frontiers of France. Soon the ideas of equality and freedom held by the French Revolutionists worked their way among all the nations of Europe, undermining the antiquated structure of a half-feudal society. As the old society started to totter and crack, dismay and confusion became apparent everywhere.

Nowhere were confusion and dismay more strikingly apparent than in France itself. After the collapse of governmental authority in the second half of 1792, furious dissensions had flared up, and savage uprisings had been reported in a hundred places. To quell these disastrous disturbances, the Convention created the Committee of General Security, which had the powers of a super-ministry of Police and acted in concert with the Committee of Public Safety. The Committee of Public Safety itself was reorganized in July, 1793. The too-easygoing Danton was expelled and replaced by the "incorruptible" and inflexible Robespierre. The Reign of Terror began.

The Revolutionists, haunted by the specter of treachery, enacted Draconian laws against all those who had any connection whatever with enemy countries. Particularly stern was the Law of the Suspects voted by the Convention at Robespierre's request on September 17, and promulgated on December 6, 1793. In compliance with that law, the Vigilance Committee of the Municipality of Paris had to check on all the residents of the capital who had recently left France to travel abroad.

As Beaumarchais was on a secret mission, no legitimate reason could be given publicly for his absence. At the end of December, 1793, his name was placed on the *émigré* list. But the *émigré* list posted by the Vigilance Committee had been made so carelessly and hastily that the Committee of Public Safety found it necessary to revise it at once. When Mme Beaumarchais pointed out that her husband was a government agent, his name was struck off the list.

In the first months of 1794, the political situation in Paris became particularly critical and tragic. Robespierre tightened his hold on the Convention. In March, Danton was sent to the guillotine. The Committee of Public Safety was now composed exclusively of Robespierre's friends, and the Committee of General Security made short work of his enemies.

Shortly after Danton's death, Beaumarchais' name was again put on the *émigré* list, this time by the Committee of General Security. Mme Beaumarchais appealed to the Committee of Public Safety, but in vain. The duplicate of Beaumarchais' order of mission, signed by Danton, probably lay somewhere in the Committee's archives. But who would bother, under the circumstances, to hunt among dusty files for a scrap of paper? Furthermore, Danton's name was an anathema to Robespierre's associates. Mme Beaumarchais, realizing that her requests and complaints were only endangering her own neck, withdrew.

Paul and Philippe Gudin then decided to burn a number of important documents in Beaumarchais' house that might be considered compromising if an inquiry was ever conducted by biased investigators. All his account books were left intact. There was no irregularity in them, and perhaps one day they might help clear him—or his memory.

Soon afterward, Paul Gudin decided to seek a safe retreat in a small town in Southern France. Mme Beaumarchais, in a similar mood, left the capital with her daughter, and settled in the near-by village of Boissy-Saint-Léger. Julie remained alone in the huge, bleak, and desolate house in the Faubourg Saint-Antoine.

Beaumarchais was now in a queer position. His order of mission had not been canceled, and consequently he was still an agent of the Committee of Public Safety. He still wrote letters to the Committee, and sometimes received replies. On the other hand, he was considered an *émigré* by the Committee of General Security. If he set foot on French soil, he would at once be arrested and executed.

He was still pathetically trying to get the Terweren guns. For some unknown reason he had been unable to obtain the money he had hoped to find in Basel. Undismayed he went back to Holland, then to London, then once more to Holland, then to Switzerland again, then to Holland.

At one phase of the war, Beaumarchais almost believed that his ordeal was at an end. The French armies were now on the offensive everywhere. General Pichegru had forced his way deep into Belgium and was within striking distance of Terweren. Beaumarchais sent frantic letters to the Committee of Public Safety, beseeching it to order Pichegru to dispatch a division across the Dutch frontier to requisition the muskets. But the Committee of

Public Safety in Paris consistenty and wisely refrained from sending commanders in the field detailed instructions on local operations, and Beaumarchais' request was simply disregarded.

Late in July 1794, Beaumarchais received heart-rending news: his sister, his wife, and his daughter had been arrested. Mme Beaumarchais and Eugénie had been jailed in the old abbey of Port-Royal, then called, without irony, Port-Libre. Julie was in the Plessis-Egalité prison. Early in June, Robespierre had had the Convention pass a new law, famous as the Law of Prairial, drastically increasing the penalties against suspects and their families. The charge against Julie, Thérèse, and Eugénie was that they were close relatives of an *émigré*—Beaumarchais. All three expected to be condemned to death.

But Robespierre himself was overthrown on July 28, and guillotined a few days later. The Reign of Terror was over. A large number of political prisoners were released without trial. Mme Beaumarchais and her daughter were set free on August 8, and Julie on October 18, 1794.

As soon as she was liberated, Mme Beaumarchais took steps to divorce her husband. This was not a mark of hostility toward her mate. Many *émigrés'* wives had saved their heads through the same subterfuge. She later said that she had considered above everything her moral duty to her young daughter. She was also perhaps not altogether averse to the idea of remaining alive herself. When she could correspond safely with Beaumarchais, she explained her move to him as follows: "As a mother, I had to use all possible means to prevent my dear child's undergoing the fate of so many innocent and honorable victims—victims who have since been rehabilitated and are remembered today with regrets and tears. But regrets, tears, and belated justice will not bring them back to life."

Mme Beaumarchais' divorce turned out to be completely unnecessary. After Robespierre's fall, being an *émigré*'s wife was no longer considered a crime. Yet, in the closing months of 1794 nobody knew if the calm was not merely a lull before another of the storms of which there had been so many in the last five years. Mme Beaumarchais did not return with Julie to the Faubourg Saint-Antoine house. During the divorce proceedings she rented a small apartment on the Rue Paradis-Poissonnière, and after the divorce was granted went with her daughter to live in her niece's house in Orléans.

Beaumarchais was still harrying the Committee of Public Safety, which had again been reorganized after Robespierre's fall, with plans, suggestions, and advice about the Terweren guns. He succeeded only in attracting attention to himself, and for a second time, Lecointre denounced him before the Convention. Lecointre's diatribe was a jumble of nonsense. He accused Beaumarchais of having been one of Robespierre's supporters, and of having absconded with enormous sums of money that had been earmarked to pay for the Terweren guns.

Lecointre's speech was published in the Paris newspapers. The English secret-service men, who naturally read the French newspapers carefully, saw in Lecointre's remarks the proof of what they had long suspected: the guns at Terweren were not destined for America but for France. In October 1794 the English decided to seize the guns.

Beaumarchais' "partner" protested in the name of freedom of

trade and American neutrality. He was courteously but firmly told by the British that "his" guns were lost in any case. The French armies, now victorious on all fronts, would certainly occupy Terweren soon. They would have no scruples about requisitioning the muskets, and paying for them in depreciated assignats. The muskets would therefore be taken to a safe place in England. Impartial arbiters would be appointed to determine the indemnity to which he was entitled, and the amount fixed would be paid to him in good pounds sterling. These fair words were backed by the menacing aspect of a trim British frigate.

Beaumarchais, who had gone to Terweren at the last moment to make a last effort, could only watch powerlessly and despondently as the British frigate sailed smoothly away. Carrying with her all his guns and all his hopes, she soon disappeared into the gray mist of the North Sea.

3. *Exiled*

THE Dutch government now examined Beaumarchais' status. Was he a refugee or a French secret agent? After some deliberation, he was given the benefit of the doubt. No action would be taken against him, but he was politely advised to leave Holland. He obeyed and went to Lubeck, in Germany.

Beaumarchais was now an exile, but he always protested that he was not an *émigré*. On December 4, 1794, he wrote his daughter Eugénie: "I shall prove that after serving the cause of liberty in America, I have, without personal ambition, served the true interests of France with all my powers. I shall prove that I am still serving her—even though I am the butt of a persecution as stupid from a political standpoint as it is nefarious. I shall prove that it is absurd to believe that a man who dedicated himself to the re-establishment of the Rights of Man in America, in the hope of thus presenting France with a great model to follow, would have become lukewarm when it came to putting these principles into practice."

Some time later he moved, for reasons unknown, from Lubeck to Hamburg. He was to remain there two years. Most of the other refugees, who were stanch royalists, refused to have anything to do with the author of *Le Mariage de Figaro.* Among the few French exiles who associated with him in Hamburg were Abbé Joseph Louis and Charles de Talleyrand-Périgord. Talleyrand, who was a consummate diplomat and an archintriguer himself, probably relished the reminiscences of the former Secret Agent who had known so many of pre-revolutionary Europe's colorful personalities. Abbé Louis, who was later to become Finance Minister during the Restoration, was mainly interested in the recollections of the great Pâris-Duverney's trusted associate.

Beaumarchais' finances were at their lowest ebb. In Hamburg, for the first time in his life since his brief boyhood escapade, he became reacquainted with poverty and want. It then occurred to him to appeal once more to the Americans, and to ask for payment of at least part of the sum due him. In 1793, the American Congress had entrusted Alexander Hamilton with the task of studying Beaumarchais' claim. Hamilton reached the conclusion that America owed Beaumarchais 2,280,000 francs. In 1794, Gouverneur Morris, who was the United States' Minister Plenipotentiary in Paris, asked the French Foreign Minister, Bruchot, if he could possibly throw some light on the murky affair of the "lost million," which had puzzled American financiers since 1786. France was then at war with England. Bruchot saw no reason to conceal the fact that Vergennes had secretly helped America prior to France's official recognition of the United States. He showed Morris the receipt for one million livres dated June 10, 1776, and signed Beaumarchais.

This revelation caused an explosion of anger against Beaumarchais in American government circles. Beaumarchais had never mentioned the receipt of such a large sum from Vergennes. He was a crook. He would be paid nothing!

It was evident that even if the "lost million" were deducted from Beaumarchais' bill, Congress still owed him about 1,280,000 francs, according to Hamilton's calculations. But Congress decided that the compound interest on one million francs from 1776 to 1794 covered the full amount of the sum due. It might have been argued that the compound interest on the 1,280,000 due and unpaid during the same period was at least equivalent to the interest on the million francs and that therefore the two amounts of interest canceled each other. But Beaumarchais was in no position to argue: he had not been informed of Morris' inquiry about the "lost million" and he did not know that Bruchot had shown the American Minister his receipt to Vergennes.

On April 10, 1795, Beaumarchais wrote the American people at large: "Americans, I have served you with indefatigable zeal and I have received, throughout my life, only bitterness as a reward for my services. I die your creditor. Allow me therefore, now that I am dying, to bequeath you my daughter, that you may endow her with a portion of what you owe me. . . . Adopt her as a worthy child of the state. . . . Let her be regarded as a citizen's daughter. But if after these efforts of mine, after all I have said . . . if I still feared you would again reject my request . . . since yours is the only country where I can go and be a beggar without shame, there would be nothing left to me but to beseech heaven to restore my health for a short time so that I could go to America. Then, once in your midst, weakened in body and mind and unable to claim my rights, I should have to be carried to the door of your National Assemblies; and there, sitting on a lowly stool, holding out the liberty cap—which no man on earth helped you to wear more than I—for all to see, I should have to cry out: 'Americans, give alms to your friend, for all his services to you have brought him naught but this reward. . . .'" *

Beaumarchais had scarcely better luck with his Terweren guns. Arbiters had been appointed by the English government, as Beaumarchais' American partner had been promised. In June 1795 the sum these arbiters declared an adequate compensation was duly paid the American by the British authorities. He in turn faithfully forwarded the whole amount to Beaumarchais. That amount, however, was ludicrously small.

Meanwhile, political agitation was gradually subsiding in France. The French Revolutionists had overcome most of their opponents both at home and abroad. The harsh measures that had undoubtedly contributed to their success were no longer needed. A revulsion against the excesses of the Reign of Terror swept over the country. The Convention was showing more and more leniency

* America's debt to Beaumarchais was finally settled, after protracted and complicated negotiations, in 1835. That year, Congress gave Beaumarchais' heirs the choice of accepting 800,000 francs as full settlement of the claim, or getting nothing at all. The heirs took the 800,000 francs.

toward the suspects. In April, 1795, Beaumarchais' ex-wife had asked for a reconsideration of her ex-husband's case. On June 30, the Committee of General Security had rescinded its previous decree against him. Yet, if Beaumarchais had returned to France then, he would have run the risk of arrest by some official unaware of the Committee's altered stand—and overhasty executions were still frequent enough in those days. All sorts of formalities had to be gone through before the exile could return to France in perfect safety.

Beaumarchais now corresponded freely with his ex-wife and his daughter. Their main topic of correspondence was not patriotic rejoicing over French victories, but concern about the housing problem, the depreciation of paper-money, and the ever-rising cost of food. Most of the French people were then very much in the same mood. France was no longer in danger. Foreign enemies had been repulsed. But there was still a great deal of poverty and distress at home. Nevertheless, the darkest clouds were perceptibly lifting. The dominant feelings throughout the nation were lassitude and relief. It was possible to hope for a better future, but the majority sought above all to escape from their current material difficulties through imagination.

To satisfy that widespread craving for escape, the management of the Opéra decided to revive *Tarare*. When Beaumarchais, who was still in Hamburg, heard of the project, he felt deeply worried. The ideas he had advocated in his libretto when a constitutional monarchy was generally considered an ideal form of government would, under the Republic, sound dangerously subversive. Thérèse, however, assured him he need have no worries. One of his friends, Framery, who had some dramatic ability, was revising the libretto, trimming off the unpalatable pieces and adding a thick, rich, republican sauce. The dish evidently pleased the audience. Thérèse reported in a letter of September, 1795, that the opera had been very well received. There had been, she said, "*une affluence prodigieuse.*"

The performance of *Tarare* drew public attention to Beaumarchais, and his case would have been settled once and for all if grave riots had not just then broken out in Paris. On October 5, 1795, a newcomer in national politics, General Bonaparte, took his first step into the hall of fame by crushing rioters with the celebrated "whiff of grapeshot." The French political world was thrown into an uproar, and the Convention dissolved on October 26, 1795, without having come to a decision on Beaumarchais.

Some time later, the new government of the Directory took up the Beaumarchais question from the beginning. New inquiries were made. New blanks were filled out. New reports were sent in. Finally, in April 1796, on the recommendation of Robert Lindet, who had been one of Danton's close friends, Beaumarchais was officially authorized to return to France.

4. All Is Well

WHEN Beaumarchais arrived in Paris, on July 5, 1796, he found André Delarue—who had not become an *émigré*, after all—impatiently waiting to be married to Eugénie. Their wedding was celebrated at once, and in June 1797 a daughter was born to them. She received the romantic name Palmyre, and soon her endearing ways sent Beaumarchais into raptures of grandfatherly enthusiasm.

After marrying off his daughter, Beaumarchais had to remarry his divorced wife. A few formalities delayed the wedding for some time; then a quiet ceremony was arranged in Paris and, immediately afterward, the Beaumarchais went to Orléans.

Beaumarchais' big house on the Boulevard Saint-Antoine had been left uncared for during several years. The garden had grown wild and the building now looked dilapidated and dismal. He tried to sell or rent it, but the mansion was too large and elaborate for its surroundings and too costly to maintain. In the end he decided to live in it himself. It took a tidy sum and nearly a year's work to put everything in order. Then, in May 1797, he and his whole family moved in from Orléans.

In 1798, the Directory created a new property tax calculated on the number of doors and windows in each house. Beaumarchais' house had two hundred windows. Yet, even under those circumstances, Beaumarchais was far from poor, for he had somehow contrived to keep a by no means inconsiderable nest egg. He could live in comfort and could afford to help old friends and even old enemies who had fallen on evil days. Paul Gudin—"My brother, my friend, my Gudin," as Beaumarchais called him in a letter of June 6, 1797—at Beaumarchais' suggestion, left his dull provincial retreat and received a commodious lodging in the Faubourg Saint-Antoine house. Mme Goëzman, whose husband had been guillotined during the Revolution, was now all but destitute. Her plight was brought to Beaumarchais' attention, and he secretly let her have regular and adequate help. Baculard d'Arnauld had lost practically all of his savings through inflation, and Beaumarchais lent him fairly important sums several times. These generous acts became known only later, when Beaumarchais' account books were examined after his death.

Beaumarchais had lost heavily through the government's manipulation of the national currency, but he was not the man to take such losses without protest. The assignats he had been given in 1792 now had practically no value at all. On the other hand, the gilt-edged securities he had deposited in Switzerland as a guarantee of his good faith had been disposed of. Furthermore, all the travels he had undertaken on behalf of the Committee of Public Safety, all the fictitious sales he had arranged, all the salaries he had paid to his agents—all these expenses had run into money. He asked the government to reimburse him fairly for his outlays.

In January 1798 the Directory appointed a commission to investigate his claims. Robert Lindet, whom he now considered, and with good reason, a personal friend, was one of the most influential members of that commission. The commission found that the government owed Beaumarchais 997,875 francs.

Then, on May 11, 1798, one of the numerous *coups d'état* which enlivened the short existence of the Directory was staged. Lindet and his group were ousted from power, and a new commission was named to study Beaumarchais' accounts. The new commission declared that the government owed nothing at all to Beaumarchais—nay, that Beaumarchais owed the government 500,000 francs. It goes without saying that Beaumarchais vigorously contested the decision and went on contesting until his death.

After his return from Orléans, Beaumarchais had met Amélie Houret again, and they resumed their liaison. He learned then how she had saved his life in August 1792 through her influence on

Manuel. Gratitude was not, however, the feeling that kept him bound to her. Even though he was now well past sixty-five, the letters he wrote her fairly reek of burning physical passion. Mme Beaumarchais was, of course, still kept in complete ignorance of the affair.

Urged on by his usual restlessness, Beaumarchais flung himself into a number of activities. *La Mère coupable* had not had, he thought, the success it deserved. The troupe of the Théâtre du Marais, which had presented it in 1792, had been too mediocre to give the play a fair chance. Beaumarchais now started to harry the actors of the Comédie Française to revive his drama. In the end, he won out. This time, the public wept copiously and applauded enthusiastically. In reaction to the brutality of the revolutionary period, France was now passing through a phase of mawkish sentimentalism, and Beaumarchais' play nicely suited this mood.

Beaumarchais then turned to politics. Since General Bonaparte was the great new star rising on the French political horizon, Beaumarchais began laying plans to be introduced to him. His son-in-law, Delarue was General Dumas' brother-in-law. General Dumas was General Desaix's intimate friend. General Desaix was closely associated with Bonaparte. Through them, Beaumarchais requested an interview of Bonaparte. Bonaparte answered: "I shall be glad to meet the author of *La Mère coupable.*" The meeting was brief. Bonaparte had little use for writers and ideologists. Somewhat disappointed, but in no way daunted, Beaumarchais tried to reach the General through his wife, Joséphine. But Bonaparte never listened to women when they tried to meddle in serious business, and Beaumarchais' efforts in that direction led him nowhere.

Beaumarchais fell back on Talleyrand. Talleyrand had risen to the position of Minister of Foreign Affairs. Beaumarchais explained to him that he, Beaumarchais, would make an excellent French Ambassador to the United States. Talleyrand was kind and courteous to his old companion in exile and did not give him a direct refusal; he merely postponed his answer—indefinitely. Beaumarchais was not one of those men on whom advancing years confer mellow authority and wisdom. His character still showed traces of immature levity, which now, more than ever, clashed with his decidedly old countenance.

Beaumarchais' sister Julie, who was then sixty-two, seems to have presented the same disconcerting contrast. Early in April 1798 she suddenly became very ill. The nature of her ailment is not known. But after a month it was obvious to all that there was no hope of recovery left for her. She knew that she was dying. On May 9, while her family and her most intimate friends were gathered around her bed, waiting for the end, she improvised and actually sang, to the tune of a popular dance, comical rhymes about her own predicament. We are assured by Beaumarchais himself that all the persons present also improvised and, to the same tune, sang merry, saucy answers to her. She died a few hours afterward.

Beaumarchais undoubtedly would have loved to die with an ironical and witty song on his lips, too. But on the morning of May 18, 1799, he was found dead in bed from a cerebral hemorrhage. He had lived sixty-seven years and three months. For the first time perhaps, his face wore an expression of serenity and calm.

Appendix:

LE NOZZE DI FIGARO AND *IL BARBIERE DI SIVIGLIA*

1. Le Nozze di Figaro

BEAUMARCHAIS' COMEDY, *Le Mariage de Figaro,* was presented in Vienna for the first time on April 7, 1784. The satirical traits that had caused great commotion in France were generally lost on the well-behaved and contented Austrians, but the play's liveliness and cheerfulness thoroughly pleased the lighthearted Viennese public.

Mozart was at that time twenty-eight years old. Three years earlier, in 1781, his patron, the Archbishop of Salzburg, had summoned him to Vienna. The Archbishop had always shown himself unappreciative and ungenerous toward Mozart. In Vienna an open breach took place between them. The young composer decided then to strike out for himself and to settle definitively in the Austrian capital, in those days one of the most important musical centers of Europe. There Mozart at once enjoyed a fair measure of success, giving from time to time concerts that were attended by the flower of the Austrian aristocracy.

The following year, on August 4, 1782, he married Konstanze Weber. Their marriage, though far from ideal, proved to be on the whole fairly harmonious. It gave the young artist a sense of responsibility he had previously lacked, a certain earnestness of outlook tinged with melancholy, and a deep insight into fundamental human emotions and feelings. Mozart was now reaching, along with maturity, the peak of his creative powers.

Soon he applied these creative powers with signal success to opera. The opera was then at a crossroads of several musical trends and genres. The most important of them, *opera seria*, had originated in Italy at the end of the Renaissance. In the seventeenth century it had spread throughout Europe, though it had everywhere retained a definite Italian flavor. The subject of an *opera seria* was sometimes a fantastic mythological legend, sometimes a heroic episode culled from Greek or Roman history. The plot, however, was only a pretext for gorgeous pageantry. The main interest of an *opera seria* lay in a succession of extremely complicated, difficult, and often truly beautiful arias, which were the delight of music connoisseurs. The melodies bore hardly any relation to the emotions they were supposed to express, but they gave the singers of the time an opportunity to perform amazing feats of vocal virtuosity.

In the second part of the eighteenth century, another form

of musical play, the *opera buffa*, came into being. Instead of mythological heroes and extraordinary events, the *opera buffa* offered characters and facts coming straight from everyday reality. The music was tuneful but plain. Gross comical effects were deliberately emphasized, not seldom falling into grotesque and rather coarse scurrility.

About the same time Gluck attempted a major reform of the whole conception of the *opera seria*. He accepted plots drawn from mythology, but he wanted them to have a broad human appeal. He contended that the arias should not be a display of vocal acrobatics, but should faithfully illustrate and accurately follow the ideas presented in the lines of the libretto. It happened that the reforms advocated by Gluck closely corresponded to eighteenth-century French musical taste. They immediately aroused passionate enthusiasm in Paris and—the earmark of any true artistic success there—also unleashed furious controversies in which all the French public took part.

Vienna welcomed Gluck's musical theories, though with somewhat more reserve than Paris. Vienna naturally partook in many aspects of the German musical tradition. Germany had produced at that time great works of chamber music and magnificent oratorios, but practically nothing worthwhile in opera. The only modest contribution of German music to the theater was the *Singspiel*—a sort of operetta in vernacular, blending familiar realism, light fun, and somewhat heavy sentimentality.

Mozart had three times tried his hand at the *opera seria*, each time with indifferent success. *Mitridate, Re di Ponto* and *Lucio Silla*, composed respectively when he was fifteen and sixteen, showed unmistakable marks of immaturity. *Idomeneo, Re di Creta*, which he completed in 1780 at the age of twenty-four, was not devoid of merit. Mozart's graceful, restrained elegance appeared in it clad in gaudy Italian style, with trimmings showing Gluck's influence. This bizarre mixture produced only a second-rate work.

An early and solitary excursion by Mozart into the field of the *opera buffa* had resulted in an unimportant sketch, *La Finta semplice.*

Mozart had also explored the possibilities offered by the German *Singspiel.* At the age of twelve, he had composed the very short *Bastien und Bastienne.* Ten years later, in 1779, he undertook a more ambitious piece of the same type, *Zaïde*, on a libretto written by Andreas Schachtner, court trumpeter at Salzburg. When Mozart went to Vienna in 1781, he showed the score of *Zaïde* to an actor of the National Theater named Gottfried Stephanie. Stephanie introduced him to the director of the theater, Graf Rosenberg, who commissioned Mozart to compose in a similar vein *Die Entführung aus dem Serail. Die Entführung aus dem Serail*, first performed on July 16, 1782, was not received with unmixed favor. Emperor Joseph II is reported to have said then: "Too fine for our ears, and a tremendous amount of notes, my dear Mozart." Subsequently *Die Entführung* was given great publicity by German critics who hailed it as the first "German" opera by a truly great composer. Yet though *Die Entführung* contains delightful music, it certainly does not count among Mozart's greatest masterpieces.

Evidently none of the various forms of musical play existing in Mozart's time had so far offered him suitable means of expression for his original genius. At this juncture, Beaumarchais' *Le Mariage de Figaro* provided him with dramatic elements that could easily be adapted to his particular needs. Mozart's *Le Nozze di Figaro* is often listed by historians as an *opera buffa.* Actually it was first presented to the public as a *commedia per musica.* Later, when the work was published in book form, the librettist, fully aware of the novelty of Mozart's attempt, wrote an Introduction wherein he spoke of "our special purpose, which was to offer a new type of spectacle." *

Mozart's librettist, Lorenzo da Ponte, was born in 1749 in the ghetto of Cenada, near Venice. His name was originally Emmanuele Conegliano. In 1763 his father, a tanner by trade, took all his family to the Bishop of Cenada, Lorenzo da Ponte, to be baptized and received into the Catholic Church. Emmanuele Conegliano's name was then changed to the Bishop's own name, and from that time on the Bishop looked after the gifted boy's education. Young Lorenzo da Ponte was soon sent to a seminary where he was ordained a priest in 1773. During the next two years he taught school at Treviso; then he drifted to Venice and engaged there in questionable intrigues and unedifying affairs, that eventually caused his banishment from the territory of the Venetian Republic. After long and uncertain wanderings, he went to Dresden and became acquainted with the Italian court poet Caterino Mazzolà. Mazzolà gave him a letter of introduction to the composer Antonio Salieri in Vienna. Thanks to Salieri's support, Da Ponte was appointed official poet at the Vienna National Theater. But the first libretto he wrote for Salieri in 1784, *Il Ricco d'un giorno,* was a failure. Salieri turned then to another librettist, and Da Ponte turned to Mozart.

Mozart had met Da Ponte in 1783 in the house of Baron

* Quoted by Alfred Einstein, *Mozart, His Character, His Work* (New York, Oxford University Press, 1945), p. 430.

Wezlar, a well-known music lover in Vienna. Da Ponte had at once promised Mozart to write a libretto for him, but their actual association began only after Da Ponte's break with Salieri. *Le Nozze di Figaro* was written and composed at the end of 1785, the work of Da Ponte on the libretto and the work of Mozart on the musical score proceeding almost simultaneously. Da Ponte was intelligent, adaptable, and friendly. He wholeheartedly accepted Mozart's personal views about the nature of the opera on which they were collaborating. According to Da Ponte's *Memoirs*, the whole opera was completed in six weeks. But in fact we know that Mozart revised his score throughout the first four months of 1786, and that he composed the overture just before the first performance, which took place on May 1 of that year.

Le Nozze di Figaro did not arouse great enthusiasm in Vienna. In Prague, it is true, success was instantaneous. But the opera did not reach Berlin before 1790, and it was rather coldly received there, though it was appreciated by the best critics. In Italy its failure was complete in 1792. In Paris it fell flat at the Opéra in 1793, and began to get due recognition only in 1815, when it was presented at a vanguard theater, the Feydeau.

This protracted resistance to *Le Nozze di Figaro* was caused to a large extent by the "new type of spectacle," which for a long time appeared disconcerting and puzzling to the general public. *Le Nozze di Figaro* did not present, as an *opera seria* would, an impressive collection of captivating though meaningless arias. It lacked the overflow of rather crude fun, often bordering on buffoonery, that was typical of the *opera buffa*. Its music was not sheer musical commentary on words "*à la Gluck.*" Its plot did not, like that of a *Singspiel*, offer a sentimental story in a familiar setting.

In fact the best characteristics of each of these established genres—the melodic beauty, the compelling verve, the psychological accuracy, the homely charm—were all to be found in Mozart's work, but in tempered proportions and blended with new elements rising out of Mozart's main innovation and purpose.

According to Da Ponte, Mozart's main innovation and purpose in *Le Nozze di Figaro* were "to present faithfully and in full colors the divers passions that are aroused" * throughout the opera in the souls of the various characters. The music, instead of being either an extraneous ornament or a goal unto itself, was intended to portray exactly not only the deep emotions but even the most elusive shades of feeling that come to light when a man or a woman, young or old, experiences love, jealousy, hope, despair, regret, gladness, melancholy, anger, envy, defeat, or triumph. All these human sentiments were strikingly conjured up by Mozart through amazingly evocative melodic inflections or subtle, elaborate contrapuntal effects.

A masterpiece of musical and psychological characterization, *Le Nozze di Figaro* necessarily implied an almost total integration between the composer's score and the librettist's text. Such an integration was possible because Beaumarchais' comedy offered a basic set of situations and characters whose cheerful liveliness against a background of melancholy was comparatively close to Mozart's own mind and mood. Yet there was too much difference between the personality of Mozart and that of Beaumarchais to allow a complete identification of their works; so Mozart and Da Ponte re-interpreted and re-arranged in terms of Mozart's own spirit the dramatic themes provided by Beaumarchais.

* Ibid.

Mozart was not interested in Beaumarchais' revolutionary message, and no political satire of any kind was allowed to appear in the opera. The general idea of a struggle between cunning and force was kept, but completely stripped of all social significance. The outline of *Le Mariage de Figaro*'s plot was retained, though reduced to mere anecdote. The pivot of the libretto is Count Almaviva, a likable profligate who runs after all the girls in sight, including, among many others, Susanna, his wife's maid-in-waiting. Susanna's engagement to Figaro causes all sorts of misunderstandings, and the opera ends in the midst of the most bewildering and entertaining confusion. The number of acts was cut from five to four, the number of characters from sixteen to twelve. The names were Italianized, but not markedly changed, except in the case of Don Guzman Brid'oison, who became Don Curzio, and of Fanchette, who became Barbarina.

But the most important transformation took place in the characters themselves. The characters created by Beaumarchais were complex human beings, with good and evil inextricably blended in their make-ups. Behind polished or amusing exteriors, they often allowed glimpses into a disturbing, secret world of morbid and turbid cravings. Mozart's music could not give an account of so baffling and unpleasant a mixture. Da Ponte and Mozart, in full agreement, simplified Beaumarchais' characters drastically. Whenever Beaumarchais had suggested harsh and discordant overtones, Mozart substituted one note, crystalline and pure.

Thus the Countess was no longer a restless woman who casts an eye upon a boy in his teens for somewhat different reasons than mere suppressed motherly instinct. She became in Mozart's opera a chaste and faithful wife, saddened by the passing of her fickle husband's love and voicing her poignant sorrow with becoming dignity and sweetness. Chérubin had been presented by Beaumarchais as an adolescent obsessed by voluptuous images, in turn too bold and too shy, awkward in spite of his sprightly naughtiness and his almost feminine charm. Mozart's Cherubino embodies the first delightful sigh of love, the first fragrant bloom of youth—a dream-figure wrapped in an atmosphere of purity and tenderness. Mozart's Figaro is not a *révolté* burning with hatred, hiding his game, biding his time, and thirsting for revenge. He displays only the most commendable feelings of respectful love for his official fiancée and of clean-cut rage against a supposedly successful rival. Likewise Bartolo and Marcelina, who when they first appear in Mozart's opera offer caricatural traits that would not be out of place in a true *opera buffa*, are soon idealized and turn into edifying models of perfect parenthood.

These alterations undoubtedly strip Beaumarchais' play of some of its dramatic significance and psychological richness. Yet Mozart was guided in all the changes he made by a deep sense of the beautiful and the universal. Beaumarchais had faced a world of particular individuals, twisted and tormented behind a deceptive façade of high breeding and gaiety. Mozart, looking at the same human landscape, saw a long and lovely vista of eternal human sentiments, sometimes droll, sometimes sad, never sordid, often enchanting, yet somehow deeply true. *Le Mariage de Figaro* provided Mozart with the fundamental pattern of reality that he needed, a reality not exempt from blemishes, but strongly colored with good humor and wit—a reality that he could understand and love. But while the warp and woof of the original French comedy remained the same, Da Ponte's libretto gave Mozart's fancy full scope to weave in and out the strong threads and the delicate tracery of his own inimitable poetic creations.

2. Il Barbiere di Siviglia

No LESS than eleven composers * have so far undertaken to give *Le Barbier de Séville* an operatic form. Yet only two of their number, Paisiello and Rossini, have succeeded in creating works of enduring value.

Giovanni Paisiello was a contemporary of Mozart. He lived in an analogous environment, composed works for a similar public, and faced the same musical problems. Beaumarchais' *Le Barbier de Séville* had been highly appreciated in St. Petersburg. To please Catherine II, and perhaps at her request, Paisiello, who had been since 1776 a resident in the Russian capital, composed in 1782 an opera on that subject. He enjoyed the collaboration of a librettist of great reputation in those days, Giuseppe Petrosellini.

Petrosellini retained all the characters and the various episodes presented in Beaumarchais' comedy, but completely changed their meaning. Practically all the wit and fun of the original disappeared in his adaptation. Figaro ceased to be the leading character. All the interest was concentrated on Bartholo and his pathetic or ludicrous efforts to keep the two lovers apart.

* Friedrich Ludwig Benda in Ham, 1782; Giovanni Paisiello in St. Petersburg, 1782; Johann Zacharias Elsperger in Sulzbach, 1783; Johann Abraham Schulz in Reinsberg, 1786; Niccolò Isouard in Valetta, 1796; Francesco Morlacchi in Dresden, 1815; Gioacchino Rossini in Rome, 1816; Costantino Dall'Argine in Bologna, 1868; Achille Graffigna in Padua, 1879; Jerónimo Jiménez in Madrid, 1901; Leopoldo Cassone in Turin, 1922.

Paisiello composed to this libretto a charming, though rather thin, musical score. His opera contains lovely arias that are remarkable mainly by their graceful simplicity. Nothing pungent, nothing roguish, nothing wayward can be found in them. They are often clever, often pretty, and they offer that slight touch of sentimentality which marked the decline of the old aristocratic society at the close of the eighteenth century in Europe.

The storm of the French Revolution and of the Napoleonic wars swept away this cultured and refined, but artificial world. A new form of society, more sanguine, more common, came into being, and along with it a new form of artistic taste. The eighteenth-century elegance, its sheer gracefulness, its love for subtle and delicate shadings gave way to a heightened sense of drama, to a search for colorful effects, and to an appreciation of movement and force.

This change in social environment and public taste did not affect at first the old distinction between *opera seria* and *opera buffa*. Yet these two genres now progressively tended to come together, each losing its most objectionable characteristics, each borrowing the best traits of the other. Thus the *opera seria*'s utter artificiality could not last in a world where conventions no longer held absolute sway, and the *opera seria* acquired certain human aspects that had previously belonged only to the *opera buffa*. On the other hand, the *opera buffa*, which appealed more than the *opera seria* to the bulk of the new public, could not remain at a low level of sketchy triviality. It increasingly aimed at more elaborate beauty and grandeur. Eventually *opera seria* and *opera buffa* were to fuse into one, giving birth to grand opera. In the first years of the nineteenth century, however, though they were still separate, each had already become broader and richer in scope.

At that time, one of the most promising young composers of Italy was Gioacchino Rossini, born at Pesaro in 1792. His father, Giuseppe Rossini, a jovial and temperamental musician, had deservedly been nicknamed *il vivazza*—"the lively one." "The lively one" had had a most agitated career. A fervent admirer of French revolutionary ideas, he had more than once got into serious trouble—even to the point of being thrown in jail—for his participation in local political coups at a time when the whole of Italy was seething with unrest.

Thus young Gioacchino grew up in an atmosphere of agitation and change, and in the midst of constant scheming and plotting. Though the rest of his life was spent in a calmer and happier period, he long retained, perhaps as traits of character inherited from *il vivazza*, perhaps as psychological results of his childhood experiences, a mercurial temperament, a bustling activity, a taste for intrigue, and an irrespressible restlessness. For many years, erratic, unstable, and always on the wing, he flitted from one city to another—Bologna, Milan, Venice, Rome, Naples—dashing off opera after opera, dickering with impresarios and indulging in light, ephemeral love affairs. He was endowed with extraordinary versatility and facility as a composer, and he enjoyed this wandering life to the full—welcoming success with glee when it came along, taking philosophically the inevitable rebuffs of fortune, watching with good-humored cynicism the motley spectacle of our crazy world, and all the time bubbling over with effervescent gaiety—truly a Figaro *redivivus*.

By 1815, when he was twenty-three, he had already composed

five *opere serie—Demetrio e Polibio, Tancredi, Aureliano in Palmira, Sigismondo, Elisabetta Regina d'Inghilterra*—and nine *opere buffe—La Cambiale di matrimonio, L'Equivoco stravagante, L'Inganno felice, La Scala di seta, La Pietra del paragone, L'Occasione fa il ladro, Il Signor Bruschino, L'Italiana in Algeri*, and *Il Turco in Italia*. Toward the end of that year, he went to Rome to supervise the production of *Il Turco in Italia* at the Teatro Valle. The impresarios of the Teatro Valle, Pietro Cartoni and Vincenzo de Santis, then asked him to compose another opera for them, in collaboration with the librettist Cesare Sterbini. He accepted at once, but the opera, *Torvaldo e Dorliska*, was a fiasco—though not a big fiasco, only a little one. Rossini, writing to his mother to let her know how his opera had fared, made a pun on the double meaning of the Italian word *fiasco*—which may signify either a failure or a certain kind of fat-bellied bottle—and simply drew on a sheet of paper that he sent her a little bottle, *un fiaschetto*.

Just at that time, Cardinal Consalvi, Roman Secretary of State, who counted among his official duties the care of all theatrical affairs in Rome, requested the Teatro Argentina—a rival of the Teatro Valle—to present a new *opera buffa* for the 1816 carnival season.

The Teatro Argentina was under the direction of Duke Francesco Sforza-Cesarini, who belonged to a noble and wealthy family, but had taken to theatrical management as a hobby. The Duke started negotiations with Rossini and suggested as a subject for an *opera buffa* a sketch written by the librettist Jacopo Ferretti. This Rossini rejected as being too vulgar. Soon, Rossini and the Duke decided to take *Le Barbier de Séville* as a basis for a libretto. How they came to that decision is not known. It may be noted that just at that time Rossini was beginning to take a special interest in a Spanish actress, Isabella Colbran, whom he was to marry seven years later, in 1822; also that one of the leading singers at the Teatro Argentina, Manuel García,* was of Spanish origin. The *Barbier*'s Spanish setting may have appealed to them, and it is possible that the choice of Beaumarchais' comedy was made, to a certain extent, under their influence. As librettist, Rossini kept Cesare Sterbini, who had already written *Torvaldo e Dorliska.*

The contract between Rossini and the Duke was signed on December 15, 1815. It was stipulated that Rossini would deliver

* Manuel García, born in Seville in 1775, made his debut as a singer (tenor) in Cadiz at the age of seventeen. In 1808 he went to Paris (Théâtre Italien) and at once attracted attention through the richness, vigor, and warmth of his voice, contrasting with the cold perfection displayed by his Italian co-singers. He moved to Italy in 1811, and the following year became acquainted with Rossini in Naples. He returned to Paris in 1816, and after a short stay in London established himself definitively in the French capital, where he powerfully contributed to the vogue of Rossini's music. A tour to America (1825–26) brought him tremendous material success and grave familial trouble as well. Upon his return to Paris he dedicated himself mainly to the teaching of singing and to the composing of operas, though he never rose above honorable mediocrity as a composer. He died in 1832. Among his children, the most famous was his daughter María (1808–36), an amazingly gifted singer (mezzo-soprano). At the time of their trip to America, when María was only seventeen, he caused her to marry a very wealthy fifty-year-old French businessman of New York named Malibran. Malibran, however, went bankrupt only a few weeks after the wedding, and was soon left by his wife, who returned to Europe. For about ten years La Malibran created an extraordinary sensation in France, in Italy, and in England by the prodigious emotional quality of her voice and the passionate intensity of her acting. She fell in love with a Belgian violinist, Charles de Bériot, and became his wife after her marriage with Malibran was annulled. She died at the age of twenty-eight as the sequel to an accident sustained while horseback riding—aggravated, it seems, by general nervous exhaustion. Manuel García's second daughter, Pauline (1821–1910) was likewise an outstanding singer (contralto), but she had a much less dramatic and pathetic life than her sister, being happily married to the director of the Théâtre Italien in Paris, Louis Viardot. García had also a son, like himself named Manuel (1805–1906), who was much less brilliantly endowed by nature as a singer (bass) than La Malibran or Mme Viardot-García. Probably for that reason, he concentrated his efforts and studies on means to improve the human voice, and he became a professor first at the Paris Conservatoire (1830–48), then at the London Royal Academy of Music (1848–95). He acquired world fame through his invention of the laryngoscope.

the first act of the opera on January 20, 1816, at the latest, and that the opera would be performed on February 5. Rossini was to receive four hundred Roman scudi for his work. He pledged himself to be present at the rehearsals, and he agreed to live, until completion of the work, in the same house as the chief singer of the Teatro Argentina, Luigi Zamboni—who was to be the first Figaro—so that he could adapt his score exactly to the singer's voice.

Sterbini lacked enthusiasm for *Le Barbier de Séville.* As a matter of fact he accepted the commission to write the libretto reluctantly, and only because both Rossini and the Duke begged him urgently to undertake the work. Yet, in contrast to Petrosellini, he was remarkably successful in retaining almost completely the original flavor of Beaumarchais' play. He shortened the dialogue, but kept its incisive sharpness and its roguish humor. The only important change he made, perhaps unwittingly, was in Figaro's character. Sterbini's Figaro is less refined, less witty, less sophisticated than Beaumarchais' Figaro. Sterbini's Figaro has the robust vitality of a true *uomo del popolo.* He is lightheaded and kindhearted, devoid of malice, yet delighted at the prospect of playing a good joke on almost anyone.

Rossini did not complete the musical score by the assigned date. He worked at it frantically for about three weeks in January and February 1816, not leaving his house and not even taking the time to shave during all that period—which later made one of his friends remark it was indeed odd that a "Barber" should have deprived him of his regular shaves. Rossini was so much pressed by time that he bodily introduced into his new work numerous important fragments he had composed for earlier operas. Thus he used as overture for his *Barbiere* the overture of *Aureliano.* The introduction to the first act came from *Sigismondo.* The cavatina sung by the Count in the first act has its origin in a rondo from *Aureliano.* Similar interpolations are to be found throughout the score.

The score of Rossini's opera offers a perfect Italian counterpart of Beaumarchais' French text. In spite of some differences arising from marked contrasts in national temperaments, the two works evidently proceed from the same inspiration and express the same spirit. The comedy and the opera present the same brisk verve, the same happy-go-lucky "philosophy," and the same brilliant, sparkling wit. At times, it is true, the Italian's music cavorts and gambols with much more abandon than strict French taste would favor. But the transposition never jars because Beaumarchais' moods and Rossini's moods fundamentally coincide.

Yet, on the day of its first performance, February 20, 1816, Rossini's opera was a complete failure. This failure, however, was mainly owing to accidental causes. Manuel García, who was taking Almaviva's part, begged Rossini to let him sing in the first act, under Rosina's window, a Spanish song of his own composition. Rossini acceded to his wish. But when García appeared on the stage, ready to sing, he noticed that he had forgotten to tune his guitar. The guitar had to be tuned on the spot, and in the process a string snapped. The public snickered, and then disliked the Spanish song. Hisses were heard. Later a cat ran across the stage, setting the galleries a-mewing. Nobody paid any attention to the music, and the first act ended in an atmosphere of hostile jocularity. Then Rossini got up from his seat and conspicuously clapped with all his might. He probably meant to applaud the talent and the pluck of the singers, who had carried on valiantly in spite of the noise, but it was believed that he was applauding his own work, and this turned the whole audience against him.

The audience's unfavorable reaction was accentuated perhaps by a cabal of partisans of the rival Teatro Valle, and certainly by a group of Paisiello's admirers, who considered it shameful that a subject already treated by the grand old master should be taken up by a young upstart. Contrary to the legend spread by Stendhal in his *Vie de Rossini,* Rossini had not written to Paisiello—then living in Naples—to ask him for permission to use *Le Barbier de Séville* for his libretto. He evidently felt justified in handling the subject anew by the fact that musical technique and taste had considerably changed in thirty-four years. Nevertheless he must have been aware of the feelings that a direct challenge to an established glory would arouse, for he did not at first give his opera the title of *Il Barbiere di Siviglia,* which Paisiello had adopted, and under which Rossini's own opera was later to acquire universal fame—but the title of *Almaviva, ossia l'Inutile precauzione.* Paisiello's friends, however, were not mollified by this courtesy, and that same evening Rossini sent his mother the drawing not of a small bottle, *fiaschetto,* but of a huge bottle, *fiascone.*

The second performance of the opera, on the following day, however, was a spectacular triumph. This time García's guitar had been tuned before the singer came onto the stage. His Spanish song had been replaced by a piece of Rossini's composition. No feline escapade distracted the audience's attention from the music, and it listened in rapture from beginning to end. Yet the opera was presented only five times in Rome that year, as the theatrical season ended with the inception of Lent on February 27. Nevertheless its success there was enough to launch Rossini's opera on a world-wide career. In the course of the succeeding years, it was presented on practically all European stages. It was received everywhere with vivid interest, but was nowhere accepted without a certain resistence. Invariably comparisons were made with Paisiello's opera, and Rossini was accused by experts of corrupting the pure old musical taste exemplified by his illustrious predecessor.

Rossini's opera was presented in London for the first time on March 10, 1818, at the King's Theatre, with only moderate success. Given in Paris at the Théâtre Italien on October 26, 1819, it was well liked by the general public, but met with cold reserve on the part of connoisseurs. However the American public, whose musical taste was less hampered by old-time prejudices than was that of European audiences, from the very start gave the opera the recognition that posterity later found it deserved. When *The Barber of Seville* was presented in an English translation at the Park Theatre, New York, on May 17, 1819, it at once made a tremendous hit. The first performance of the opera in America in Italian was sung at the same theater by a company under Manuel García's direction on November 29, 1825.

By that time *Il Barbiere di Siviglia* had been acknowledged by all as one of the finest Italian operas and as Rossini's masterpiece. Rossini embarked afterward on more ambitious and complicated works, but he never recaptured the *Barbiere*'s enchanting vein of youthful exuberance and merry, mischievous fun—fundamental aspects of his own character, for which he had found perfect expression in Beaumarchais' comedy.

Appendix

In 1822 Rossini visited old Beethoven in Vienna and spoke to him about his own musical ambitions and plans. Beethoven kept repeating: "Compose another *Barbiere di Siviglia,* compose another *Barbiere di Siviglia.*" But this Rossini could never achieve: Beaumarchais had written only one *Barbier de Séville.*

BIBLIOGRAPHY

ARNETH, ALFRED VON: *Beaumarchais und Sonnenfels* (Vienna: Braumüller, 1868)

BETTELHEIM, ANTON: *Beaumarchais, eine Biographie* (Frankfurt a/Main: Rütten & Loening, 1886)

BONNEFON, PAUL: *Beaumarchais* (Paris, L'Artiste, 1887)

CORDIER, HENRI: *Bibliographie des œuvres de Beaumarchais* (Paris: Quantin, 1883)

DALSÈME, RENÉ: *La Vie de Beaumarchais* (Paris: Gallimard, 1928)

FRISCHAUER, PAUL: *Beaumarchais, der Abenteurer im Jahrhundert der Frauen* (Zurich: Allgemeine Verlagsgesellschaft, 1935)

GAIFFE, FÉLIX: *Le Mariage de Figaro* (Amiens: Malfère, 1928)

GUDIN DE LA BRENELLERIE, PAUL: *Histoire de Beaumarchais* (Paris: Plon, 1888)

HALLAYS, ANDRÉ: *Beaumarchais* (Paris: Hachette, 1897)

HUOT, PAUL: *Beaumarchais en Allemagne* (Brussels: Lacroix, Verboeckhoven & Cie, 1869)

JOHNSON, MARGARET L.: *Beaumarchais and His Opponents* (Richmond, Va.: Whippet & Shepperson, 1936)

JONES, FLORENCE NIGHTINGALE: *Beaumarchais and Plautus; the Sources of the Barbier de Séville* (Chicago: Scott, Foresman and Co., 1908)

KITE, ELIZABETH S.: *Beaumarchais and the War of American Independence* (Boston: Richard G. Badger, 1918)

LAFON, ROGER: *Beaumarchais, le brillant armateur* (Paris: Société d'éditions géographiques, maritimes et coloniales, 1928)

LATZARUS, LOUIS: *Beaumarchais* (Paris: Plon, 1930)

LESCURE, MATHURIN DE: *Etude sur Beaumarchais* (Paris: Perrin, 1887)

LINTILHAC, EUGÈNE: *Beaumarchais et ses œuvres* (Paris: Hachette, 1887)

LOMÉNIE, LOUIS DE: *Beaumarchais et son temps* (Paris: Calmann Lévy, 1880)

MARSAN, JULES: *Beaumarchais et les affaires d'Amérique* (Paris: Champion, 1919)

RIVERS, JOHN: *Figaro, the Life of Beaumarchais* (London: Hutchinson and Co., 1922)

VALLES, CHARLES DE: *Beaumarchais magistrat* (Paris: Olivien, 1928)

INDEX

Index

Index

Index

INDEX

Index

Index

INDEX

A NOTE ON THE TYPE

The text of this book was set on the Monotype in Bodoni, *so called after Giambattista Bodoni (1740–1813), son of a printer of Piedmont. After gaining experience and fame as superintendent of the Press of the Propaganda in Rome, Bodoni became in 1766 the head of the ducal printing house at Parma, which he soon made the foremost of its kind in Europe. His* Manuale Tipografico, *completed by his widow in 1818, contains 279 pages of specimens of types, including alphabets of about thirty foreign languages. His editions of Greek, Latin, Italian, and French classics, especially his Homer, are celebrated for their typography. In type-designing he was an innovator, making his new faces rounder, wider, and lighter, with greater openness and delicacy.*

The book was composed, printed, and bound by KINGSPORT PRESS, INC., *Kingsport, Tennessee.*